Hg2|London

Dean Street Townhouse

A Hedonist's guide to…

London

Edited by Fleur Britten

A Hedonist's guide to London
3rd Edition

MANAGING DIRECTOR – Tremayne Carew Pole
MARKETING DIRECTOR – Sara Townsend

DESIGN – Nick Randall
MAPS – Richard Hale & Amber Sheers
REPRO – Advantage Digital Print
PRINTER – Leo Paper
PUBLISHER – Filmer Ltd
Sleep by Talib Choudhry and Fleur Britten
Eat by Lucas Hollweg, Kate Spicer and Joe Warwick
Drink (Bars) by Nick Hackworth, Simon Kurs and Fleur Britten
Drink (Pubs) by Jennifer Coyle, Ollie Wright and Mary Meyer
Snack by Helen Brown, Ruby Warrington and Fleur Britten
Party by Fleur Britten and Guyan Mitra
Culture by Fleur Britten
Shop by Daisy Finer and Fleur Britten
Play by Fleur Britten and Helen Brown
Info by Fleur Britten

Photography – Ed Lane Fox, Leila Miller, Tremayne Carew Pole, John Spaull,
Danir Fabijana, Visit London, Mark Whitfield, John Trampner, Jason Lowe, Ed-
die MacDonald, Stephen McLaren, Angell, Manuela Luise
Additional research – Anita Bhagwandas, Christy Thatcher

Email – info@hg2.com
Website – www.hg2.com
Published in the United Kingdom in January 2011 by
Filmer Ltd
10th Floor, Newcombe House,
45 Notting Hill Gate, London W11 3LQ

ISBN – 978-1-905428-49-6

Hg2|London

How to...

A Hedonist's guide to London is broken down into easy-to-use sections: Sleep, Eat, Drink, Snack, Party, Culture, Shop, Play and Info. In each section you'll find detailed reviews and photographs. At the front of the book is an introduction to London and an overview map, followed by introductions to the main areas and more detailed maps. On each of these maps, the places we have featured are laid out by section, highlighted on the map with a symbol and a number. To find out about a particular place simply turn to the relevant section, where all entries are listed alphabetically. Alternatively, browse through a specific section (e.g. Eat) until you find a restaurant you like the look of. Surrounding your choice will be a coloured box – each colour refers to a particular area of the London. Simply turn to the relevant map to find the location.

Book your hotel on Hg2.com

We believe that the key to a great London break is choosing the right hotel. Our unique site now enables you to browse through our selection of hotels, using the interactive maps to give you a good feel for the area as well as the nearby restaurants, bars, sights, etc., before you book. Hg2 has formed partnerships with the hotels featured in our guide to bring them to readers at the lowest possible price. Our site now incorporates special offers from selected hotels, as well information on new openings.

The concept

Ever had the feeling, when in an exciting new city, that its excitements were eluding you? That its promise failed to be delivered because you lacked the keys to unlock it? That was exactly what happened to Hg2's founder, Tremayne Carew Pole, who, despite landing in Budapest equipped with all the big-name travel guides, ended up in a turgidly solemn restaurant when all he wanted was a young, cool locals' hangout. After a wasted weekend, he quit his job and moved to Prague to write the first Hg2 guide. That was back in 2004, and since then, Hg2 has gone on to publish 22 city guides globally, all with the same aim in mind: to offer independent, insiders' advice to intelligent, urbane travellers with a taste for fine design, good food, the perfect Martini, and a city's inside track. Our take on hedonism is not just about pedal-to-the-metal partying, but a respect for the finer things in life.

Unlike many other guidebooks, we pride ourselves on our independence and integrity. We eat in all the restaurants, drink in all the bars, and go wild in the nightclubs – all totally incognito. We charge no-one for the privilege of appearing in the guide, refuse print advertising, and include every place at our own discretion. With teams of knowing, on-the-ground contacts, we cover all the scenes but the tourist trap scene – from the establishment to the underground, from bohemia to the plutocrats' playgrounds, from fetish to fashiony drag, and all the places between and beyond, including the commercial fun factories and the neighbourhood institutions. We then present our findings in a clean, logical layout and a photograph accompanying every review, to make your decision process a quick, and effective one, so you can just get amongst what suits you best. Even the books' design is discreet, so as to avoid the dreaded 'hapless tourist' look.

Updates

Hg2 has developed a network of journalists in each city to review the best new hotels, restaurants, bars, clubs, etc, and to keep track of the latest openings. To access our free updates as well as the digital content of each guide, simply log onto our website www.Hg2.com and register. We welcome your help. If you have any comments or recommendations, please feel free to email us at London@hg2.com.

The Hg2 London team

The editor, **Fleur Britten**, is an editor at Sunday Times Style magazine, as well as author of A Hedonist's Guide to Life, A Hedonist's Guide to Milan, Debrett's Etiquette for Girls, and On The Couch: Tales of Couchsurfing a Continent. She fled to London as soon as it was legal, and it has been hard to prise her from the capital ever since. For this guide, she has enlisted the expertise of Sunday Times colleagues past and present (**Lucas Hollweg**, **Kate Spicer**, **Talib Choudhry**, **Ruby Warrington**, **Mary Meyer**, **Simon Kurs** and **Helen Brown**), as well as some of Hg2's most trusted London-based writers (**Guyan Mitra**, Hg2 Lisbon; **Joe Warwick**, Hg2 Eat London; and **Nick Hackworth**, Hg2 Istanbul).

The Zetter

◼ London

Virgin visitors to London might expect to find it teeming with red buses, black cabs and bobbies on the beat, variously dotted around the Monopoly board, where trips to Buckingham Palace and Big Ben are followed by fish and chips and a nice cup of tea. These tourist emblems live on in London, remaining as rare constants in a city that embraces progress. Though, yes, Old Kent Road really is still on the lowest rung of the property ladder and Mayfair the highest.

Most Londoners are quietly proud of their Britishness, and, provided it continues to generate tabloid headlines while holding no real power, the monarchy remains popular. While London's historical VIPs – Shakespeare, Dickens, Newton, Darwin, etc – lend the city wisdom and influence, it is the people on the ground past and present that afford London its individuality: the Dickensian waifs and strays, the East End gangsters and pearly kings and queens, those naughty punks, goths and sceney club kids with lampshades on their heads, and a multi-ethnic influx of immigrants – Eastern Europeans (with a huge Polish contingent), Afro-Caribbeans, Africans, Asians etc. As many as one-third of Londoners are now not British-born, in part due to Labour's pro-immigration policy of the Noughties, and out of some 12 million in Greater London (some 609 square miles), its non-white population is the largest of any European city (London is also its most populous). Like New York, London is less of a melting pot, more a mosaic of cultures free to retain their own identity, thanks to the (albeit controversial) policy for multiculturalism (the controversy being that it has arguably created a cultural apartheid). Where Christianity once dominated, London is now a pluralist society with huge communities of Hindus (the largest outside India), Jews, Muslims, Sikhs, Buddhists and a seemingly endless supply of Hare Krishna converts proselytising up and down Oxford Street. But while London can seem unfriendly, insular and competitive, all over are village communities, from the quaint Englishness of Primrose Hill to the curry-pushing enclave of Brick Lane.

London is a global city – ie, along with New York, Tokyo and Paris (so go the textbooks), it has a direct effect on global affairs, culturally, politically and socio-economically. It's also become the most unequal city in the West (the richest tenth with an average wealth of just under £1 million, the poorest with only £3,400). Since the Labour government introduced a lax tax set-up for non-domiciles, London's super-rich scene is now characterized by international bankers, Russian oligarchs, and Chinese and Indian entrepreneurs. New tax rules have now been implemented and some of the super-rich have scarpered, but most have made their homes here, possibly having grown accustomed to the capital's world-class culinary, arts, fashion, music and sports scenes.

With the City recognised as the world's leading financial centre (alongside New York), fingers were pointed in its direction for abusing financial product for maximum gain. Whosever fault it was, the recession created a vacuum ripe for revolution. And so, with a Blitzy Keep Calm and Carry On spirit, bullshit was called on so much of London's showy excesses (bankers especially becoming *personae non gratae*). London got real, true value became valued, and people increasingly pursued their passion projects and social enterprise over profiteering and white-collar enslavement. Many argue the recession has been a force for good, culling London's chinks, forcing a recalibration of ideals, and rehabilitating London as the innovator, with developments such as pop-up shops, underground restaurants and resourceful endeavours that are cafés/galleries/shops by day, wild clubs by night, re-energising the city.

The UK may have the world's sixth largest GDP, but a new, unfamiliar coalition government sworn in in summer 2010 (with Conservative David Cameron as prime minister and Liberal Democrat Nick Clegg as his deputy) spells an uncertain political and economic near-future. However, hope is ahead with the mayor Boris Johnson gearing London up to the 2012 Olympics. No doubt it will be criticized for being billions over budget, but it will bring energy, visitors and a new addition to London's skyline – Turner Prize-winning Anish Kapoor's Orbit Tower, a 115m-high sculpture (the UK's largest) variously compared to a treble clef, a helter-skelter and, according to BoJo, a 'super-sized mutant trombone'.

That only adds to an iconic skyline that gracefully blends old and new. For London is a capital that thrives on the clash of opposites. The bankers will always sit

encore
Tickets

CONDITIONS OF SALE

1. Tickets cannot be exchanged or cancelled.

2. Encore Tickets Ltd acts as an agent only and has no control over the event.

3. Tickets are sold subject to the producer/promoter's right to make alterations to the advertised cast or programme because of circumstances which are beyond their control, without being obliged to refund monies or exchange tickets.

4. Personal arrangements including travel and accommodation relating to the event are the ticket-holders' own risk and in no event shall Encore Tickets Ltd, the venue or the producer/promoter be liable for any wasted expenditure beyond the ticket price and booking fee.

5. The ticket holder has a right only to a seat of a value corresponding to that stated on the ticket. Both Encore Tickets Ltd and the venue management reserve the right to provide an alternative seat to that stated on the ticket.

6. Every member of the audience must be in possession of a valid ticket which must be produced to gain entry to the venue and as thereafter requested by a member of the theatre's staff or authorised representative.

7. This ticket may not be sold or re-sold by anyone other than Encore Tickets Ltd or one of their authorised sub-agents; nor may it be transferred for profit or commercial gain. If this happens this ticket becomes invalid and the venue management reserve the right to refuse entry to the event or to eject the ticket-holder from the venue.

8. Latecomers may not be admitted into the auditorium if the performance has started. Whilst most venues will attempt to seat customer during a suitable break in the performance, this cannot be guaranteed, and we ask you to ensure that you are at the venue in plenty of time for the advertised performance time which is shown on the face of this ticket.

9. Children under the age of 3 will not be admitted to any theatre. For more information about specific age restrictions for individual shows please contact us.

10. Flexitickets can only be utilised prior to 72 hours before performance.

Encore Tickets Ltd. Encore House, 50-51 Bedford Row, London WC1R 4LR
Helpdesk Tel No. - 0207 492 1583

Please check your ticket carefully as mistakes cannot be rectified afterwards

Should you have any queries please e mail helpdesk@encoretickets.co.uk

encore
Tickets
020 7492 1500

Encore Tickets Booking Ref: 4131699

KING, JAMES

2 tickets
Shaftesbury Theatre
Fri 6 DEC 13 07:30 PM

This is not a ticket

See reverse for terms & conditions

in disagreement with the bohemians, the Establishment versus the underground, tradition versus experiment – call it creative tension, and for that, London will always be dynamic. Its liberal, progressive outlook makes for a modern metropolis, happy to adopt a new set of emblems – namely, 'Chelski' Football Club, chicken tikka masala (though perhaps that was more to do with our erstwhile cooking talents), and maybe even a super-sized mutant trombone.

London Overview

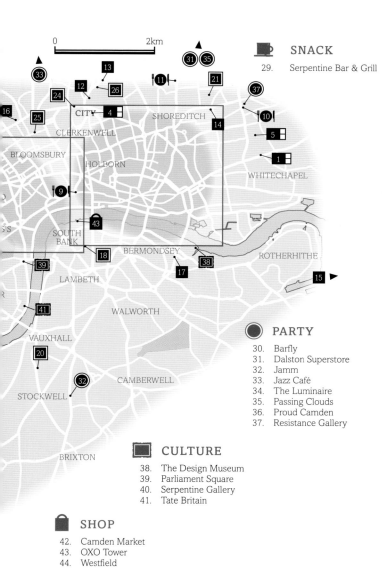

SNACK

29. Serpentine Bar & Grill

CITY
SHOREDITCH
CLERKENWELL
BLOOMSBURY
HOLBORN
WHITECHAPEL
SOUTH BANK
BERMONDSEY
ROTHERHITHE
LAMBETH
WALWORTH
VAUXHALL
CAMBERWELL
STOCKWELL
BRIXTON

PARTY

30. Barfly
31. Dalston Superstore
32. Jamm
33. Jazz Café
34. The Luminaire
35. Passing Clouds
36. Proud Camden
37. Resistance Gallery

CULTURE

38. The Design Museum
39. Parliament Square
40. Serpentine Gallery
41. Tate Britain

SHOP

42. Camden Market
43. OXO Tower
44. Westfield

0   2km

Central London

Where is the centre of London? What exactly comprises 'central London'? Frankly, there are several versions of the truth, not least thanks to estate agents and landlords trying to muscle in on its commercial clout. Central London essentially constitutes the borough of the City of Westminster, and is hemmed in by the river (south), the City (London's financial centre; east), Regent's Park (north) and Park Lane (west). And if you were to follow a road sign that read, 'Central London: 20 miles' for precisely 20 miles, you'd eventually find yourself at Charing Cross Station where a stone monument of a mounted King Charles I marks this apparent centre. It is from here that all mileages to London are measured (it's not the geographical centre, simply fuzzy British logic), and all London's residential streets are allegedly numbered so that number 1 is nearest Charing Cross, though we can't profess to have tested this comprehensively or indeed to believe it entirely.

London's dark heart is known as the West End – an imprecise zone that is neither west nor an end, but that buzzes with pleasure-seekers (note though that its pace of life is fast and tourists are often on the receiving end of pavement rage for walking too slowly). It includes the consumer frenzy of high-streety Oxford Street and Regent Street, the infinitely more exclusive Bond Street, Covent Garden's theatreland and seedy Soho. Covent Garden (once 'Convent's Garden' where monks grew vegetables and which until recently had a huge fruit and veg market) is now an entertainment and shopping destination with theatres and street performers galore, decent boutiques, and lots of dawdling tourists unfeasibly fascinated by those silver-frosted living statues.

Soho, a historic network of narrow streets, harbours numerous wanton scenes (gay, sex, nightlife – sometimes all at once), the creative industries (advertising, TV and film) and an extended family of colourful characters that exist outside convention and inside its boozers (a recent renaissance has seen a new wave of hip, pro-

14

gressive eateries, bars and hotels). Also in the West End are Leicester Square (aka Cinema Central and Tourist Hell – a pedestrianized square full of naff nightclubs, cut-price ticket booths, rip-off restaurants, sweaty steakhouses and preying pickpockets) and Piccadilly Circus, London's answer to Time Square, with vast neon advertising hoardings, a statue of Anteros (the Greek god of requited love, often mistaken for his – possibly more appropriate – twin brother Eros, god of love and lust), and lots of traffic. People even say 'Oooh, it was just like Piccadilly Circus' to mean extremely busy. Avoid both. Just north of Leicester Square is London's compact but authentic Chinatown, the main drag being Gerrard Street with ersatz oriental gates, phone box pagodas, and ornamental lions, dragons and lanterns. Beyond the West End, the capital is back to business. The legal quarter lies just east in Holborn, and has done since medieval times when barristers worked and lodged in public houses, so-called the Four Inns of Court (Lincoln's Inn, Gray's Inn, Inner Temple and Middle Temple). The latter two were owned by the Knights Templar and are now the haunt of Da Vinci code-crackers; to normal people, their relevance is simply that all four are now geographical reference points.

To the north of the West End are Bloomsbury and Fitzrovia. Bloomsbury is considered London's intellectual land, home to the University of London, The British Museum and, in the early 20th century, the Bloomsbury Group, an elite circle of artists and writers which included Virginia Woolf, EM Forster and John Maynard Keynes. Blue plaques punctuate Bloomsbury's elegant Georgian terraces to commemorate other brainy residents – Dickens, WB Yeats and Edgar Allen Poe. Just west of Bloomsbury, to the west of Tottenham Court Road (the golden mile of electrical bargains), is Fitzrovia (aka Noho, as in North of Soho), which has become a zone for TV and post-production companies, and also includes a little-known Spanish quarter, which, true to form, hosts flamenco, tapas bars and late-night raucousness.

Central London

SLEEP

1. Dean Street Town House
2. Haymarket Hotel
3. Hazlitt's
4. Myhotel Bloomsbury
5. The Sanderson
6. Soho Hotel
7. St. John Hotel
8. St. Martin's Lane
9. W Hotel

EAT

10. L'Atelier du Joel Robuchon
11. Barrafina
12. Bob Bob Ricard
13. HIX Soho
14. J. Sheekey
15. Polpo
16. Yauatcha

DRINK

17. Benugo Bar Kitchen @ BFI
18. Bloomsbury Bowling
19. Dick's Bar @ El Camino
20. Mark's Bar

SNACK

21. Balans
22. Dehesa
23. Fernandez & Wells
24. Princi
25. Terroirs
26. Tierra Brindisa
27. Villandry
28. Wahaca

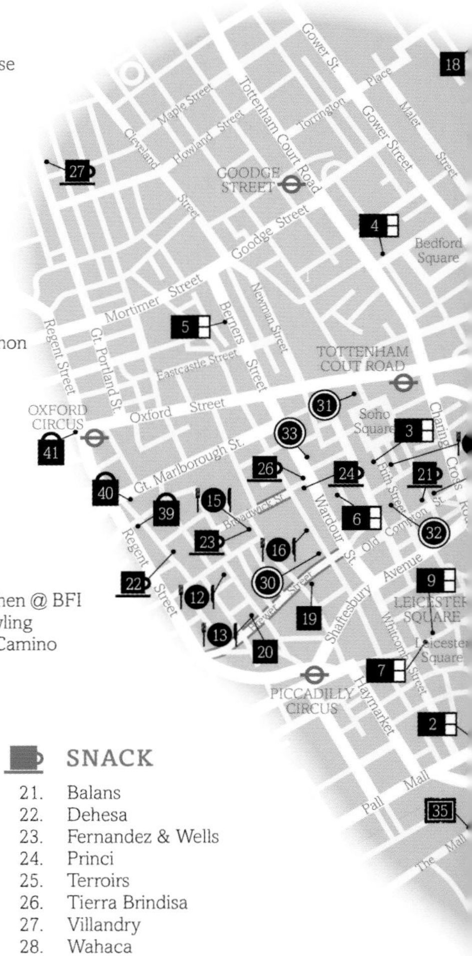

0   250m   500m

⊖ Underground
   Station

PARTY

29. Den & Centro
30. Madame Jojo's
31. Punk
32. Ronnie Scott's
33. St. Moritz

CULTURE

34. British Museum
35. ICA
36. Photographers' Gallery
37. Sir John Soane's Museum
38. South Bank Centre

SHOP

■ Broadwick Street
■ Brewer Street
■ Earlham Street
■ Floral Street
39. Hamley's
40. Liberty
■ Monmouth Street
■ Neal Street
■ Shorts Gardens
41. Top Shop

■ Mayfair & North

Flanking the south of the West End is the political powerhouse of Westminster, the royal seat in St James, and Mayfair. Monopoly's premier property zone, Mayfair, remains a des res for old money and new (particularly Russians and Arabs), understandably charmed by its palatial properties, the quaint bistros and bars of Shepherd Market, and its proximity to London's best auction houses, commercial art galleries and Bond Street boutiques (as well as the recent arrival of its own growing collection). It's only fitting that such privilege is cushioned by a generous buffer of royal parkland, namely St James's Park, Green Park and Hyde Park. North of Mayfair is Marylebone, at once a villagey residential area, a destination for medical excellence with Harley Street's numerous private dental and cosmetic clinics, and a stronghold of independent endeavour with boutiques, coffee shops and eateries. North London proper starts at King's Cross (beyond this map). In Victorian times it was an industrial area serviced by Euston, King's Cross and St Pancras stations, but its redbrick warehouses were eventually abandoned by all but prowling prostitutes and junkies. King's Cross is now undergoing a major urban regeneration spearheaded by the arrival of uber-architect Norman Foster's Eurostar rail link at St Pancras station, opened late 2007. It's arguably failed to attract the hyped draw, but it's a radical improvement.

To its northwest is Camden, a training-ground for London teenagers riding out their angry goth phase, and a stomping-ground for subversives of all ages (punks, emos, crusties); shopping for bootleg CDs and vintage clothes at Camden market is a rite of passage for any young Londoner and naive tourist; a Hollywood-style Walk of Fame for legendary rockers that is promised for 2011 doesn't bode well for tourist traffic. Camden recently enjoyed a moment of cool when a hedonistic clique of indie rock stars – the Camden Caners – were papped snogging/falling out of/kicking off outside its grungey pubs, but then big investments in 'hip' hangouts followed, undoing the glamour of rebellion. Still, it tidied up the scuzz.

Just west is the vastly prettier and posher Primrose Hill – a picturesque hilltop park with views over London, sandwiched between London Zoo and its own village. Cosy gastropubs, expensive Victorian townhouses and a chichi celebrity scene have made it a fashionable destination, though now loaded bankers have bought into it, forcing up property prices and, some say, pushing out its soul. Bridging Camden and the East End is Islington, a buzzy, young area lined with independent boutiques, bars and restaurants. Its fine Georgian houses are largely populated by trendy New Labour-orientated professionals (Tony Blair himself until recently), but its nightlife has become such a mecca that at weekends, it can seem like one big stag party. The neighbourhoods of Holloway, Archway, Highbury and Kentish Town sit just north of Islington and Camden and are largely residential – rent is cheaper, horizons are rugged with industrial wastelands, and there are plentiful pockets of ethnicity – just the edge to attract a cool, creative crowd.

But it is the venerable villages of Highgate and Hampstead, on either side of Hampstead Heath's rolling hills, that lend North London its intellectual and artistic associations. Famous Hampstead inhabitants have included Sigmund Freud, Robert Louis Stevenson, John Constable and George Orwell. Highgate – the highest point in London – has been home to Samuel Taylor Coleridge, JB Priestley and Yehudi Menuhin, while Highgate Cemetery is the final home for Karl Marx, Douglas Adams and George Eliot, and most recently, punk pioneer Malcolm McLaren. North London is host to a strong Jewish community, most concentrated around Golders Green, in whose cemetery are buried Jewish people such as Marc Bolan, Peter Sellers and Sigmund Freud. Many live in North London's most expensive areas including 'Millionaires' Row', aka The Bishops Avenue near Highgate. Increasingly also a lair also for London Arabs, it's rather like Hollywood's Bel-Air, with faux Grecian temples here, mock Tudor mansions there and one-upmanship all around.

Mayfair & North

SLEEP

1. The Arch London
2. Athenaeum
3. Brown's
4. Claridge's
5. The Connaught
6. The Dorchester
7. Langham
8. La Suite II
9. The May Fair Hotel
10. No. 5 Maddox Street

EAT

11. Automat
12. Cecconi's
13. Corrigans
14. Galvin Bistro de Luxe
15. Locanda Locatelli
16. Murano
17. Nobu Berkeley
18. La Petite Maison
19. Scott's
20. Sketch
21. The Wolseley

DRINK

22. Claridge's Bar
23. Duke's Hotel Bar

PUBS

24. The Punch Bowl

SNACK

25. Claridge's
26. Inn the Park
27. Sketch Parlour

0   250m   500m

⊖ Underground
   Station

Cavendish
Square

Oxford Street   OXFORD
                CIRCUS

Regent Street

Cavendish
Square

22

36

18

18

20

27

12

Berkeley
Square

11

3

31

17

9

GREEN
PARK

28

21

Piccadilly

33

Piccadilly

23

PARK
NER

Green
Park

26

30

St. James's
Park

PARTY

28. Mahiki
29. Whisky Mist

CULTURE

30. Buckingham Palace
31. Royal Academy

SHOP

■ Bond Street
■ Bruton Street
■ Conduit Street
■ Savile Row
■ Jermyn Street
■ South Molton Street
■ Marylebone High Street
32. Selfridges
33. Fortnum & Mason
34. Gray's Antique Markets

■ Chelsea & South

Kensington, Chelsea and Fulham remain the territory of the Sloane, that upper-middle-class horsey type identified in the 1980s and named after one of their favourite haunts, Sloane Square. Extending from Sloane Square is the King's Road where the Swinging Sixties – and Mick Jagger, Twiggy and Mary Quant – once swung, and where, in the 1970s, punks roamed, lured by Vivienne Westwood and Malcolm McLaren's emporium called (for controversy's sake) SEX. These days, the youthquake has passed and the scene is rather more Chelsea Pensioners (those scarlet-uniformed war veterans who retire to the Chelsea Royal Hospital) and Sloanes (not dissimilar to their 1980s counterparts, if now more posh-chav in appearance – stripey blonde hair and lots of slap) who can afford to live in the area's (or their parents') beautiful townhouses. Some of Britain's most expensive real estate is in nearby Belgravia – grand, stuccoed houses painted regulation cream gloss, inhabited by international embassies, international bankers using million-pound pads as mere pied-à-terres, and international playboys, often of Russian extraction. Next door, Knightsbridge – certainly no knockdown neighbourhood having recently claimed the world record for property price at £6,000 per square foot – is home to Harrods, the designer boutiques of Sloane Street, and the kind of person who enjoys boasting that Harrods is their local. Summer sees something of a supercar circus (lurid Lamborghinis) as affluent Arabs escape the Middle East heatwaves to drop some cash here. Just west is South Kensington, also posh and pricey but with the added gravitas of 'Albertopolis', a loose campus of national museums and colleges commissioned by Prince Albert in the 1850s.

Most of South London lies south of the river (beyond the map). Known as 'Saarf London' because of its working-class majority, it's arguably the underdog in terms of wealth and status. Fans maintain that inhabitants are salt-of-the-earth, hard-working types and not the bourgeois snobs of the north (NB: petty north–south rivalry endures). Its critics – usually North Londoners – say it's an ugly, unsafe suburban sprawl with terrible transport links. In reality, it's this and more – its lag stems from pre-bridge medieval times when North London was developed and South London languished – few historic monuments were built here. The South Bank, however, is London's most important contemporary culture centre, and is lined with galleries, concert halls and theatres.

Just beyond the riverbank, Waterloo, Southwark, Borough and Bermondsey have all seen recent gentrification, with industrial-age factories converted into chic loft spaces, and the concomitant foodie/drinkie scene to cater for them. Further south, Elephant and Castle, Vauxhall and New Cross (an area that includes Monopoly's cheapest street, Old Kent Road) are more 'earthy', with gloomy tower blocks and grim shopping centres. Some delight in these last bastions of pre-gentrification – New Cross and Deptford have enjoyed recent cachet, briefly rivalling the sceney draw of Shoreditch; non-believers call it plain inner-city decay. Upstream are Battersea and Clapham, residential neighbourhoods with plenty of lively hangouts to service its young (and mostly conventional) graduate community. With Battersea Park (and its boating lake, zoo and river views) and Clapham Common (with its summer concerts), the quality of life is good and the reason why many good-time South Africans and Australians settle here.

Brixton, Camberwell and Peckham are the antidote to that safe and squeaky grad scene. You'll find West African communities in Peckham, Jamaicans in Brixton, and a mixture in Camberwell; these areas are also popular with the liberal middle classes and the politically correct social-worker cliché who wants to unite with their brothers and sisters, preferably in a communal squat over a Camberwell Carrot (a fat spliff). Music is instrumental to the area, especially Brixton, whose black-and dance-music scenes attract both diehard and tryhard clubbers. Brixton is not all so mellow, however – the area is charged with attitude. An increasing Yardie presence, a high incidence of gun, drug and street crime, and a history of race riots lend a tough tone. Camberwell and Peckham, with the nearby Camberwell College of Arts, share a more easy-going, artistic feel, though all – run-down and rough yet dynamic and diverse – provoke extreme reactions either way. Rather like the north–south divide, in fact.

Chelsea & South

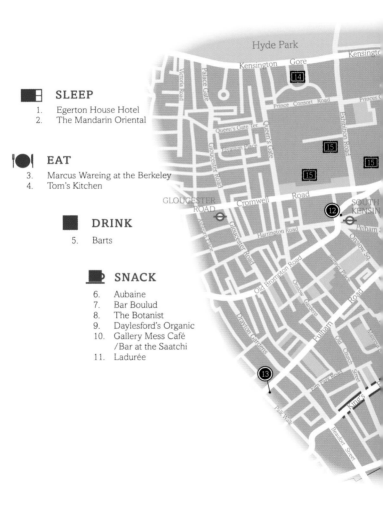

SLEEP

1. Egerton House Hotel
2. The Mandarin Oriental

EAT

3. Marcus Wareing at the Berkeley
4. Tom's Kitchen

DRINK

5. Barts

SNACK

6. Aubaine
7. Bar Boulud
8. The Botanist
9. Daylesford's Organic
10. Gallery Mess Café
    /Bar at the Saatchi
11. Ladurée

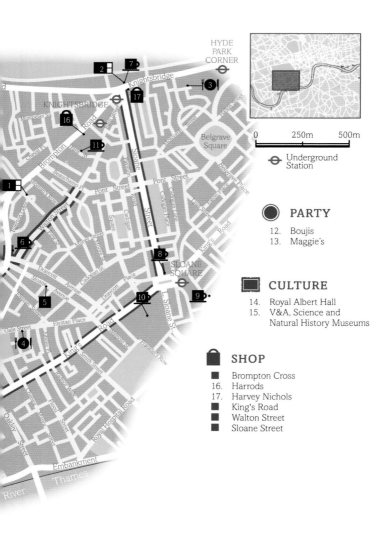

HYDE PARK CORNER

KNIGHTSBRIDGE

Belgrave Square

SLOANE SQUARE

0   250m   500m

⊖ Underground Station

⬤ PARTY

12. Boujis
13. Maggie's

▦ CULTURE

14. Royal Albert Hall
15. V&A, Science and Natural History Museums

🛍 SHOP

■ Brompton Cross
16. Harrods
17. Harvey Nichols
■ King's Road
■ Walton Street
■ Sloane Street

Notting Hill & West

The expression 'that's so West London' has come to describe a look that is pretty, safe and moneyed (mostly uttered by the edgier, and possibly chippier – ie, less loaded – East Londoners). It's usually directed at West London's dominant breed, a sibling of the Sloane – posh, conservative (and Conservative) and English. The heartbeat of this bourgeoisie radiates from Notting Hill, where stuccoed mansions provide the kind of comfort to which these Londoners are accustomed (not least to the 'Notting Hill Set', the inner circle of the Tory party itself – Cameron, Osborne and Vaizey; Notting Hell, by Rachel Johnson, sister of Boris and Tory insider, satirises the scene). In truth, there are other power tribes in Notting Hill: in the 1950s, West Indian immigrants took root here and still now, local Caribbean culture continues to be a proud part of street life. The annual Notting Hill Carnival in August – launched in the 1960s to promote harmony between the immigrant communities and the English majority – is still Caribbean in flavour, with steel drum bands, jerk chicken street stalls and exotically dressed dancers on floats. The privileged throw parties on their decked terraces overlooking the riffraff – rather less integrationist but, frankly, London's biggest street party needs all the space it can get.

In the 1960s, Notting Hill was a haven for bohemians and many still live here, now with their grown-up posh-hippy offspring. Other settlers – from Morocco, Spain, Portugal and Greece – have added a welcome Mediterranean flavour with vibrant bistros and colourful food markets, but in many ways Notting Hill remains fraffly English – hence a good location for a Hollywood romcom about a Hollywood star who falls in love with an archetypal bumbling British chap (Hugh Grant, who else?). And the film? Notting Hill, of course. That location manager had a gift of a job – Notting Hill's middle-class bohemia makes for a perfectly picturesque set thanks to the romance of Portobello Road, a cute, characterful lane lined with candy-coloured cottages, and buzzing with antiques shops and its famous street market. However, the steady encroachment of bland-tasted bankers has seen the high-end global brands move in, and individuality increasingly driven out. Just west (beyond this map), Holland Park is a grown-up, more affluent version of Notting Hill, with the same grand stucco-fronted, pillar-porched Victorian townhouses, without the ethnic diversity or retail scene (and Holland Park actually exists, a 22-acre public garden that's appropriately genteel, with an orangery, open-air theatre, cricket pitch and peacocks).

Further west, the BBC's TV studios take out a large proportion of Shepherd's Bush, the rest a home for Polish, East African and West Indian communities (and lots of Brits). Its neighbour, Hammersmith, is right on the river with historic pubs

aplenty; both are a mix of expensive townhouses and sorry social housing. Plenty of other ethnic enclaves characterize West London – Bayswater's hookah cafés and shwarma shops service a lively Lebanese, Egyptian and Algerian community; St John's Wood is a wealthy Jewish district (also home to EMI's Abbey Road recording studio and that famous zebra crossing, hence a place of pilgrimage for Beatles fans), as is Maida Vale – a gorgeous, spacious residential area scored with the scenic canals of Little Venice (named by the poet Robert Browning), while Earl's Court has become a refuge for backpacking Antipodeans, and Kilburn for the Irish.

West London also has a rich royal legacy, as Britain's kings and queens have historically looked west for their parks and palaces. Hyde Park, acquired by Henry VIII as a hunting ground, spreads westwards from Marble Arch to Kensington; the west section of Hyde Park, Kensington Gardens, is home to Kensington Palace, the one-time residence of the Prince and Princess of Wales (Charles moved to St James's after divorcing Diana); further out is Hampton Court, Henry VIII's splendid Tudor palace on the Thames, and Richmond Park, London's largest open space with 2,350 acres, and a royal park since the 13th century. Windsor Castle, the Queen's weekend retreat, is 20 miles west in the Berkshire countryside. No wonder, then, that the posh chose this royal corridor to take up residence.

Notting Hill & West

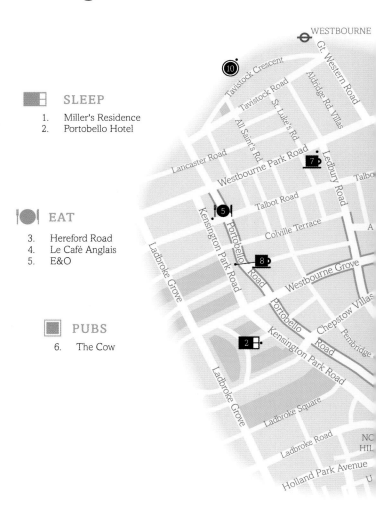

SLEEP

1. Miller's Residence
2. Portobello Hotel

EAT

3. Hereford Road
4. Le Café Anglais
5. E&O

PUBS

6. The Cow

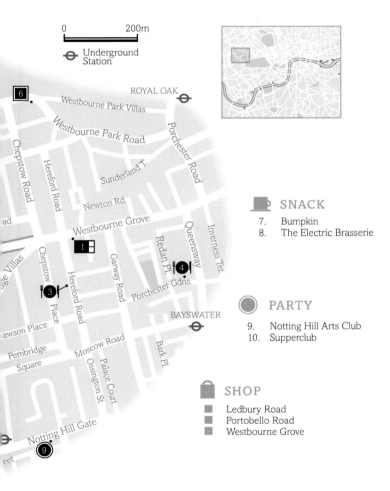

0   200m

Underground
Station

ROYAL OAK

Westbourne Park Villas

Westbourne Park Road

Chepstow Road

Hereford Road

Sunderland T.

Porchester Road

Newton Rd.

Westbourne Grove

Queensway

Redan Pl.

Inverness Ter.

ad

e Villas

Chepstow Place

Hereford Road

Garway Road

Porchester Gdns.

BAYSWATER

awson Place

Pembridge Square

Moscow Road

Palace Court

Ossington St.

Bark Pl.

Notting Hill Gate

eet

SNACK

7.   Bumpkin
8.   The Electric Brasserie

PARTY

9.   Notting Hill Arts Club
10. Supperclub

SHOP

■   Ledbury Road
■   Portobello Road
■   Westbourne Grove

■ The City & East

All eyes have gazed on the dynamic east in the last few years, with the self-consciously cool creative camp gravitating towards Shoreditch, Hackney and Dalston, and ever more stratospheric skyscrapers being built in the City and Canary Wharf. London's eastern promise begins in Clerkenwell, where abandoned warehouses, 18th-century French Huguenot residences and watchmakers' workshops have been converted into loft accommodation, photographic studios, media offices, style bars, gastropubs and nightclubs. Just south is Fleet Street, forever the namesake of British journalism, and although all the newspapers have now dispersed, some of the original buildings and legendary pubs frequented by legendary hacks still remain. Just east, the City of London contains the 'square mile' of London's financial quarter. During the week, it's eyes down, full throttle in hive-like endeavour where the Stock Exchange is the queen bee; by the weekend, it's a ghost town. Alongside the City's contemporary architecture (famously, the Gherkin and Lloyds of London) are some of the oldest parts of London, adding some much needed soul to City soullessness – scores of 17th-century Wren-designed churches that shot up after the Great Fire of London (including St Paul's Cathedral), the medieval Tower of London and relics of Roman walls.

The East End (that starts on the west side with Spitalfields, Hoxton and Shoreditch – the latter two being used interchangeably though which actually occupy the west and east hub respectively) is London's HQ of cool (if its smug residents, with their experimental haircuts and clashing thrift chic, are to be believed). In the early 1990s, the area was essentially a wasteland of disused industrial structures and rundown council estates. Impoverished artists moved in, bringing with them cachet and counterculture, and other creatives soon followed (notably the dot-com entrepreneurs, ad execs, rock'n'roll rebels). Cheap rents also lured an influx of immigrants – Bangladeshis populate Brick Lane (aka Banglatown, now famed for its curry houses and bilingual street signs); the Vietnamese settled around Kingsland Road, and Afro-Caribbeans in Hackney and Dalston. Then came gentrification and the trendies, spawning an economy seemingly fuelled solely by art galleries, bars, clubs and hairdressers – and then the chains, yet more chains, and the bridge and tunnellers. On a Saturday night, Hoxton and the 'Ditch can feel more like Leicester Square – London's centre of gravity has definitely shifted east.

And so, as investment continues to pour in, with new private members' clubs and glossy, over-designed bars and hotels, the avant-garde marches on – Dalston (north of Shoreditch), Stoke Newington (even more north), London Fields (northeast) and Clapton (even more northeast) all hold a certain cachet, but it's Dalston, having made it to the pages of Vogue Italia as creative crucible numero uno (a gritty grungeville where fashion designers Christopher Kane, Marios Schwab and Gareth Pugh operate from), that wins the prize. Meanwhile, the East End's artistic community has come of age, with the burgeoning commercial art scene of Hackney's Vyner Street and Herald Street. The East's crown of cool endures, albeit now ripe for parody with all those tragic tryhards. But the real tragedy is that the original working-class East Enders – or Cockneys, born within earshot of Bow Bells, the church bells of St Mary-le-Bow – have gradually been displaced by soaring property prices paid for by middle-class 'Mockneys'. To that, they probably retort, 'What a load of pony and trap.'

Further east is the City's younger brother, Canary Wharf (beyond this map) – a financial development built on old docklands that includes three of London's tallest buildings: the totemic office blocks of One Canada Square (London's tallest at 235m), and HSBC and Citigroup Towers. The entire area is designed with one thing in mind – maximizing profits, minimizing distraction – so there's little to see. Just east is the infamous Millennium Dome, the Labour Party's colossal white elephant, now a rather more successful nightclub and gig venue, The O2, and for the 2012 Olympics, will host the gymnastics and basketball. The 500-acre Olympic Park sits in Stratford, due east of Hackney and built on waste- and industrial land, bringing yet more urban regeneration, focus and human traffic to East London. The equestrian stuff will take place in Greenwich, London's southeast pocket, due south of Stratford. As the city's maritime zone, it's home to the stately Old Royal Naval College and the famous 19th-century tea clipper, the Cutty Sark. Also here is the chance to walk the line of longitude that marks GMT – evidence that London really is centre of the universe.

The City & East

SLEEP

1. Andaz
2. Boundary Rooms
3. Hoxton Urban Lounge
4. Malmaison
5. The Rookery
6. Shoreditch Rooms
7. The Zetter

EAT

8. Bistro Bruno Loubet @ the Zetter
9. Boundary Restaurant
10. Brick Lane
11. Caravan
12. Club Gascon
13. The Luxe
14. Magdalen
15. The Modern Pantry
16. Moro
17. Pizza East
18. St. John
19. White Chapel Gallery Dining Room

DRINK

20. Callooh Callay
21. Favela Chic
22. Lounge Bohemia
23. The Rake
24. Roxy Bar & Screen
25. Vinopolis
26. Vinoteca

PUBS

27. The Coach & Horses
28. The Eagle
29. The Fox & Anchor
30. The George & Dragon
31. The Golden Heart
32. The Jerusalem Tavern
33. Ye Old Mitre

32

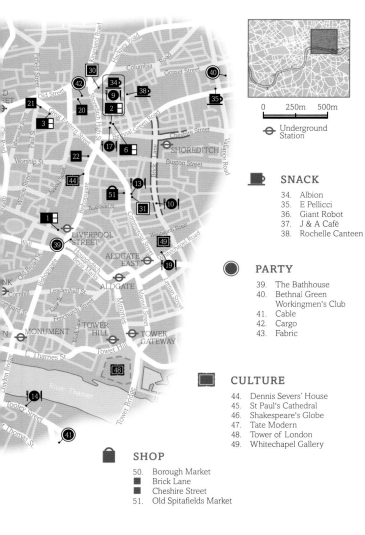

0   250m   500m

⊖ Underground
    Station

☕ SNACK

34. Albion
35. E Pellicci
36. Giant Robot
37. J & A Café
38. Rochelle Canteen

⬤ PARTY

39. The Bathhouse
40. Bethnal Green
     Workingmen's Club
41. Cable
42. Cargo
43. Fabric

▣ CULTURE

44. Dennis Severs' House
45. St Paul's Cathedral
46. Shakespeare's Globe
47. Tate Modern
48. Tower of London
49. Whitechapel Gallery

🛍 SHOP

50. Borough Market
■   Brick Lane
■   Cheshire Street
51. Old Spitafields Market

sleep...

In such straitened times, there seems to be an awful lot of money available for new developments, with structural uprisings all over town. And largely, it's out with the big and in with the small, as the post-capitalist consumer demands something with more feeling, less phoney flashiness. Hail the micro-boutique hotel, where the staff know your name, actually care if you're cold, thirsty or in dire need of a nightcap in the middle of the night, and maybe even eat their breakfast with you, like a real-life family. As the desire for genuine, homely service trumps the need for ego-boosting grandeur, it makes sense to scale down guest numbers (while of course building in exclusivity). Similarly, there's a return to the comforts of nostalgia, with hot water bottles and board games at Nick Jones' Shoreditch Rooms, and the rise of inns and (luxury) rooms above pubs, at St John Hotel, The Fox & Anchor, and Gordon Ramsay's gastropub York & Albany, which has the ambience of a friendly country house.

There's also a welcome return (amongst the enlightened) to the old-fashioned virtues of good value and honesty – minibars have become more beneficent (for example, at Athenaeum and Andaz), and more and more hotels are doing away with different high and low season prices, offering a more democratic and transparent wysiwyg room rate (namely, at Rough Luxe, 40 Winks and St John). Some are simply offering much more reasonable pricing, albeit for small rooms (at Dean Street

Townhouse and Shoreditch Rooms). Good value is imparting on design, which is increasingly (though not always) a case of design with a little 'd'– the simplicity of austerity chic is pushing out the aggressive over-design and unnecessary accoutrements such as tricksy lighting walls that are impossible to turn off.

And predictably, as with London's housing market, interest has taken a considerable swing eastwards, with a veritable mushrooming of luxury hotels and a new centre of design excellence where, not so long ago, were halfway houses, homeless hostels, brothels and strip joints. Actually, many remain, apparently lending that gritty 'edge' to the likes of Shoreditch Rooms, Conran's Boundary Rooms, 40 Winks in Stepney Green and Town Hall Hotel and Apartments in Bethnal Green. Which brings us to another trend: the self-contained apartment with 24-hour room service – your home from home that delivers the luxury and reputation of a hotel, with the freedom of your own kitchen and space, now at a much more reasonable price – perfect for private types who'd need a disguise just to get down the hotel corridor, or indeed who'd prefer to walk it naked (also Anouska Hempel's La Suite II and No. 5 Maddox Street).

To clear the way for the new guard, we've pulled out a lot of the big old ladies like the Ritz and the Lanesborough, that now seem less relevant with their ostentation and fussy formality (and prohibitive prices). Some of London's oldest hotels will always be timeless, however. Claridge's and Brown's conjure up a glamorous, old-world feel reminiscent of empire and PG Wodehouse's Jeeves and Wooster, and are both beautiful and atmospheric.

Meanwhile, London's design hotels (The Sanderson, St Martin's Lane and newcomer W Hotel) – perhaps unfairly renowned for employing models for staff and (therefore) for lofty service – all clamour for the holy trinity of the hotel industry: the hottest restaurant, the coolest bar and the hippest guests. Not that the hip hotel bar is exclusive to contemporary hotels: the classics alike know a good branding exercise when they see one. Hotel bars are often more beautifully designed, and attract more beautiful people, than the rooms themselves – see and be seen at The Langham's Artesian Bar, Claridge's Bar, Soho Hotel's Refuel and The Sanderson's Long Bar. But to really generate a scene, the haute hotels are starting to throw wild parties, for example at St Martin's Lane (with the arrival of members' club Bungalow 8), Andaz, W Hotel and Claridge's, even. Benders in hotels are good for business.

The rates quoted here range from the price of a standard double in low season to a one-bedroom suite in high season (May–September, Christmas and Easter); prices include VAT though many hotels will quote prices without it. If you're a British or EU citizen, you'll have to factor it in, so we have for you. However, you can often find rooms at cheaper prices than rack rates if you book through www.Hg2.com.

the best hotels…

Top Ten:
1. Claridge's
2. Dean Street Townhouse
3. The Haymarket Hotel
4. Shoreditch Rooms
5. The Connaught
6. Town Hall
7. Brown's
8. York & Albany
9. St John Hotel
10. Mandarin Oriental

Style:
1. The Boundary Rooms
2. Town Hall
3. Haymarket Hotel
3. Miller's Residence
4. 40 Winks

Atmosphere:
1. Shoreditch Rooms
2. Dean Street Townhouse
3. The Soho Hotel
4. The Hoxton Hotel
5. Claridge's

Location:
1. The Athenaeum
2. Mandarin Oriental
3. Brown's
4. The Haymarket Hotel
5. The Connaught

■ **40 Winks** *(top)*
109 Mile End Road, Stepney
Green, E1
Tel: 020 7790 0259
www.40winks.org
Rates: single £90; double £130

Welcome to the wildcard. With none of the conventions of a conventional hotel (no spa, no room service, no reception desk even), and with just two bedrooms sharing one (stunning) bathroom, 40 Winks, located in the pound-shop environs of Stepney, is a world away from Hiltonified homogeneity. The personal home (and showcase) of your host and interior designer David Carter, this impeccable Queen Anne townhouse built in 1717 is enchantingly decorated with whimsy and history (antique toy dogs, mannequins' arms, a Beatles drum). In fact, so desirable is it that its very existence as a hotel (since spring 2009) was prompted by photographic crews repeatedly asking if they could stay the night (yes, as a shoot location, it's appeared in countless magazines). The real luxury here is the emotional engagement, that antidote to robotic customer care. The experience is more like a sleepover with your long-lost eccentric uncle; Carter even admits to being embarrassed about charging guests. So it's shoes off and slippers on, DIY tea and coffee plus kitchen access, reading in the garden, and nightcaps in the drawing room. Your stay may even coincide with his pyjama parties with bedtime stories and gin in teacups. It's a tiny revolution.

Style 9, Atmosphere 8, Location 6

■ **Andaz** *(bottom)*
40 Liverpool Street, EC2
Tel: 020 7618 5000
www.andaz.com
Rates: £165–300

Whoa! Where's the front desk? Where's the concierge? You're really offering graffiti tours? Andaz – the first of a brand new Hyatt chain – is getting brave with its concept. What was until 2007 The Great Eastern Hotel has done away with standard practice: removing all physical barriers, things are meant to be a bit more personal ('andaz' meaning personal style in Hindi). And inventive – hence ideas like East End street-art tours and tranny parties (the theme is always resolutely fashionable). For all that, it's still a grand old station hotel (and rather corporate, for practical reasons): behind the Victorian redbrick façade lies a sleek, modern lobby, vast atrium and exposed glass lift shafts, which sit alongside original 1880s staircases and stained-glass windows. The 267 five-star rooms (including 25 suites) feature clean lines, dark woods, cream tones and chrome accents, while seven bars and restaurants ably service the needs of the itinerant. But back to that innovation: Andaz is keen that everything is all-inclusive, so extras such as softies from the mini-bar, local calls and WiFi are all free. Perhaps that's because they now have nothing to hide behind when guests balk at big bills.

Style 8, Atmosphere 7, Location 7

The Arch London *(left)*
50 Great Cumberland Place, W1
Tel: 020 7724 4700
www.thearchlondon.com
Rates: £176–£353

Enviable setting, tick. Grand period building, tick. Tasteful interiors, tick. Restaurant serving modern British food, tick. Yes, this 82-room, five-star hotel (taking out seven Georgian town-houses and two mews homes) has all a self-respecting new London hotel requires (it opened late 2009). It also has a few extras to distance it from the crowd. Located near Marble Arch and the chic shops of Bond Street and Mount Street yet in a quiet side-street, the hotel's bar and restaurant HUNter 486 (somewhat laboriously named after the 1950s district dialling code for Marylebone) packs a sophisticated punch with a cosy, informal feel (all blazing wood fired ovens, leather banquettes and refectory-style tables). Then there's the glam Martini Library (think jewel-coloured wingback chairs set beside period fireplaces) where

guests can sip cocktails while poring over a Taschen tome, and Le Salon de Champagne, a series of intimate floor-to-ceiling booths designed for quaffing fizz in stylish seclusion. Rich fabrics and boldly patterned 'feature walls' lure guests back to their rooms, but the striking black granite bathrooms are the main attraction here, with invigorating rain showers, televisions by the baths and products by cult New York brand Malin + Goetz. Tick, tick, tick.

Style 8, Atmosphere 7, Location 9

 The Athenaeum *(middle)*
Hotel & Apartments
116 Piccadilly, W1
Tel: 020 7499 3464
www.athenaeumhotel.com
Rates: £220–450

Talk about a room with a view: the five-star Athenaeum's bedrooms either back onto the royal parks or smart Mayfair, while floor-to-ceiling windows, mirrored walls and Juliet

40

balconies (in parkview rooms) help to bring the outside in. Even the Art Deco building's elegant façade is awash with verdant greenery thanks to an eight-storey 'vertical garden'. Once the Athenaeum Club (where MPs and Lords made merry in the name of promoting wisdom) and then, when owned by a film company, a Hollywood hangout (for the likes of Brando, Bacall, Beatty), it's been a family-run hotel since the 1990s, though the A-listers never left thanks to its friendly atmosphere and apartments with private entrances (mostly surprisingly good value given the location). Even standard rooms feel special; contemporary styling, Bose sound systems and 42-inch plasma TVs, and free 'extras' (unlimited soft drinks and nibbles from the huge minibars, newspapers, WiFi) make for a stylish home-from-home. The all-day restaurant serves trad British dishes and a delightfully frothy, award-winning Ladurée afternoon tea, while there's more manly fare in the Whisky Bar, with over 270 varieties of the stuff as well as virtually ever other beverage known to man. After which, a bit of park air might be welcome.

Style 8, Atmosphere 7, Location 10

 The Boundary Rooms *(right)*
2 Boundary Street, E2
Tel: 020 7729 1051
www.theboundary.co.uk
Rates: £200–£350

Sir Terence Conran might be in his late seventies, but he's still got it. Each of the 12 rooms of his latest venture is individually decorated in homage to a legendary designer or design movement. So, the Charles & Ray Eames room is chock-full of Mid-century modern classics such as Eames' iconic lounger and ottoman, as well as more subtle nods (the patterned bath tiles, for example, are based on one of their storage units). Rooms inspired by Eileen Gray and Mies van der Rohe are similarly impressive. All rooms are ultra-spacious (the smallest is 31 sq m, or

334 sq ft), while four of the five suites run over two floors. Design excellence permeates the whole building, from the underground boreholes which provide water for eco-air conditioning to the lift's graphic murals by Brit artist Adam Simpson. Admire them as you ride to the rooftop garden where sail-like canopies and an open wood fire mean you can view the east London rooftops in leisurely fashion. You can also dine alfresco in the adjacent 48-seat grill, or at the basement restaurant (see Eat) for fine British and French cuisine. It's a haven for design snobs and foodies alike. As Conran ever was.

Style 9, Atmosphere 8, Location 8

....

Brown's *(top)*
33 Albemarle Street, Mayfair, W1
Tel: 020 7493 6020
www.brownshotel.com
Rates: £295–1,500

Opened in 1837 by James Brown, butler to poet Lord Byron, this was London's first luxury hotel and has been a haven for the rich and famous ever since. Following a £24 million refurbishment, Brown's was reopened in winter 2005 by hotel supremo Sir Rocco Forte and his interiorista sister, Olga Polizzi. Her redesign of the 11 adjoining Mayfair townhouses is an update rather than a reinvention – The Albemarle restaurant still has its dark wood panelling, intricate Jacobean plaster ceiling and famous carving trolley, but has been refreshed with moss-green leather banquettes, sparkling 1930s-style lanterns and the culinary direction of British revivalist Mark

Hix. The English Tea Room (where old money mixes with the chattering classes, and which won the Tea Guild's Top Afternoon Tea, 2009) and lobby are similarly trad-with-a twist. However, Polizzi has completely modernized the 117 five-star guestrooms (including 29 suites), chucking out the chintz in favour of a subtle mixture of Art Deco, contemporary furniture and original British artworks (by the likes of Tracey Emin and Bridget Riley). The basement spa and Donovan Bar (a homage to the famous fashion photographer) are glamorous new additions that are always picture-perfect not least thanks to their well-heeled regulars.

Style 8, Atmosphere 8, Location 9

....

Claridge's *(bottom)*
Brook Street, Mayfair, W1
Tel: 020 7629 8860
www.claridges.co.uk
Rates: £490–1,185

With a guest register that includes Queen Elizabeth II, Winston Churchill and Jackie Onassis, Claridge's is London's most loved luxury hotel. And with its welcoming committee of whatever-madam-desires doormen (and a 5% discretionary service charge on the bill), international flags flying and attendant paparazzi, arriving does feel like something of an arrival. That it was the hotel of choice for many a royal exile during World War II is testament to its majesty. The jewel in the hotel's crown is the stunning Art Deco lobby, topped by a vast Dale Chihuly chandelier made of 300 hand-blown glass pieces, while its salon, the Foyer, is the place for afternoon tea (see

Snack). Many of the hotel's 203 spacious, five-star rooms have an Art Deco theme, others take inspiration from the opulence of pre-revolutionary France, and since summer 2010, 20 rooms and suites feature the bold stamp of fashion designer Diane von Furstenberg. There are other names to drop: Gordon Ramsay oversees the restaurant (whacking his name on it), David Collins designed the Claridge's Bar and The Fumoir (see Drink). Kate Moss celebrated her infamously debauched 30th birthday here, while Little Britain comedian David Walliams married his supermodel wife Lara Stone in May 2010. It's a shorthand for pure class.

ing extras. Its curiously shaped 1920s lift (used to transport stretchers when the building was a hospital) is a quirky historical throwback, while the softly lit tapas bar is a thoroughly modern innovation. A note of caution: avoid the two basement bedrooms, which reverberate with Underground rumblings, and the top floor, inaccessible by lift. This is not the place to stay if you want to be in the heart of the action, but the slightly offbeat location (only in fact a 15-minute tube journey from Oxford Circus) means that the luxurious rooms are very reasonably priced. Minnie the cat can be persuaded into pet duty at no extra cost.

Style 9, Atmosphere 9, Location 9

Style 8, Atmosphere 7, Location 7

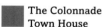 **The Colonnade** *(top)*
Town House
2 Warrington Crescent,
Maida Vale, W9
Tel: 020 7286 1052
www.theetoncollection.com
Rates: £141–200

This charming 19th-century stuccoed townhouse lies in the gorgeous residential area of Little Venice where canals are lined with colourful narrowboats and pretty foliage. The boutique hotel's 43 four-star rooms (including seven suites, two of which are named after one-time visitors, Sigmund Freud in 1938 and JFK in 1962) are full of period charm and individually decorated, featuring four-poster beds, rich fabrics and antiques. Many also have small terraces with canal views. Frette bed linens, bowls of apples and Highland Aromatics' wildflower toiletries in the reasonably sized bathrooms are pleas-

The Connaught *(bottom)*
Carlos Place, Mayfair, W1
Tel: 020 7499 7070
www.the-connaught.co.uk
Rates: £339–1,400

For over a hundred years, the five-star Connaught has been synonymous with royalty, glamour and celebrity – a fact which made Marc Jacobs' insanely decadent bash in 2007 the perfect way to mark its closure for a £70 million refurb. A crack team of craftsmen and architects (including British interior designer Guy Oliver) was drafted in to revive period details and sympathetically integrate 21st-century comforts. The 88 guestrooms skillfully balance pale period colours, damask silks and antique furnishings with new bespoke pieces, abstract paintings and discreet technology. Beds are dressed in Italian linen and caramel cashmere blankets, while the white marble bathrooms boast both cast-iron tubs and separate showers. French chef and Alain Ducasse protégée Hélène Darroze has been awarded a Michelin star for her eponymous restaurant at the Connaught, Aman Resorts opened their first UK spa and pool here (see Play), while the jewel-coloured Coburg Bar (a reference to the hotel's original name) has been strewn with crystal chandeliers, velvet armchairs and Julian Opie art: the perfect place to sip an appletini after a hard day's shopping in nearby Mount Street (home to Marc Jacobs), which, like the rest of this pretty pocket of Mayfair, is enjoying a renewed buzz.

Style 9, Atmosphere 8, Location 9

Dean Street Townhouse *(top)*
67 Dean Street, W1
Tel: 020 7434 1775
www.deanstreettownhouse.com
Rates: £90–270

Can Soho House supremo Nick Jones do no wrong (or leave no stone unturned)? His latest venture, opened in 2009 is a 39-room hotel/bar/restaurant/media magnet back at his starting point, Soho. And appropriately, the two genteel Georgian townhouses it inhabits come loaded with soul and stories dating back to the 1730s. The aristocrats, artists, drunkards have come and gone, but its most famous incarnation was as the legendary Gargoyle Club, founded in 1928 and the hangout of politicians, libertines and artists such as Henri Matisse who dreamt up some of the lavish interiors. A little of that old-time decadence has been recaptured in the all-day dining room (think 21st-

century gentlemen's club) where the in-crowd indulges in English comfort food or chatters by the bar. The décor in the guestrooms is in keeping with the building's history (hand-painted wallpaper, four-poster beds, rich upholstery), but there are also luxurious concessions to modernity (Sony flatscreen TVs, free WiFi, and bathrooms stocked with Cowshed lotions, Jones' spa; see Play). Rates start at just £90 for the 'broom cupboard'-sized room, and all beds are either king-size or super king-size. Though one would hope that, in true Soho tradition, guests don't retire aware of such minutiae.

Style 7, Atmosphere 9, Location 8

The Dorchester *(bottom)*
Park Lane, W1
Tel: 020 7629 8888
www.thedorchester.com
Rates: £425–17,000

Built in 1931, the elegant and highly refined Dorchester Hotel was deemed regal enough to host Prince Philip's stag party. The 250 five-star rooms may have a cosy country-pile feel (hand-woven carpets, four-poster beds), but high-tech business and entertainment centres are discreetly hidden inside antique armoires. A team of e-butlers are also on hand to help captains of industry (or Joe Bloggs) with any technical questions. Downstairs, guests can take afternoon tea in the elegant Promenade lobby (marble columns, floral arrangements). For something more substantial, the Grill Room serves traditional, and expensive, British fare; while the additions

of China Tang (Chinese) and Alain Ducasse (Modern French) have turned the hotel into a dining destination in itself. But the perfect place to sip Bellinis after a hard day's shopping in Mayfair is the mirror-panelled Dorchester Bar, while hidden away in the Crystal Room is – wait for it – Liberace's rhinestone and glass baby grand, the perfect Dorchester mascot. The reopening of the Dorchester Spa with its Art Deco sumptuousness and indulgent treatments is the perfect treat for those in needing to unwind after a hard day's shopping.

Style8, Atmosphere 7, Location 8

Egerton House Hotel *(top)*
17 Egerton Terrace,
Knightsbridge, SW3
Tel: 020 7589 2412
www.egertonhousehotel.com
Rates: £311–617

Contemporary isn't a word you'd use to describe this five-star townhouse hotel. Instead, the management aims to transport guests back to a more discerning age with impeccable, old-school service. Guests are greeted with a chilled glass of champagne (or a more genteel pot of tea) by a butler only too happy to unpack your luggage should sir or madam so wish. At bedtime, you'll find Fragonard candles gently flickering in your room and a warm bathrobe, slippers and an evening newspaper by the super-comfy Savoir bed. The 28 guestrooms are decorated in lavish period fashion (richly patterned fabrics, antique furniture, frothy curtains) and the walls are lined with

original engravings and lithographs by the likes of Picasso and Matisse. However, there are also a few discreet high-tech additions such as video-iPods (pre-programmed with content of your choice) and flatscreen TVs in both the bedroom and bathroom. But it's unlikely you'll spend much time channel-hopping. As well as London's most famous museums, department stores Harrods and Harvey Nichols and the designer boutiques of Sloane Street are a short stroll away. Not sure what to buy? The hotel's personal shopper will come with you. It's all part of the service.

Style 7, Atmosphere 7, Location 9

Haymarket Hotel *(bottom)*
1 Suffolk Place,
Trafalgar Square, SW1
Tel: 020 7470 4000
www.firmdale.com
Rates: £250–1,750

Opened in 2007, the latest five-star thoroughbred in the Firmdale stable contains all the Kemp ingredients that have proved so popular with the creative industries in their sister hotels (Charlotte Street, Covent Garden et al), plus a few added attractions. Its 55 super-plush guestrooms and suites are individually decorated in trademark eccentric English elegance, bathrooms are kitted out in granite and oak and supplied with generous baskets of products from English perfumer Miller Harris, and the thoughtfully designed communal areas feature quirky, witty artworks by a host of contemporary artists. But it's the glamorous 18ft

swimming pool (cleverly illuminated with coloured lighting) and adjacent long pewter bar that take centre stage (to the chagrin of those after an early night at weekends in ground-floor rooms – take heed). It's a more mannerly affair upstairs in the Brumus bar and restaurant which serves Italian fare throughout the day. The hotel's super-central location (a stone's throw from Piccadilly Circus and Trafalgar Square) is either a huge plus or pain depending on your sensibilities. But if the commotion of the capital gets too much, you can always take a stroll through nearby St James's Park, or a cleansing dip.

Style 9, Atmosphere 8, Location 9

....

Hazlitt's Hotel   *(top)*
6 Frith Street, Soho, W1
Tel: 020 7434 1771
www.hazlittshotel.com
Rates: £220–395

Set in a trio of townhouses built in 1718, Hazlitt's is located in the frenzied centre of Soho, and is named after a former resident, the celebrated early 19th-century essayist William Hazlitt ('The art of life is to know how to enjoy a little and to endure very much'). The charming Georgian property (complete with wonky stairs and creaky floorboards) was converted into a small and cosy four-star hotel 20-odd years ago and furnished in charming period style, with plush antiques and classical paintings that complement the ornate, high ceilings and beautiful fireplaces. Each of the 23 rooms is named after Hazlitt's friends and conquests, which included Jonathan Swift and Lady Frances Hewitt. There are

numerous atmospheric nooks for reading one of the many signed first editions bequeathed by visiting authors in homage to the essayist, plus a fully stocked honesty bar. With its discreet Frith Street entrance, the rooms are also prized by celebrities seeking privacy. The downside? There is no lift, air-conditioning or restaurant on site (room service is available), although its excellent location means that there are innumerable eateries nearby. Just be sure to ask for a room that doesn't overlook the street if you require perfect silence to aid slumber.

Style 9, Atmosphere 8, Location 8

....

The Hempel   *(bottom)*
31–35 Craven Hill Gardens, Bayswater, W2
Tel: 020 7298 9000
www.the-hempel.co.uk
Rates: £179–599

London's first minimalist hotel was opened back in 1997 by designer Anouska Hempel (aka Lady Weinberg, wife of city financier Sir Mark Weinberg). The discreet, easily missed 'H' outside the portico-ed front door sets the tone – a sparse, white reception (all polished Italian plaster and Portland stone) is flanked at either end by long, low fires with flickering blue flames. Walls are – shock – devoid of ornament and only a handful of decorative touches break the clean lines – a roughly carved Indian door used as a table, imaginatively arranged groups of orchids. Each of its 36 five-star rooms and six self-contained apartments are similarly spare. Beds are set on platforms or suspended from ceil-

ings; bathtubs are hewn from blocks of black granite or pale limestone. That's not to say that rooms are monastic – Frette bed linen, plump armchairs and Diptyque candles are comforting additions, as is its large, serene garden. The problem faced by era-defining design hotels is that nothing dates faster than modern design – new ownership has ushered in a basement art gallery and chucked out the 'so 1990s' fusion food for a new modern European restaurant, 'No. 35'. Yet its loyal fanbase grasps this minimalist masterpiece's enduring draw: sumptuous simplicity and Zen tranquillity in a noisy world.

Style 7, Atmosphere 6, Location 7

The Hoxton *(top)*
Urban Lodge
81 Great Eastern Street, EC2
Tel: 020 7550 1000
www.hoxtonhotels.com
Rates: £1–£169

Put simply, The Hoxton Urban Lodge aims to offer a boutique experience on a high-street budget. In 2006, the suits behind the Pret A Manger chain applied the same money-spinning philosophy to hospitality that transformed the humble sandwich. So far, so unappealing? Don't be put off: the results are surprisingly upmarket. Look past the explosion of 'eclectic' design motifs (mock baronial fireplaces, ugly papier-mâché bird light fittings) cluttering the huge lobby and you'll find that The Hoxton is a jolly nice place to stay. Rooms are undeniably cosy: red fabric lamps cast a warm glow over simple, curvy furniture, Frette bed linen and flatscreen TVs, and while

bathrooms are devoid of actual tubs, slate-tiled power showers feel suitably stylish. The absence of mini-bars is a minor quibble but the atmospheric lobby bar's comprehensive cocktail list should adequately quench thirst; besides, half the point is that Hoxton is on your doorstep. The other half is budget: you'll be lucky to win in its Ryan Air-style '£1 sale' (five rooms sold each night in low season for a quid), but with rooms available at £59 every night of the year, The Hoxton is undeniably bargainous.

Style 7, Atmosphere 9, Location 8

The Langham *(bottom)*
1 Portland Place,
Oxford Circus, W1
Tel: 020 7636 1000
www.langhamhotels.com
Rates: £179–599

The Langham opened in 1865 as London's largest grand hotel, offering – gasp – the combination of hot and cold running water, and England's first hydraulic lift. After it was bombed in World War II, the building was used as office space by the BBC, until the early 1990s when Hilton International took it over and refurbished it (the BBC's radio HQ, Broadcasting House, is still over the road). However, this is not just another conveyor-belt chain hotel (now that Hilton has long gone and another, £80 million refit was completed in 2009). The stone façade mimics a Florentine palace (think gargoyles, cupolas and columns), while the public rooms reflect the power and majesty of the British Empire at its height (huge Murano chandeliers, elegant wallpaper recreated from the original design, and an eminence-inspiring tea salon). Its 380 five-star guestrooms are less opulent but nonetheless tastefully furnished with pale French provincial furniture and striped or floral fabrics. David Collins – the man all London establishments call when in need of a fix – turned his hand to the style-and-substance Landau restaurant and the Artesian Bar, where Art Deco meets Orientalism meets masterful mixology meets the masters and mistresses of the media universe.

Style 8, Atmosphere 6, Location 8

Malmaison *(top)*
18–21 Charterhouse Square, Clerkenwell, EC1
Tel: 020 7012 3700
www.malmaison-london.com
Rates: £125–£325

The thing about McMaison, oops, Malmaison is that as a British chain in 12 cities, you know what you're getting – a good thing to some people, not to others. But for all its homogeneity, what the 'Mal' sets out to do – namely, affordable chic – it does it well. Like all the other casts of the national mould, its 97 rooms feature dark minimalist design with 'moody' spotlighting, plus entry-level luxuries of Egyptian cotton bed linen, fluffy robes and techy toys (the hotel has a free DVD and CD library for in-room entertainment). Its biggest danger is its safety: monochromed this, slate-floored that, and lilac, dove and earth tones sitting politely in muted harmony – to 'rock' it up, there are antique Napoleon and Malmaison portraits (Chateau Malmai-

son being his grand residence outside Paris – the chain's original reference point for 'iconic style'). For that, just look out of the window: housed within the shell of a Victorian redbrick nurses' residence for St Bartholomew's Hospital, it overlooks a private park in the quaintly cobbled square – be sure ask for a square-facing room.

Style 7, Atmosphere 7, Location 8

Mandarin Oriental *(bottom)*
Hyde Park
66 Knightsbridge, SW1
Tel: 020 7235 2000
www.mandarinoriental.com/london
Rates: £295–1,500

Following a £57 million makeover, the palatial Franco-Flemish architecture (redbrick, Portland stone and turrets) of the erstwhile Hyde Park Hotel, where Queen Elizabeth II learned to ballroom-dance, reopened its doors in 2000 as the five-star Mandarin Oriental. The marble-clad, chandelier-bedecked interior is grandly Victorian in feel and HRH would surely approve of the still-sparkling ballroom (such is the royal connection, its parkside entrance is only accessible with permission from the Royal Household). Many of the 200 richly decorated rooms (Irish linen sheets, goose-down pillows, fresh orchids) have fine views of Hyde Park (don't forget to request one, unless you'd sooner window-shop at Harvey Nichols) and original paintings on the walls – at a combined value of over £5 million. The Michelin-starred restaurant Foliage and the stylish Mandarin Bar (housing London's largest humidor and hotel wine cellar) are now joined

by French/New York sensation Daniel Boulud's Bar Boulud (see Snack), and, from December 2010, Heston Blumenthal's much anticipated first London restaurant, while its immaculately appointed spa (see Play) is among the best in the UK. The Mandarin, its amenities and six-star service attract a sophisticated, older crowd happy to pay the price of a regal experience.

Style 8, Atmosphere 8, Location 9

<hr />

![ ] **The May Fair Hotel** *(left)*
Stratton Street, W1
Tel: 020 7769 4041
www.themayfairhotel.co.uk
Rates: £260–1,950

Don't be surprised if you spot a gaggle of paparazzi camped outside this 410-bedroom behemoth (of the Radisson Edwardian chain). They're waiting for the never-ending stream of celebrities who stay here. Perhaps it's the location (yes, Mayfair) that attracts them, perhaps the recently souped-up five-star facilities? Or could it be the hotel's covert policy of giving them one of their 12 superluxe suites? The management has been working hard to regain its original glamour (when even King George V himself opened the hotel in 1927). Has it worked? Well, it's certainly glitzy, with partygoers splashing the cash at the May Fair bar and Palm Beach casino in its Art Deco ballroom. Guestrooms are tasteful and contemporary, with an emphasis on texture over colour (think beige/mocha fabrics with zebrano wood panelling). Beds come with Vi-Spring mattresses, bathrooms boast oval Sicilian marble tubs, and in-room technology comes care of Bang & Olufsen. The Amba restaurant serves up British dishes with aplomb, but better still, the concierge can help secure a table at Scott's, Cipriani or Nobu Berkeley opposite. They can also organise a private jet faster than you can say visiting oligarch. Plus delivering the real-time contents of Heat magazine.

Style 7, Atmosphere 7, Location 9

Miller's Residence   *(middle)*
111a Westbourne Grove,
Notting Hill, W2
Tel: 020 7243 1024
www.millershotel.com
Rates: £175–235

This quirky, 18th-century-style B&B is run by antiques enthusiast, author and sybarite Martin Miller; that he also lives here gives the four-star hotel its name, and, yes, it is his collection of antiques and *objets d'art* that decorates it, while one of his five daughters, Cara, runs it. Behind an anonymous red door lies a candlelit staircase leading up to a theatrical 40ft-deep drawing room, upholstered in rich red velvets and overflowing with curios. Visitors are welcomed by a roaring wood fire and are free to help themselves to the gregarious owner's well-stocked bar (including Martin Miller's Gin – yes, by his own hand). On the upper two floors are six rooms and two suites (both with kitchens, lounges and dining tables) named after the English Romantic poets, each with an appropriate verse on the door and opulent décor reflecting their life. The Byron room, for example, is hung with landscapes of Venice, where the poet famously swam the Grand Canal. Miller's resonates with character, romance and old-world charm – the perfect choice for romantics seeking refuge from 21st-century life, or, like Gavin Rossdale and Stella McCartney, a flamboyant backdrop for a riotous party.

Style 9, Atmosphere 8, Location 8

myhotel Bloomsbury   *(right)*
11–13 Bayley Street,
Bloomsbury, WC1
Tel: 020 7667 6000
www.myhotels.co.uk
Rates: £169–269

When it opened in 1999, myhotel's minimalist white walls and feng shui philosophy were the talk of the town. Now, as the pendulum swings ever closer to maximalism, flashes of bright colour and softer textures have been introduced to temper the asceticism.

Its four-star rooms are tasteful, tranquil and bright, if on the small side, while clever design in the compact, white-tiled bathrooms (filled with BeeKind products) helps to create space. On the ground floor, Mybar is fitted out with modern design classics (Saarinen Tulip tables, Tom Dixon lights); the basement library houses arty tomes, complementary refreshments and two workstations – popular with the high proportion of corporate clients here. There is also a gym and treatment room, Mysnug, a cosy area that screens black-and-white movies, and its new restaurant Pinchito Tapas. A second branch is in Chelsea (35 Ixworth Place, SW3; 020 7225 7500). Both hotels ask guests to complete a form before arrival to help personalize their stay (feather or foam pillows, classical or pop music, etc) and rooms are customized accordingly. This clever gimmick helps Myhotel to feel like your hotel as soon you arrive.

Style 7, Atmosphere 7, Location 7

No. 5 Maddox Street *(middle)*
5 Maddox Street, Mayfair, W1
Tel: 020 7647 0200
www.no5maddoxst.com
Rates: £258–720

No. 5 Maddox Street is a discreet Mayfair hideaway that combines the luxury of 24-hour room service and a daily maid with the privacy and space of an apartment. Located just off Regent Street, it has 12 five-star one-, two- and three-bedroom suites with private kitchen facilities. All have understated design schemes (neutral tones, bamboo flooring, faux sable throws) and a stock of groceries ranging from 'good' (organic pasta) to 'bad' (peanut butter) to 'baddest' (Ben & Jerry's ice-cream); you can also order in restaurant meals or catering to feed entire parties. Also provided are kimono robes for lounging around, in-suite treatments from Thai massage to pilates and pedicures, and rentable bikes for exploring the city. Many suites have decked balconies while two have planted terraces, offering sanctu-

ary from the busy city below (read: it's not exactly about the views here). As the only public spaces are the tiny (but tasteful) reception and steep, five-floor stairwell (no lift), there's no communal buzz to talk of, and best to think of it as your personal pied-à-terre.

Style 7, Atmosphere 5, Location 9

Portobello Hotel *(left)*
22 Stanley Gardens, W11
Tel: 020 7727 2777
www.portobello-hotel.co.uk
Rates: £190–300

The décor may be whimsical and chintzy, but this privately owned bolthole has been servicing all manner of wild celebrities for over 35 years. A persistent rumour that Johnny Depp filled the Victorian bath in room 116 with champagne for Kate Moss, only to have a maid inadvertently drain it, is just one of the many stories feeding the mythology of Portobello Hotel. The 24 small-ish four-star rooms have a bohemian feel – each brimming with flowing drapes and eclectic antiques. Many have free-standing bathtubs in open alcoves next to sumptuous four-poster or circular beds. This hotel is the distilled essence of Notting Hill – insouciantly stylish with a sexy edge to traditional English foundations. After a heavy night, guests can refuel with breakfast in bed – his'n'hers trays serve porridge and a fry-up for him, muesli and a passion fruit salad for her. The restaurant is tiny, but nearby Julie's is under the same ownership, scene-filled and worth a visit; a stay also includes complimentary day membership to Boho party paradise The Cobden Club. Assuming you can be bothered to get out of bed, that is.

Style 8, Atmosphere 8, Location 8

The Rookery *(right)*
12 Peter's Lane,
Clerkenwell, EC1
Tel: 020 7336 0931

www.rookeryhotel.com
Rates: £189–301

The creation of friends Peter McKay and Douglas Blain (who also own Hazlitt's in Soho and who, as founding members of the Spitalfields Trust, are passionate about preserving Georgian property), The Rookery shares Hazlitt's historic charm despite its associations being rather less intellectual – it was once a brothel. Following extensive restoration to three adjoined (and near-derelict) 18th-century houses, The Rookery boasts 33 beautifully decorated four-star rooms (carved antique headboards, plush furnishings, claw-footed baths), mostly named after the building's residents over the last 250 years. The Rook's Nest, the most luxurious of the hotel's three suites, has magnificent views across London's rooftops from St Paul's to the Old Bailey, a vast four-poster, and a bathtub in the corner of the bedroom. Like Hazlitt's, The Rookery has gone for period-drama atmosphere over hi-tech mod-cons – think crooked floors, polished oak panelling, open fires and flagstone floors, and instead of a dining room or bar, there's breakfast in bed, or in the Conservatory, and an honesty bar. Plus the odd American wooed by the novelty of history.

Style 8, Atmosphere 8, Location 8

Rough Luxe   (top)
1 Birkenhead Street, WC1
Tel: 020 7837 5338
www.roughluxe.co.uk
Rates: £177–300

Note the oxymoron in the name. The wallpaper is peeling. There's no lift. Some rooms are unashamedly tiny. You might get a desk or wardrobe, you might not, and definitely not a fridge. That – obviously – is the 'rough' bit (or a very studied 'design' take on it). And the luxe? The London-based designer/owner Rabih Hage's impressive art collection throughout includes a portrait of Gilbert & George and Massimo Listri's transfixing trompe-l'oeil photographs of Italian palazzi. The bathrooms feature limestone tiling, chrome fittings and handmade Arran Aromatics toiletries (though not all nine Grade II-listed rooms are – shudder – ensuite). There's free WiFi. But most important is the sense of informal intimacy: there's no 'Sir' or 'Madam' and, if you like, plenty of long chats over the hotel's fine wine collection, perhaps in the pleasant private courtyard, or the basement breakfast room (they'll fetch champagne if desired because there's obviously no bar). The resident managers Antonio and Leo bring a continental *mi casa es su casa* vibe – if you want to cook in the (tiny and 'ironic' 1960s) kitchen, you can. But with such a clever concept, everything 'rough' just becomes art form.

Style 8, Atmosphere 7, Location 7

St John Hotel   (bottom)
1 Leicester Square, WC2
020 7251 0848
www.stjohnhotellondon.com
Rates: £200–750

Laughingly close to the mighty W Hotel is a David to W's Goliath. And if the folk behind St John – namely, the celebrated chef Fergus Hender-

son (see Eat) and business partner Trevor Gulliver – weren't so gracious, they might well laugh at W. Here, with zero aims on being 'boutique', 'grand' or 'superlative' is an intimate, 15-room inn (one suite) opened autumn 2010, almost like the olden days where staff know your name (something hotel manager Matthew Rivett relishes after 10 years at the Ritz). Except, of course, that it's very modern indeed – with signature St John whitewash, plus – gasp – some colour, with bold rubber flooring. But it's also modern in concept, with democratically fixed rates, an emphasis on value that promises a cuppa won't cost a tenner, and crisp rooms where everything can be laundered – none of this dust-gathering scatter-cushion fuss. Henderson is a qualified architect so it's a good fit, but food takes centre stage, with a formalish restaurant serving proper dinner till 2am and such Britishy things as (Henderson's take on) elevenses and afternoon tea, plus a lounge bar for diners and residents. But such is St John's following, whatever they do, they'll be laughing.

Style 8, Atmosphere 8, Location 8

St Martin's Lane   *(top)*
45 St Martin's Lane,
Covent Garden, WC2
Tel: 020 7300 5500
www.stmartinslane.com
Rates: £205–800

Opened in 1999, the five-star St Martin's Lane is slightly older – and less exclusive – in feel than its sister hotel The Sanderson, but remains equally

stylish. Its towering yellow-glass revolving doors (London's tallest) succinctly illustrates that staying here is a Statement. Giant chess pieces, gilt chairs and molar-teeth stools (all by St Martin's designer, Philippe Starck) are scattered across a soaring, dramatic lobby, while recessed niches are painted a welcoming deep yellow. Flashes of mood-altering colour are a recurring theme at St Martin's – each of the 204 bedrooms has an interactive light installation, allowing guests to bathe the space in a spectrum of colours at the flick of a switch. While not afraid of bold gestures, Starck has been careful not to over-design: there are pristine white beds, Lucite chairs and onyx desktops with floor-to-ceiling windows overlooking busy Covent Garden. If that induces agoraphobia, there's plenty to stay in for – including excellent champagne cocktails at the Martini advert-esque Light Bar, Asian/Cuban fusion food at its restaurant Asia de Cuba, and celeb-spotting as they spill out of the basement outpost of Amy Sacco's illustrious New York nightclub, Bungalow 8.

Style 8, Atmosphere 8, Location 8

The Sanderson   *(bottom)*
50 Berners Street, Fitzrovia, W1
Tel: 020 7300 1400
www.sandersonlondon.com
Rates: £225–800

When the partnership between hotelier Ian 'Studio 54' Schrager and design guru Philippe Starck produced The Sanderson in 2000, the media swooned, celebrities rocked up and aesthetes applauded. Inside a grey 1950s office block (the one-time Sanderson wallpaper factory), Starck has created a trippy, witty, modern dreamscape with floaty drapes and eclectic statement pieces – Cocteau-esque furniture, Louis XIV-inspired settees and carved African armchairs – set against a pure white canvas. The Long Bar, an 80ft glowing onyx rectangle, and the Malaysian restaurant Suka attract bright young girls and rich businessmen who mingle with a complicit sense of quid pro quo; the Purple Bar – a heady speakeasy-style Martini bar – is reserved for members and residents. A courtyard garden is open to the sky for most of the year while the cloud-like Agua spa is another oasis of calm. Moodily lit mauve corridors lead onto 91 five-star rooms, all without any internal walls – bathrooms are encased in clear glass boxes and levels of privacy are controlled with electronically operated white silk drapes. In-room sets of weights perfectly symbolise this appearance-focused establishment.

Style 8, Atmosphere 8, Location 8

....

Shoreditch Rooms *(top)*
Shoreditch House,
Ebor Street, E1
Tel: 020 7739 5040
www.shoreditchhouse.com
Rates: £75–115

The glacially-cool reputation of members' club Shoreditch House has been built on exclusivity and aspiration, so it is refreshing that its latest venture has a more egalitarian ethos. 26 small-but-perfectly-formed bedrooms are now open to all, costing from under £100. Better still, hotel guests have access to the club's facilities, including summer's Scene Central: its rooftop swimming pool. Bedrooms are elegantly decorated with simple, muted furnishings, wood-panelled walls and stylish 'traditional' bathrooms (though it's luxe rain showers over baths, plus Cowshed toiletries – there's a Cowshed spa on-site), plus thoughtful touches such as retro radios, vintage books, kettles and hot water bottles. The idea is to create a cosy home-from-home, which isn't too difficult given that all of the rooms are very compact. That said, it's unlikely that you'll spend much time there anyway – Shoreditch House is about the three Ps (partying, pampering and people-watching). The upper floors see the members' club action (bar, restaurant and pool) – there might be an awesome view of the city up top, but that's nothing compared to the fascinating sight of preening media wannabes, fashion folk and visiting A-listers.

Style 8, Atmosphere 9, Location 8

....

The Soho Hotel *(bottom)*
4 Richmond Mews, Soho, W1
Tel: 020 7559 3000
www.firmdale.com
Rates: £294–3,232

The five-star Soho was opened to much fanfare in autumn 2005 by Tim and Kit Kemp, the glamorous hoteliers fast monopolizing the industry in London. Although being their largest offering (with 91 rooms), it still has a boutique feel thanks to signature warm and

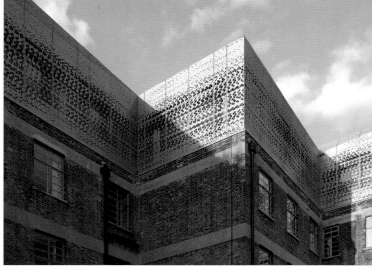

witty pastels and homely florals, and despite being in the centre of Soho, the hotel is set back in a quiet cul-de-sac. Purpose-built with a redbrick warehouse vibe on the site of a former car park, rooms are well proportioned and suffused with light; large granite and oak bathrooms feature Firmdale's standard bounty of Miller Harris toiletries. The ground-floor drawing rooms and library offer comfort and seclusion, while the bar/restaurant, Refuel, is packed with dressed-down media types from the power-breakfast hour till the final cocktail. As Soho's hippest haute hotel, the local film-industry crowd have embraced its public spaces while Hollywood execs have taken to block-booking the six top-floor apartments (the £3,232-a-night Terrace Suite, with views as far as Canary Wharf, has been lauded as the world's most glamorous hotel suite) and Hollywood A-listers have been known to prowl at large.

Style 8, Atmosphere 9, Location 8

....

■ **La Suite II**   *(top)*
24 Nottingham Place, W1
Tel: 020 7487 8100
www.lasuitehotel.com
Rates: £175–300

Design maven Anouska Hempel's trademark minimalism is instantly evident upon entering this Marylebone townhouse. A dramatic four-storey void spliced by a blade wall forms the spine of the central staircase and the 16 all-white, four-star suites have been artfully softened using beams of acid yellow light. Despite the flashy

design flourishes, function and form are equally important in this boutique bolthole aimed at style-conscious business travellers. Guestrooms have been based upon Japanese homes and feature floating walls which slide and pivot to transform the space into work, rest or sleeping areas. Each suite also has a tiny yet super-stylish kitchen, a slick bathroom with backlit mirrors and a 'media wall' housing every conceivable piece of electronic kit a travelling entrepreneur might need, plus a built-in PlayStation console for precious downtime. There's no hotel bar or restaurant (just the lobby which offers free cappuccinos and fruit, and a restaurant delivery service) – this is a sanctuary for silence. There's even a lending library (also in the lobby), with a fashionable selection of art, design and photography tomes. It's all very neat, high-tech and Zen-lite (so Hempel); romantics and pleasure-seekers should head elsewhere.

Style 8, Atmosphere 6, Location 9

....

■ **Town Hall**   *(bottom)*
Patriot Square, E2
Tel: 020 7871 0460
www.townhallhotel.com
Rates: £241–405

If you'd rather keep your eating habits (or dinner guests) private, look no further than Town Hall, opened in 2010 with some 92 apartments with their own discreet kitchens, and just six hotel rooms without. Set in Bethnal Green's long-abandoned yet stately Edwardian civic hall, the transformation evidently took much to-ing and fro-ing with

English Heritage – as a Grade II-listed building, structural changes were limited, so Paris/London-based design firm Rare Architects have restored many of the Art Deco public spaces to breathtaking effect, including an ornate cupola in the first-floor hallway and the gorgeous marble hall. Meanwhile, they have used box-like frameworks to 'drop' bedrooms and glass-cube bathrooms (with L'Occitane products) into the old chambers and offices, capitalising on their lofty proportions; rooms in the newly built top floor have a more contemporary feel, though don't feel as grand or unique as those with original features. Great swathes of elegant plasterwork, vintage furniture and a sprinkling of artwork by a new wave of YBAs make for a spectacular end-result. There's also a swimming pool, gym, bar and the destination restaurant, Viajante, run by El Bulli-trained chef Nuno Mendes (see Eat), making dining decisions very difficult indeed.

Style 10, Atmosphere 8, Location 7

....

W Hotel *(top)*
10 Wardour Street,
Leicester Square, W1
Tel: 020 7290 7231
www.wlondon.co.uk
Rates: £316–5,875

Someone forgot to tell Starwood, the giga-chain behind W hotels, about the recession. Going for pre-bust bling, with, for example, a 600-piece disco-ball 'cloud', is a £300 million, 194-bedroom, five-star blockbuster (literally, having taken out the block where the Swiss Centre once stood). Seemingly modelled on a colossal ice cube, the entire building is covered in a curved glass veil that by night glows according to the mood of the 'light DJ' (appropriate given the hotel is more like a nightclub). As well as the usual W treats – the Wyld Bar/club, lounge bar, restaurant, spa/gym and the W store (selling, predictably, skimpy party dresses), plus – phew – calmly designed rooms with feather-top mattresses, 350 thread-count Egyptian cotton sheets and goose-down duvets – it also promises insidery access to London Fashion Week and film previews in its own 48-seat cinema. Unashamedly appealing to the jet-set, perhaps it doesn't matter that, despite opening in October 2010, it's somewhat out of step with the zeitgeist, since the jet set will always appreciate W's wow-factor (even with 'extreme Wow' suites). No doubt a whole host of celebrities will find their spiritual home here.

Style 8, Atmosphere 8, Location 8

....

York & Albany *(bottom)*
127–129 Parkway, NW1
Tel: 020 7387 5700
www.gordonramsay.com/
yorkandalbany
Rates: £206–676

Given his inclination for outbursts, you'd sympathise if York & Albany's neighbours were somewhat disgruntled to have angry uberchef Gordon Ramsay arrive late 2009, with his first venture into hotels. But most are apparently pleased that the John Nash-designed Regency mansion-turned-Victorian pub that stood empty for 20

years has finally been put to good use. And besides, at the helm is Ramsay's altogether more amiable protégée Angela Hartnett MBE. As such, the 10 Russell Sage-appointed rooms (all different, all with king-size beds, Victorian antiques and discreet modern luxuries) are in much demand with gastro-tourists hungry for Hartnett's food morning, noon and night – on the ground floor is her upscale gastropub (complete with Sunday roasts, Monday pub quizzes, and a mean range of pizzas) and the retro-styled Nonna's deli for picnics on Regent's Park and Primrose Hill. When not at Murano (see Eat), Hartnett will happily oblige an audience, even taking a Saturday masterclass (£350). And because Hartnett is rather more popular than some chefs, her loyal team has stuck with her since Connaught days – including restaurant manager Odessa and hotel manager Fran, making for a homely, first-name feel. And not an f-word in sight.

Style 9, Atmosphere 8, Location 8

 The Zetter   (opposite)
86–88 Clerkenwell Road, EC1
Tel: 020 7324 4444
www.thezetter.com
Rates: £153–360

When restaurateurs Mark Sainsbury (son of Lord Sainsbury) and Michael Benyan – the backers behind Moro (see Eat) – opened the four-star Zetter in 2004, their aim was to offer comfort and style without the usual hefty London price tag. Mission accomplished: the 59 rooms are at once effortlessly stylish and reasonably priced. Housed in a converted Victorian warehouse in the heart of Clerkenwell, the slickly casual hotel retains many original 19th-century features, counterbalanced by a contemporary-meets-kitsch décor. Flashes of vintage wallpaper, chintzy carpet and classic 1960s furniture sing out in a predominantly calm design scheme. You'd expect a great restaurant from this dining duo, and indeed, in spring 2010, Bistrot Bruno Loubet (see Eat) opened to critical acclaim. For post-dinner drinks, retire to the high-camp retro cocktail lounge, Atrium. When that shuts, try the alcoholic vending machine, and then sink into bed with one of the secondhand Penguin classics provided. Not sleepy? From the comfort of your room, you can surf the web, rock out to one of the 4,000 music tracks available or flick the lighting panel to 'porno pink'. Enough said.

Style 8, Atmosphere 8, Location 8

the best of the rest...

the Firmdales...

Classic Kemp style means bold and beautiful contemporary English décor where none of the five-star rooms are the same. Expect Frette bed linen, oak and granite bathrooms, Miller Harris toiletries, gorgeous public rooms including libraries and drawing rooms with log fires, an honesty bar, and brasseries good enough to attract the locals.

Charlotte Street Hotel
15 Charlotte Street, Fitzrovia, W1
Tel: 020 7806 2000
www.charlottestreethotel.co.uk
Rates: £300–887
52 rooms with a Bloomsbury Set theme; with a red-leather basement cinema and buzzy brasserie, it's a magnet for media darlings

Covent Garden Hotel
10 Monmouth Street, WC2
Tel: 020 7806 1000
www.coventgardenhotel.co.uk
Rates: £300–395
Its sceney brasserie and 58 rooms and suites have endured as a London bolthole for fashion mavens and celebrities for over a decade

The Knightsbridge Hotel
10 Beaufort Gardens, SW3
Tel: 020 7584 6300
www.knightsbridgehotel.com
Rates: £258–595
44 rooms in a quiet tree-lined street, a stone's throw from Knightsbridge's exclusive boutiques; sets out to be (relatively) affordable

Number Sixteen
16 Sumner Place,
South Kensington, SW7
Tel: 020 7589 5232
www.numbersixteenhotel.co.uk
Rates: £229–329
An ultra-stylish take on a B&B with 42 rooms, an airy conservatory and a pretty, tree-filled garden; useful for museum buffs

for good value...

22 York Street
Marylebone, W1
Tel: 020 7224 2990
www.22yorkstreet.co.uk
Rates: £120
Homely 10-room B&B, run by Liz and Michael Callis in a Georgian townhouse, with a warm (if aged) French farmhouse feel

Bermondsey Square Hotel
Bermondsey Square, Tower Bridge Road, SE1
Tel: 020 7378 2450
www.bermondseysquarehotel.co.uk
Rates: £99–359
79 contemporary four-star rooms and suites including one with a rooftop hot tub in the gentrified locale of Bermondsey

Harlingford Hotel
61 Cartwright Gardens, WC1
Tel: 020 7387 1551
www.harlingfordhotel.com
Rates: £112–£120
A sweet three-star hotel in Bloomsbury with 44 interior-designed rooms, some overlooking the private gardens and tennis court, all with exclusive access to it

The Mandeville Hotel
Mandeville Place, Marylebone, W1
Tel: 020 7935 5599
www.mandeville.co.uk
Rates: £176–388
This edgy-pretty four-star hotel is some way towards the economy of

scale – with 142 (often small) rooms, it's a place for good deals when shopping in Marylebone village, St Christopher's Place and Selfridges is a priority

The Sumner
54 Upper Berkeley Street,
Marble Arch, W1
Tel: 020 7723 2244
www.thesumner.com
Rates: £165–182
Sober and understated, with 20 four-star rooms with a modern luxe design scheme; plus a log fire in the sitting room, air con, honesty bar and free WiFi

Hotel Indigo
16 London Street, W2
Tel: 020 7706 4444
www.hotelindigo.com
Rates: £159–297
Budget boutique hotel near Paddington, with 63 fresh and modern four-star rooms from the Holiday Inn group

the grande dames…

Corinthia Hotel London
Whitehall Place, SW1
Tel: 020 7930 8181
www.corinthialondon.com
Rates: £516–1,763
('plus service charge')
Opened late 2010, The Corinthia comes with big ambitions: 300 spacious, five-star rooms on the Thames and London's largest spa in the restored shell of the Ministry of Defence.

The Lanesborough
Hyde Park Corner, SW1
Tel: 020 7259 5599
www.lanesborough.com
Rates: £582–840
The archetypal grande dame with the double privilege of overlooking both Green Park and Hyde Park, the five-star Lanesborough's 49 rooms and 46 suites are large and opulent and its butlers bow and scrape to all legal whims

The Savoy
Strand, WC2
Tel: 020 7836 4343
www.the-savoy.com
Rates: £411–1,763
The 121-year-old five-star landmark on the river finally returns late 2010, with an extravagant £200 million refurbishment of its Edwardian and Art Deco influences in its celebrated Savoy Grill (run by the Gordon Ramsay group), American Bar and 268 rooms

homely hotels…

Fox & Anchor
115 Charterhouse Street, Clerkenwell, EC1
Tel: 0845 347 0100
www.foxandanchor.com
Rates: £117–294
Six rooms above a boozer (see Pubs), but very much with 21st-century standards: Miller Harris toiletries, Bose speakers, copper baths, plus a meaty fry-up in the mornings in keeping with its proximity to Smithfield Meat Market.

The Orange

37 Pimlico Road, SW1
Tel: 020 7881 9844
www.theorange.co.uk/sleeping.html
Rates: £182–225
Restaurant-quality room-service because these four king-sized rooms, luxuriously appointed with aircon, blonde woods and crisp linens, are above the Orange gastropub (run by the Thomas Cubitt management; see PUBS)

San Domenico House

29 Draycott Place, SW3
Tel: 020 7581 5757
www.sandomenicohouse.com
Rates: £235–310
Oodles of romantic charm in 15 individually themed rooms, with four-poster beds, 19th-century furniture, and toile de Jouy fabrics

for romantic affairs...

Blakes

33 Roland Gardens, South Kensington, SW7
Tel: 020 7370 6701
www.blakeshotels.com
Rates: £265–565
The theatrical first venture of Anouska Hempel – heavily swagged rooms with a sumptuous, boudoir feel, trompe-l'oeil murals and fantastical beds bedecked in exotic silks

The Gore

190 Queen's Gate,
South Kensington, SW7
Tel: 020 7584 6601
www.gorehotel.com

Rates: £159–411
Stuffed with antiques, curios and over 5,000 pictures, it has the air of an eccentric country house with 50 four-star trad-with-a-twist rooms

The Pelham

15 Cromwell Place, London SW7
Tel: 020 7589 8288
www.pelhamhotel.co.uk
Rates: £200–294
The Gore's sister hotel, acquired from the Kemp-ire, is predictably a fresher, more contemporary affair, with 52 five-star rooms conveniently located for museum action

temples to modernity...

Baglioni

60 Hyde Park Gate, Kensington, SW7
Tel: 020 7368 5700
www.baglionihotellondon.com
Rates: £260–385
66 five-star rooms, with sleek, modern furniture and a palette of black and gold with flashes of scarlet, plus B&O phones and Gaggia coffee machines

The Halkin

5 Halkin Street, Belgravia, SW1
Tel: 020 7333 1000
www.halkin.como.bz
Rates: £225–385
A prevailing sense of stealth wealth over 41 five-star muted bedrooms in soft, earthy tones with strong black accents, Bulgari toiletries and high-tech controls, plus Armani-uniformed staff

High Road House
162 Chiswick High Road, W4
Tel: 020 8742 1717
www.highroadhouse.co.uk
Rates: £140–160
The Soho House for the nappy valley
– Nick Jones' 14-room media haunt
designed by Ilse Crawford with fresh
colours and eclectic furniture

Sanctum Soho Hotel
20 Warwick Street, Soho, W1
Tel: 020 7292 6100
www.sanctumsoho.com
Rates: £200–681
The spiritual home of Spinal Tap,
the 30-roomed five-star Sanctum is
pitched as a playpen for rock stars,
complete with Wii consoles, round
beds, a cinema and a roof terrace with
24-hour cocktail bar and hot tub

For Something A Little More Personal…

If staying in a hotel makes you feel like the outsider, and you're ready for something a little more intimate short of a one-night-stand, check out **www.Airbnb.com**, a global listing service including nightly rentals in London of people's own bedrooms and apartments of all standards from suburban bedsits to design-porn loft apartments (variously with or without the owner present, from $38). Referred to as 'Ebay for space', it's an online marketplace for private accommodation where user-generated reviews lend an honest impartiality. The five-star version of that is 'the unhotel', **www.onefinestay.com,** which uses Londoners' empty homes (all of a fine aesthetic standard), and delivers the service of a hotel: The White Company toiletries in bathrooms, maid service if desired, and 24/7 concierge if required (from £125). And the free version is **www.couchsurfing.com** – there are some 10,000 Londoners happy to host a stranger in their own home. All 'couches' (be it the sofa in the living room, the spare bedroom, floor space, or even tent space) come with positive, neutral or negative references (or none at all), so with good sense, it's difficult to place yourselves in grave danger – though getting your own space is also unlikely. The network also delivers an instant social life – local drinks and dinners, house parties, film screenings, sporting appreciation, and Londoners happy to meet for a drink to share a few insiders' tips (you don't actually have to face the intimacy of wandering around in your towel in front of strangers – you can do all this from your hotel).

The will to open doors to strangers really does come from altruism, a readiness to share what's theirs, and an up-for-it sociability. The rewards for the traveller are priceless – you'll see how a real Londoner lives (or African, or American, or Antarctican – every continent and practically every country is represented), what they eat for dinner, how they like to party. You'll meet their friends, maybe their family, and you'll return with a depth and connection to London (or Brooklyn, or Berlin, or Barcelona) that no concierge, no matter how obliging, can deliver.

Pizza East

eat…

The days when eating out in London meant enduring overcooked meat and boiled-to-oblivion vegetables are, for the most part, long gone. You may, if you look hard enough, find better French cuisine in Paris and more authentic dim sum in Hong Kong, but for the sheer breadth of dining experiences on offer, London now leads the way (if we say so ourselves). Prices can be high, but then so too is quality – only the tourist traps of the West End still charge astronomical prices for truly appalling food.

As for trends, high-end modern French remains eternally popular (purveyed by Britain's three-Michelin-star superchef Gordon Ramsay and the world's most Michelin-starred chef Joel Robuchon), although there has also been a welcome return to simplicity, with the likes of Racine, newcomer Bruno Loubet and the inevitable proliferation of Galvin offering upmarket reinventions of Gallic bistro classics. There is some exceptional Italian (notably at Locanda Locatelli and Murano), some thrilling new-Indian (at the Cinnamon Club), and some pretty good Spanish (at Barrafina and Brindisa). In fact, whether you want contemporary oriental, modern British, North African or just plain cosmopolitan, you'll find it somewhere in London – and increasingly, three times a day as the fashionable power breakfast is added to the menu (try The Wolseley, Automat and Cecconi's).

There's also a trend towards 'diffusion' restaurants, with top chefs (read: brands) such as Gordon Ramsay and Tom Aikens branching out with pubs, bistros and even a hotel (Ramsay), and two new outlets at Somerset House (Aikens). But perhaps most excitingly, a renaissance for robust yet simple British food is afoot. Championed by the likes of St John, HIX Soho and Magdalen, it makes a virtue of the unpretentious, and while it sometimes borrows from France, Italy and Spain, its heart – and ingredients – are firmly rooted in home soil. Saint Fergus Henderson of St John (who quietly advocated nose-to-tail cooking) has arguably spawned a cultural shift, with disciples at Hereford Road and The Anchor & Hope – his genius is in bringing a kind of exoticism from our own land. Meanwhile, a bright bunch of new-wave Kiwis – Anna Hansen at Modern Pantry, Miles Kirby at Caravan – are cooking modest yet imaginative food (having both worked with Kiwi godfather Peter Gordon of Providores), combined with an inimitable Kiwi service that's relaxed yet efficient (you should see what the Antipodeans are doing with coffee; see Snack). Even honorary Brit John Torode's effortless Aussie bonhomie at his new joint The Luxe can't help but cheer the atmosphere.

Ramsay's new resto, Pétrus, didn't make the grade because we felt it didn't chime with the times (see The Death of Fine-Dining). It does however, like Gordon Ramsay at Claridge's, feature the 'chef's table' – essentially a reality-TV-like viewing platform positioned right inside the kitchen. It's an admittedly thrilling place to be, but more endearing are London's other eminent chefs who have resisted going global to do smaller, more meaningful projects – such as Mark Hix who stepped down from heading up Caprice Holdings (owners of The Ivy, Scott's etc) to run his own kitchens, and Sir Terence Conran, who has put his clout behind a 'personal' food and design project with his wife.

Other well-known names have been omitted from these pages. Where are those hardy perennials The Ivy, Le Gavroche, Le Caprice? The answer is, first, we thought you might know about them already. But, secondly, we've tried to recommend places where you don't necessarily have to book months in advance to get a table. So Sheekey's, for example, is owned by the same group as The Ivy, and is just as exciting, but a reservation is easier to come by. In most cases, booking ahead is still essential, but it is always worth calling at the last minute to check for cancellations. Third, we've conceded, with a comprehensive roundup at the end of this section.

London restaurants tend not to have extended annual closing periods; with the exception of Christmas Day and possibly Easter Sunday, many are open year round. Though if you want to eat on a public holiday, do call to check they're open. Restaurants are rated here in three categories: food (quality of the cooking and presentation), service (efficiency and warmth) and atmosphere. The price has been calculated on the cost of three à la carte courses for one with half a bottle of wine. An optional service charge (12.5% is generally the norm) is usually added to the final total. If you're paying by credit card, make sure you aren't paying the charge twice – unless, of course, you want to.

The Death Of Fine-Dining

London foodies are over astronomical gastronomy. Post recession, luxury is – gasp! – out of fashion and the Towers of Babel have been toppled. Instead of the studied fanciness, oppressive formality and cheffy faffing of more ostentatious dining, diners are choosing something altogether more honest, better value and spirited. The economic downturn has not stemmed the flow of new restaurants (nearly half of the following reviews are new entries), but it has radically changed their philosophy.

So it's fine-cooking over fine-dining – in all sorts of fresh guises. It explains the popularity of the modern bistro model, where layers of imagination have been applied to a humble onion soup, say (at Bistrot Bruno Loubet). There's the tiny but mighty Polpo (that's proved so successful that a second, Spuntino, was inevitable). Perhaps the very epitome of the new mood, Polpo mixes New York's egalitarian walk-in culture with Venice's friendly tapas-style sharing plates, all at honest, good-value prices. Wine is served in modest carafes (as at Arbutus and Terroirs; see Snack) – an effective shorthand for saying that good times are rated over, say, Pétrus.

Similarly, the trend for sharing tiny plates (Polpo, Bocca di Lupo, Caravan) and massive roasts alike (HIX Soho, Magdalen, The Anchor & Hope) only helps to jolly the experience, gets people talking about food, and finally allows us to make the kind of mess that the starchy white tablecloths forbade. And all-day dining? It's down with rules, and up with eating what and when you like. The rise of bar-eating (especially lovely for two) – at J Sheekey's new oyster bar, Bocca di Lupo, Barrafina, Polpo (again) – also serves to break down the barriers; the bar is basically the chef's table, without costing hundreds of pounds for the privilege.

But there is a new variety of privilege afoot – it's very democratic, exceptionally good value and very friendly indeed. It's the underground restaurant movement, where amateur chefs open up their own kitchens to cook for cash, and of course, the love of it. Given that these are not businesses, they are prone to come and go, so the best way to find them is online – though when you have, do book ahead. Some have even been so successful that they've gone overground, for example Nuno Mendes' Viajante. Perhaps Gordon Ramsay should open up his home.

the best restaurants...

Top Ten:
1. Bistrot Bruno Loubet
2. Polpo
3. HIX Soho
4. Boundary Restaurant
5. St John
6. Viajante
7. The Wolseley
8. Modern Pantry
9. Corrigan's
10. Scott's

Food:
1. Marcus Wareing
2. Bistrot Bruno Loubet
3. Murano
4. Viajante
5. St John

Service:
1. Viajante
2. Boundary Restaurant
3. Modern Pantry
4. Caravan
5. Scott's

Atmosphere:
1. Polpo
2. HIX Soho
3. Pizza East
4. The Wolseley
5. Barrafina

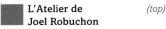 **L'Atelier de** *(top)*
Joel Robuchon

13 West Street, Covent Garden, WC2
Tel: 020 7010 8600
www.joel-robuchon.com
Open: daily, noon–3pm, 5.30–11pm
(10.30pm Sun)

French **£80**

The superchef is becoming a global brand: working the same formula already applied to Paris, Tokyo, New York, Vegas and Hong Kong comes L'Atelier de Joel Robuchon, where guests sit at a sultrily illuminated counter as tapas-style French dishes with Italian and Spanish influences are prepared by the chef in front of them (hence l'atelier, or workshop). Of course, 'chef' is unlikely to be Robuchon himself, on account of prior commitments, but since he's the world's most Michelin-starred chef, London is evidently pleased to have him – or his brand. The concept might lack the stars or culinary acrobatics of his more prestigious sisters, but it still provides a spellbinding insight into Robuchon's magic, and can be good value if you have the discipline to stick to the set menus; largely though, it's stonkingly expensive, not least since portions are decidedly nouvelle. Upstairs, La Cuisine is a more formal affair: the food more fiddly, the bill more immoderate, the charm somewhat dimmed. For that you need to skip upstairs again to Le Bar where a dramatic fireplace, seductive cocktails and more await, including a new roof terrace and Robuchon's take on afternoon tea – quite the fit for this fuss-food.

Food 9, Service 8, Atmosphere 7

 **Automat** *(bottom)*
33 Dover Street, Mayfair, W1
Tel: 020 7499 3033
www.automat-london.com
Open: 7am–11am, noon–midnight
Mon–Fri; 10am–11pm (10pm Sun)
Sat/Sun

American **£48**

There's no doubting Automat's A-list aspirations. This upmarket take on an American diner is the brainchild of Carlos Almada, the jet-set Argentine restaurateur behind New York's 1990s fashionista favourite Man Ray. Almada has always cultivated a starry following, and when Automat opened in 2005, there was no shortage of famous faces to wish him well; Alexander McQueen held a party here before the doors even opened. The celeb count has fallen off a bit since, but the place still draws a glamorous crowd, all happily chowing down on upscale comfort food (there's lobster and fish cakes as well as mac'n'cheese and chicken noodle soup). Add in a buzzy brasserie vibe, sparky staff and a kitchen that works seamlessly from breakfast to dinner, and this Mayfair slice of the Big Apple has considerable appeal. Most seating is out back in a bright, white-tiled cafeteria-like room with an open kitchen, but if you want to get intimate, book a booth in the 'dining car', where dark leather seats and a polished wooden ceiling give the luxurious feel of a 1920s railway carriage. The real ticket, though, is to one of Almada's after-dark parties in the basement den.

Food 7, Service 7, Atmosphere 8

eat...

Barrafina *(left)*
54 Frith Street, Soho, W1
Tel: 020 7813 8016
www.barrafina.co.uk
Open: noon–3pm, 5–11pm Mon–Sat;
1–3.30pm, 5.30–10.30pm Sun
Spanish £37

Sam and Eddie Hart's original restaurant Fino (33 Charlotte Street, W1; 020 7813 8010) was a shoo-in for the title of best Spanish in town. Now, though, it just feels like a warm-up for the main event. That being Barrafina: everything about the restaurant – which the brothers opened in 2007 – is bang on, from the food to the concept to the décor. Modelled on the iconic Barcelona tapas joint Cal Pep, there's an L-shaped metal bar with just 23 stools and an open kitchen, where chefs furiously chop and cook. The zippy menu is heavy on grilled seafood – clams, langoustines, and giant prawns – plus tuna tartare, fabulous Spanish ham and pitch-perfect renditions of tapas-bar staples such as *croquetas* and egg tortillas. It's a turn-up-and-wait number – sometimes even for 30 minutes (at peak times the place attracts queues of voracious media folk) – but cold Seville beer and the smell of pristine shellfish being given a dose of flame and garlic mean it's hardly an onerous experience. In summer, battle it out for one of the eight al fresco tables and watch the beau monde go by.

Food 9, Service 8, Atmosphere 8

Bistrot Bruno Loubet *(middle)*
at The Zetter
86-88 Clerkenwell Road, EC1
Tel: 020 7324 4455
www.bistrotbrunoloubet.com
Open: 7–10.30am, noon–2.30pm, 6–
10.30pm Mon–Fri; 7.30–11am, noon–
2.30pm, 6–10.30pm Sat/Sun
French £43

The fact that this place is constantly

stuffed to the gills with extremely grateful guys who have been waiting their whole (soon-to-be short) lives for Loubet's perfect, French heart-attack food should not put you off. After a decade in Australia, most chefs return with a lightened style. Not Loubet, who returned with a menu of traditional bistro food cleverly reinvented with layers of meaning, but never pointlessly monkeyed with. Let's call it 'posh rough', as Loubet outstandingly combines rustic comfort with elegance – onion soup comes with emmenthal soufflé atop, while ingredients like quinoa feature alongside more recognisably French dishes like snails and crepes suzettes. Thus it opened (in spring 2010) to massive applause and it's why most nights you can find a restaurant critic eating in here for fun. And don't expect the turgid interiors of most hotel restaurants; go-to guy Russell Sage has done an expert make-under of the space, with salvaged wood furniture and crisp white walls. The wine list is robust and interesting for all pockets, with a strong focus on southwest France. Service can be bossy, but overall, this is one hot ticket for all but the miserable weight watcher.

Food 9, Service 7, Atmosphere 9

....

Bob Bob Ricard   *(right)*
1 Upper James Street, Soho, W1
Tel: 020 3145 1000
www.bobbobricard.com
Open: noon–11.30pm Mon–Fri; 11am
–11.30pm Sat; 11am–10.30pm Sun
Eclectic   **£50**

'Press for Champagne!' Actually, don't, because it's much quicker just to flag down one of the kitschly attired waiting staff (pale pink waistcoats for boys, turquoise blazers for girls), but these service buttons in each teal-toned booth are emblematic of Bob Bob Ricard's amalgam of charm and originality. Named after its two best-friend

owners, Richard Howarth and Leonid 'Bob' Shutov ('Bob' has a two-thirds share, hence Bob Bob), BBR combines wit, luxury and start-up enthusiasm to create an enchanting dining experience. The Wolseley was undoubtedly mentioned to arch-designer David Collins who created a grand salon to the theme of the Orient Express-meets-American diner (Art Deco lighting, fixed dark-wood tables in booths, velvet curtains for intimacy). The feel-good factor extends to the food: think diner classics (burgers, milkshakes, knickerbocker glories), life's luxuries (caviar, lobster, chateaubriand) and original dishes not found elsewhere – 'Bob' is Russian so there's *vareniki* and *pelmeni* (Russian ravioli, essentially – appealing to the novi Ruskis). There's also a price guarantee on wine where mark-up is capped at £50, unlike its competitors. This doesn't mean, insists the management, that people get more drunk here. It's far too civilised for that.

Food 7, Service 9, Atmosphere 7

Boundary Restaurant *(left)*
2–4 Boundary St, Shoreditch, E2
Tel: 020 7729 1051
www.theboundary.co.uk
Open: 6.30–10pm Mon/Sat; noon–3pm, 6.30–10.30pm Tues–Fri; noon–4pm Sun
French/English £40

When Terence Conran sold his restaurant empire, everyone assumed that that was it – the man who had democratised British design with Habitat and made eating out pleasurable again with his slick restaurants was taking a bow. Then he opened the Boundary, his first private venture since Bibendum in the 1980s. This well-run, multi-purpose space is a personal project between him and his wife Vicki, and represents all that the couple loves: contemporary British art (largely from his private collection), hotel rooms designed after

the great modern architects, and the sort of fresh, seasonal British food they grow and eat on their Berkshire estate. The menu is brief, straightforward and executed just-so, like a velvety wild garlic soup or simply, smoked eel. Shellfish, game and charcuterie are all outstanding; the French dishes are rich, heavy treats, and service is personable and impeccable. It's hard to find a single gripe – except perhaps that the basement room is not ideal for sunny lunches. But watching handsome head chef Henrik Ritzen work the turquoise-tiled kitchen like a very muscular ballet dancer is a lively diversion from the sunshine.

Food 9, Service 10, Atmosphere 8

Brick Lane & around *(right)*
E1
Bangladeshi/Indian/Pakistani

Running through the heart of London's Bangladeshi community, Brick Lane is, on the face of it, a pretty good place to go looking for curry. The street is home to a seemingly endless array of Indian restaurants, all gaudily lit in the hope of attracting passing punters, and when business is slack, touts are sent out onto the pavement to charm diners inside. If all you're after is something hot and spicy to round off a night on the beers, then take your pick – the food tastes much the same in all of them, due to the widespread use of generic sauces. But don't expect anything particularly good or authentic. For that, head off the main drag to **New Tayyabs** (83 Fieldgate Street, E1; 020 7247 9543), where the excellent North Indian and Pakistani grills and *karahi* (wok) dishes constantly play to a packed house. A little further afield is the **Lahore Kebab House** (2 Umberston Street, E1; 020 7488 2551), an extremely basic Pakistani canteen serving some of the East End's best curries and kebabs – all at ludicrously low prices.

Le Café Anglais *(top)*

8 Porchester Gardens, Bayswater, W2
Tel: 020 7221 1415
www.lecafeanglais.co.uk
Open: daily, noon–3.30pm, 6.30–11pm (11.30pm Fri/Sat, 10.15pm Sun)

European **£45**

It's worth riding out the shame of stepping into Whiteleys shopping mall to enter the foodie heaven of Roux-trained chef-with-brains Rowley Leigh – he who in 1987 gave London the agenda-setting restaurant Kensington Place (don't bother – he's left). Le Café Anglais is a homage to European cuisine (French, British, Italian) of yesteryear – there are plenty of historical references for foodie nerds to decipher, plenty of old-fashioned dishes to bewilder the young (eggs en gelée, anyone?) and a kitchen-full of complex, grown-up flavours (game, eel, kippers etc – Leigh's moreish parmesan custard with anchovy toast has taken on cult status), cooked up with plenty of acclaimed, creative ambition. That, and a French-heavy wine list, is served up by friendly if at times confused staff in a pleasingly spacious, sweeping Art Deco salon filled with light and crispness. Special events, such as bridge classes and Le Ciné Anglais (an open film and supper club) ensure a steady flow of fans and midlife plutocrats, from eminent political writers to aging lothario pop stars, many of whom count themselves friends of one of the industry's most likeable men. Not that there's much competition.

Food 8, Service 6, Atmosphere 8

Caravan *(bottom)*

11 Exmouth Market, EC1
Tel: 020 7833 8115
www.caravanonexmouth.co.uk
Open: 8–11am, noon–11pm Mon–Fri; 10am–4pm, 5–11pm Sat; 10am–4pm, 5–10pm Sun

Kiwi/Eclectic **£31**

This Farringdon newcomer (opened spring 2010) is headed up by a pair of Kiwis whose combined CVs include time with fashionable caterers Urban Caprice and head-cheffing for fellow New Zealander and Pacific Rim godfather, Peter Gordon, at the Providores. Almost instinctively, they have covered about all that's current on the foodie scene in their glass-wrapped corner spot on Exmouth Market. An all-day menu. A combination of snacks, small plates and grown-up main courses (accompanied by a snappy, similarly well-chosen wine list). An Antipodean fastidiousness about coffee (they roast their own beans in the basement and do proper drip-fed filter for those that sneer at the Americano, with a choice of single-origin coffees to satisfy the most discerning of caffeine geeks). And of course, friendly Kiwi efficiency on the floor, and that know-how in the kitchen – named to reflect the globe-trotting pick'n'mix menu, Caravan mixes Asian with European influences, delivering, for example, Sichuan pepper squid with chilli mayonnaise, veal schnitzel with gypsy potatoes. But it's perhaps at breakfast or over a relaxed weekend brunch that its charms are best appreciated, and its coffee most needed.

Food 8, Service 9, Atmosphere 8

Cecconi's *(top)*
Burlington Gardens, Mayfair, W1
Tel: 020 7434 1500
www.cecconis.co.uk
Open: daily, 7am (8am Sat/Sun)–1am
(midnight Sun)
Italian £44

This Mayfair Italian has been through many changes in the last two decades. From being the favoured haunt of the rich and royal during the 1980s, its fashionable credentials went rapidly downhill when the original owner, Enzo Cecconi (the erstwhile youngest ever manager of Venice's Cipriani), sold up in 1999. Now though, Cecconi's is riding high again under the ownership of Nick Jones, the brains behind Soho House members' clubs in London and New York. He summoned his long-time collaborator, the interiors guru Ilse Crawford, who created a graceful, classic space with striped black-and-white marble floors, mirrored walls, and those gorgeous spearmint leather chairs. The all-day menu – courtesy of chef Simone Serafini – offers decent Italian classics, from lobster spaghetti to osso bucco, plus a concession to British breakies in the morning, and a range of Venetian-style *cicchetti* (tapas) to be taken at the grand island bar, as in Venice. But the food isn't really the point. This is a restaurant where the beautiful people go (Jones has since opened an LA outpost) and its proximity to the designer boutiques of Bond Street and art galleries of Cork Street ensures it vibrates with a glitzy cross-generational crowd.

Food 7, Service 7, Atmosphere 8

Club Gascon *(bottom)*
57 West Smithfield, EC1
Tel: 020 7796 0600
www.clubgascon.com
Open: noon–2pm, 7–10pm (10.30pm
Fri/Sat). Closed Sat lunch and Sun.
French £75

Housed in a former Lyon's Coffee House on the edge of Smithfield meat market, Pascal Aussignac's restaurant is a temple to Gascon gastronomy, the robust cooking of southwest France (cassoulet, duck, foie gras etc). Aussignac's thoughtful reinvention makes for a modern and mind-blowing menu that now boasts a Michelin star and, offering no fewer than 10 variations of foie gras, it's become a mecca for it. Having been instrumental in the industry's sharing revolution, dishes come tapas-sized so that everyone gets to try a bit of everything (five or six dishes per person make up a full meal), though you can still keep it all for yourself with an à la carte menu. The elegant room and good French wine list make it a popular spot for business lunches, but in the evenings true gastronauts take over. If you don't want the full blowout, there's Cellar Gascon, a wine-tasting and tapas bar next door and a deli/café on the other side of the market (Comptoir Gascon, 61 Charterhouse Street, EC1; 020 7608 0851). The same team is behind Le Cercle in Chelsea (1 Wilbraham Place, SW1; 020 7901 9999), a more modern space, equally modern concept.

Food 9, Service 7, Atmosphere 7

Corrigan's *(left)*
28 Upper Grosvenor Street,
Mayfair, W1
Tel: 020 7499 9943
www.corrigansmayfair.com
Open: noon–3pm, 6–10.30pm
Mon–Fri; 6–11pm, Sat; noon–4pm,
6–9.30pm Sun
European   **£45**

Corrigan's comes from the heart. The smart yet substantial modern European food with a strong British/Irish bent is worthy of Michelin praise, but Richard Corrigan, a big Irish character often seen chatting and drinking in his dining room after service, isn't one for pandering to the whims of inspectors. He does what he wants, be that punchy curry flavours or a delicate Cornish crab jelly. The menu is strong on flesh, with, for example, deconstructed steak and kidney pie, or linguine cooked in red wine with pecorino and bone mar-

row, but he's also a natural host, so when Stella McCartney comes in – a strict veggie – he'll do her something special (though for fish, best head to his other institution, Bentley's Oyster Bar, 11 Swallow Street, Piccadilly, W1; 020 7734 4756). Designer Martin Brudnizki (also responsible for St Pancras Grand, Scott's and HIX Soho) has preserved the grandeur of what was once the Grosvenor Hotel's fine-dining room, adding some masculine modernity – a dark, oak-panelled room with a New York steakhouse vibe (Mayfair hedgies love its clubby atmosphere). Corrigan likes his restaurant to be used so it's equally good for a quick bite at the bar or meandering indulgence, though service can be over-familiar if you're used to formality – Corrigan's warmth is evidently infectious.

Food 9, Service 7, Atmosphere 8

E&O
(right)

14 Blenheim Crescent,
Notting Hill, W11
Tel: 020 7229 5454
www.rickerrestaurants.com
Open: noon–3pm, 6–11pm Mon–Fri;
noon–11pm Sat; 12.30–10.30pm Sun

Pan-Asian   **£42**

E&O (standing for Eastern and Oriental) is the restaurant that first ignited the trend for pan-Asian dining in London. While other places now arguably outperform Will Ricker's smart Notting Hill hangout on the food, its merit as a social stalwart (where louche lunches last the afternoon) keeps the reservations line busy. The menu runs the gamut from dim sum, tempura and sashimi to fragrant soups and salads, all stunningly presented and with tantalizing layers of flavour. Oversized lampshades and muted colours give the dining room a chic contemporary feel, while model-turned-waiter staff and a supporting cast of faux-boho Notting Hillites mean there are few better places for edging in on West London's moneyed scene. There might be more suits in evidence these days, but early visits from the likes of Nicole Kidman (who once named it her favourite London restaurant), Elton John and Madonna have ensured that E&O remains see-and-be-seen central for famous faces and locals alike. If you can't make it to Notting Hill, check out E&O's sister restaurants, Eight Over Eight (392 King's Road, SW3; 020 7349 9934) and XO (29 Belsize Lane, NW3; 020 7433 0888). Same beautiful food, different beautiful people.

Food 8, Service 8, Atmosphere 9

Galvin Bistrot de Luxe *(top)*

66 Baker Street, Marylebone, W1
Tel: 020 7935 4007
www.galvinrestaurants.com
Open: daily, noon–2.30pm (3pm Sun),
6–10.30pm (9.30pm Sun)
French £53

Move over, Albert and Michel Roux. With over 50 years of cheffing experience between the two Galvin brothers (Chris was head chef at the Wolseley; Jeff cooked at L'Escargot), they have proved themselves the standard-bearers for London's cuisine bourgeoise revival. Their visionary reworking of unpretentious French bistro classics (steaks, stews and braises, confits, terrines et parfaits) has also proved recession-resistant, and they've been quietly spreading their influence over the capital ever since opening their Marylebone flagship in 2005 (all wood panelling and leather benches in a nostalgic nod to French brasseries). After 'Galvin', as the original brasserie is known, and its more casual onsite wine bar Le Bar, came Galvin at Windows, for food with a view from the top of the Hilton (22 Park Lane, W1; 020 7208 4021), and, in 2009, Galvin La Chapelle and its lower-key, lower-cost annexe Café de Luxe. Set in the stunning downtown-style conversion of the Grade II-listed St Botolph's Hall (steel, glass and brick under soaring vaulted ceilings), La Chapelle is wooing City suits, and, as such, the service is tuned towards obsequiousness. But such is their following, quality control is involuntarily outsourced to its steadfast devotees, who grumble when dishes are replaced, or if that formula shifts,

or (be warned) when other diners complain.

Food 8, Service 7, Atmosphere 7

HIX Soho *(bottom)*

66 Brewer Street, Soho, W1
Tel: 020 7292 3518
www.hixsoho.co.uk
Open: daily, noon–3pm, 5–11pm (bar open: daily, noon–midnight)
British £42

Mark Hix is friends with interesting and important people, including every contemporary British artist you've ever heard of, several of whom – Damien Hirst, Sarah Lucas, Tim Noble and Sue Webster – have provided Hix with art, including bespoke mobiles which hang over the noisy, café-style dining room designed by Martin Brudnizki. Even ex-Blur bassist Alex James provides the cheese. Hix has a devoted following among the in-crowd, who crowd around his restaurants (also Hix Oyster & Chop House, 36 Greenhill's Rents, EC1; 020 7017 1930, and, tellingly, within Selfridges: HIX Restaurant and Champagne Bar; 020 7499 5400). Hix's passionate menu is hearty, manly, fleshy, juicy, a little bit messy and British. It's a foodie dream – spring leek and nettle soup with mendip snails, cod tongues with hazelnuts – though Hix is not afraid to serve fish and chips with a bottle of Sarson's. This confidence is madly cool and uniquely relaxing, making for a 'pick up the bone and eat with your fingers' good time, not a cathedral-like hush of wonder over the smoothness of a velouté. It's a fitting (if unwitting) tribute that legendary bon viveur Keith Floyd ate Hix's cooking for his last supper before suffering a fatal heart attack.

Food 8, Service 6, Atmosphere 9

....

Hereford Road *(top)*
3 Hereford Road, Bayswater, W2
Tel: 020 7727 1144
www.herefordroad.org
Open: noon–3pm, 6–10.30pm Mon–Sat; noon–4pm, 6–10pm Sun
British   **£30**

A more plain-speaking, well-delivered and honestly British menu is not to be found in West London. Because of course most of the area's good restaurants are rubber-necking heaven, but on a quiet street on the Bayswater/Notting Hill borders is a little-known treasure opened in 2007 where people come to sit in plain, unfussy booths, enjoy its easy ambience and that deceptively difficult art of great ingredients cooked simply. The chefs cook at the grill inside the door, including head chef/owner Tom Pemberton who amply displays the skills of a man trained under Fergus Henderson at the near-mythical St John, where nose-to-tail eating and forgotten veggies became a matter of pride (see separate entry). Taking resolutely local and seasonal ingredients (including game, offal and lesser spotted curiosities such as Ticklemore cheese), Pemberton adds quirky, British twists. Cauliflower soup comes with skate cheeks, moules marinières becomes cockles, cider and lovage (the daily changing menu is posted online). It's all cooked with care and confidence, yet without fuss;

service is efficient and low-key, but the final treat is the bill, which comes in way lower than expected for food of this distinction (especially so with its shared roasts). Thank God it's too understated for Notting Hill's jewellery-shaking set.

Food 8, Service 7, Atmosphere 7

....

J Sheekey *(bottom)*
28–32 St Martin's Court,
Covent Garden, WC2
Tel: 020 7240 2565
www.j-sheekey.co.uk
Open: noon–3pm, 5.30pm–midnight Mon–Sat; noon–3.30pm 6–11pm Sun
Fish/Seafood   **£50**

Like the legendary Ivy, Sheekey's (nobody calls it 'J Sheekey') is owned by millionaire-restaurateur Richard Caring, and to those in the know, this is by far the better restaurant. Despite being located down a theatreland alleyway, it is every bit as glamorous in its own way as its more famous sibling. The mirrored windows in Sheekey's Dickensian façade do a fine job of preserving the identities of those inside, the series of elegant wood-panelled rooms makes it a great spot for intimate dinners, and without the preying paparazzi outside, high-profile diners are spared the indignity of being snapped as they leave. On the food front, the simple fish-based menu (including perennial favourites such as potted shrimps and skate in brown butter) is everything you could wish for – right down to the sort of traditional puddings that reduce grown-up British schoolboys to tears of nostalgic

joy. And, if that weren't enough, in late 2008, J Sheekey Oyster Bar opened just next door, serving market-fresh oysters, cockle and mussel meunière, gravadlax and the like, and champagne to help it down. Best of all, it is way easier to get a table at Sheekey's than at The Ivy. But then you didn't want to go there anyway, did you?

Food 9, Service 8, Atmosphere 8

Kitchen W8   *(top)*
11 Abingdon Road,
Kensington, W8
Tel: 020 7937 0120
www.kitchenw8.com
Open noon–2.30pm, 6–10.30pm
Mon–Sat; 12.30–3pm, 6.30–9.30pm
Sun

European   **£48**

A partnership between veteran restaurateur Rebecca Mascarenhas (of Sonny's in Barnes) and the Michelin-starred Philip Howard (chef-patron of The Square), Kitchen W8 has settled rather nicely into Kensington since opening in autumn 2009. Mascarenhas previously ran the site with varying degrees of success, as 11 Abingdon Road and Bistrot Eleven, and despite the new cream and retro-wallpapered interior, it's still somehow a hard room to love. Not so the food, which, with Howard protégé Mark Kempson behind the stove, is clever, accomplished and creatively presented in dishes such as a tartare of Ayrshire beef with pickled radish, truffle cream and deep-fried quail egg. While the location might cry neighbourhood restaurant, albeit in one of London's most affluent neighbourhoods, the cooking is ambitious

Michelin star-chasing stuff – with Howard involved, it was never going to be another bistro. The set lunch, Sunday lunch and early evening dinner menus offer an affordable way in for those that don't own their own Kensington mews.

Food 8, Service 7, Atmosphere 6

Locanda Locatelli   *(bottom)*
8 Seymour Street,
Marylebone, W1
Tel: 020 7935 9088
www.locandalocatelli.com
Open: daily, noon–3pm (3.30pm Sat/Sun), 6.45–11pm (11.30 Fri/Sat, 10.15pm Sun)

Italian   **£60**

There has been a fashionable buzz about Giorgio Locatelli's Michelin-starred new-wave Italian ever since it opened back in 2002 and it's still up there as one of the capital's culinary hotspots. Locatelli is Britain's finest Italian chef, with a knack for taking fabulous ingredients and lifting them to almost poetic heights. His simple brilliance is sometimes lost on those more used to the overt fireworks of French cuisine, but at its best – in the likes of veal shank ravioli or quail risotto – his food is nothing short of genius. Even better, you get to eat in David Collins' Euro-smart interior, one of the most understatedly luxurious dining rooms in town, with lighting so flattering it would make even Jackie Stallone look good. Waiters are super-informed, happily pointing diners in the direction of new experiences, and it's not uncommon for Giorgio himself to do a spot of meeting and greeting later in the evening. Getting a table isn't easy, and early sittings are limited to two hours. But persevere – for food this good, it's worth it.

Food 9, Service 8, Atmosphere 8

 **Lutyens** *(top)*
85 Fleet Street, EC4
Tel: 020 7583 8385
www.lutyens-restaurant.com
Open 7.30am–10pm Mon–Fri
French **£52**

The second instalment of Terence Conran's comeback after The Boundary (see separate entry) is his latest love-letter to the classic French bistro, opened late 2009. Housed in a handsome Fleet Street building and named after Edwin Lutyens, the revered British architect who laid out New Delhi, it occupies the two lower floors of the 1930s Lutyens-designed former Reuters HQ. The menu, overseen by David Burke, who started working for Conran back at Bibendum under Simon Hopkinson, should appeal to anyone with a love for polished French classicism in familiar dishes of snails, lobster mousse, rabbit wrapped in bacon, skate wing with brown shrimps and butter, and Peach Melba. But it's also all very new Conran, which is to champion excellent food alongside highbrow design (the room includes some Lutyens furniture, as well as Conran's subtle references to Art Deco and Modernism). Rather grandly billed as a 'Restaurant, Bar, Members' Club & Cellar Rooms', its aspirations mostly hold up thanks to its setting, crisp linen and smart service, and (perhaps un-

fortunately) its popularity with power-wielding City chieftains.

Food 7, Service 8, Atmosphere 6

The Luxe *(bottom)*
109 Commercial Street, Spitalfields, E1
Tel: 020 7101 1751
www.theluxe.co.uk
Open: noon–3pm, 6–11pm Mon–Fri; 6–11pm Sat; noon–5pm, Sun
British **£40**

John Torode, the Aussie judge off Masterchef, the one the housewives love, returns to restaurant-land with a relaxed space edging Old Spitalfields Market. It's one of those one-stop, never-leave places with coffees, sarnies and flowers from a dramatic ground-floor birdcage, live music in the basement bar, and on the first floor, Torode's surprisingly elegant and calm restaurant. Set around a central open kitchen, the room retains its 19th-century form with exposed red brick, oval windows and parquet flooring; silk chinoiserie wallpaper and old aviaries outside reference the songbirds once bred in the eaves. Torode knows his meat (the menu at his other restaurant, Smiths of Smithfield, references every cut's heritage as if it's hoping to marry a prince) – most meat here is cooked in a wood oven, the sign of a purist, and, as such, is not really messed with. The menu sees British-meets-Asian dishes like split pea soup with potato *pakora*, or resolutely Brit and meat-mad, like liver and bacon with obscenely buttery mash. If John's in, he may personally and enthusiastically recommend un-

usual wines like Kung Fu Girl Riesling, while his sommelier rolls his eyes affectionately. Cute things like that make The Luxe a unique and friendly place.

Food 7, Service 8, Atmosphere 8

Magdalen *(top)*
152 Tooley Street,
London Bridge, SE1
Tel: 020 7403 1342
www.magdalenrestaurant.co.uk
Open: noon–2.30pm, Mon–Fri;
6.30–10pm, Mon–Sat
British   **£45**

London has a growing cohort of British revival restaurants, but Magdalen is undoubtedly one of the best. The two-storey corner site – just a turnip's throw from Borough farmers' market – is done out in that gents' club mix of dried ox-blood walls, white linen and dark-wood bistro chairs that has become the uniform of born-again Brit eateries. Then again, perhaps Brit isn't quite the word. The food here is a deliciously, peasanty amalgam of seasonal ideas from English, Italian and southwestern French cooking, similar to that championed by nearby gastropub, The Anchor & Hope (see Pubs). In practice, that means droolsome meat dishes of, say, braised hare or slow-cooked lamb shoulder, plus potted crab, skate and caper salad, or cuttlefish with chickpeas and gremolata; there's always a roast or two intended for sharing (like you-know-which pub). It's pretty much a family outfit, the kitchen run by James Faulks (ex of, surprise, surprise, The Anchor & Hope, as well as Heston Blumenthal's Fat Duck), with his father Roger and wife Emma, who does the

puddings. The downstairs tables are kept for walk-ins, but it's best to book – the place is justifiably popular.

Food 8, Service 8, Atmosphere 7

Marcus Wareing at the Berkeley *(bottom)*
Wilton Place, Belgravia, SW1
Tel: 020 7235 1200
www.marcus-wareing.com
Open: noon–2.30pm, 6–11pm Mon–Fri; 6–11pm, Sat
European   **£75**

When Wareing acrimoniously split from his one-time friend and boss Gordon Ramsay to go solo in 2007, the foodie gossips went into overdrive. Ramsay reclaimed the name of the restaurant that had earned Wareing two Michelin stars, Pétrus, but the Berkeley Hotel kept the man, and very wisely so. Sitting in the plush, David Collins-designed purple velvet dining room is like being nestled in a chocolate box, and food and service is formal, with amuse bouches and gentlemen pouring wine with one hand behind their back, as you'd expect from a Michelin-starred hotel restaurant. But Wareing has attracted a crowd that breaks the stiff, French restaurant mould. It's less the concierge-sent tourists and expense-account white males, more all ages, women, families, friends, making for an unusually mellow energy. And, of course, the food is beautifully balanced, highly accomplished and thoroughly modern. Expect gasps of pleasure at the French/Italian cheese trolley, giggles at the OTT bonbon trolley that tinkles round with coffee, and intent interest on a serious 1,000-strong cellar

that's as sound on entry-level wines as on the £25,000 1961 Pétrus.

Food 9, Service, 9, Atmosphere, 7

 The Modern Pantry *(top)*
47 St John's Square, Clerkenwell, EC1
Tel: 020 7250 0833
www.themodernpantry.co.uk
Café open: 8am–11pm Mon–Fri; 9am–11pm Sat; 10am–10pm Sun
Restaurant open: noon–3pm Tues–Fri, 6–10.30pm Tues–Sat

Fusion £44

It's a good start: Modern Pantry sits on Clerkenwell's golden triangle of restaurants with Bistrot Bruno and Giant Robot (see separate entries). It's also thoroughly modern, and as if the grey-painted brick, shiny copper lampshades, melamine tables and smiley, good-looking staff were imagined by Wallpaper's style fascists – this place is not luxurious (now deemed a good thing), and is innately chic. So are its customers, who tend to be youngish and open-minded – no traditionalist would dare the menu's unusual flavours. Named one of The Daily Telegraph's top five female chefs of the decade, as well as New Zealander of the Year 2010 (the nation that invented the tricky fusion genre) is its accomplished chef/owner Anna Hansen, who can be seen at the pass every day preparing what only she describes as 'everyday cooking'. Her 'everyday' is our 'exciting': Duke of Berkshire pork cheeks come with crispy trotter, tonka beans and pickled bean sprouts; chorizo, date and feta fritters with rose yoghurt. Conservative eaters should try the down-stairs café for great salads, and, on a Friday, its famous fish and chips. See – she can even do the trad stuff.

Food 7, Service 9, Atmosphere 8

Murano *(bottom)*
20 Queen Street, Mayfair, W1
Tel: 020 7592 1222
www.gordonramsay.com/murano
Open noon–2.30pm; 6.30pm–10.30pm Mon–Sat

Italian £70

Still Gordon Ramsay's apparently willing handmaiden at the time of writing, despite rumours that she might be looking to go solo if she can somehow negotiate a way to take her Mayfair restaurant with her, Angela Hartnett's Murano suffers in the same way as many restaurants in Ramsay's empire. Service is unnecessarily fussy and, at times, plain poker-up-the-arse stuffy. Despite a name that conjures up images of the beautifully colourful Venetian glass, the interior is – a couple of chandeliers aside – afflicted with familiar upscale beigeness. Not so the food – Hartnett is a very fine cook and few do fancy Italian with the flair she manages in dishes such as braised rabbit pappardelle with confit lemons, Taggiasca olives, mint and rocket, and confit halibut in olive oil with celeriac fondant, fregola and ginger, and crab vinaigrette; the wine list cherry-picks Italy's finest with a few quality bottles from elsewhere. But like all Italian luxury goods (and Ramsay output), it doesn't come cheap. We can't help but will Hartnett away from her svengali.

Food 9, Service 6, Atmosphere 6

eat...

Moro *(top)*
34–36 Exmouth Market,
Clerkenwell, EC1
Tel: 020 7833 8336
www.moro.co.uk
Open: 12.30–2.30pm, 7–10.30pm
Mon–Sat (tapas all day)
Spanish/Moroccan £42

Until husband-and-wife team Sam
and Samantha Clark opened their An-
dalusian-inspired restaurant in 1997,
Exmouth Market was off the radar
as far as most food lovers were con-
cerned. These days, people travel from
across town to sample their authentic
food. And you can't blame them. Influ-
enced by the two Sams' travels through
southern Spain and North Africa in
a campervan with a small gas hob, it
is as mouthwatering as it is inventive
(they've since published two cook-
books on Moorish cuisine). The decep-
tive simplicity is matched by the no-
frills dining room – bare wooden floors,
tightly packed tables and a zinc-topped
bar along one side for tapas and sherry (13 available by the glass), plus an
open kitchen where the Clarks are kept
busy over the charcoal grill and wood-
fired oven (the bread here is sublime).
Despite their success, the pair remain
charmingly unassuming – something
that has obviously rubbed off on the
front of house. Service, though not always the most efficient, is friendly to a
fault, ensuring that a meal at Moro is
always a relaxed experience.

Food 8, Service 7, Atmosphere 8

 **Nobu Berkeley** *(bottom)*
15 Berkeley Street, Mayfair, W1
Tel: 020 7290 9222
www.noburestaurants.com
Open: noon–2.15pm, 6–11pm
(midnight Thurs/Fri) Mon–Fri; 6pm–
midnight Sat; 6–9.15pm Sun. Bar open
until 2am.
Japanese £80

For anyone who has eaten at Nobu
Matsuhisa's other restaurants, the food
here will hold few surprises. It's the
same phenomenally good – and phenomenally expensive (note the unprec-
edented 15% service charge) – Japa-
nese-Peruvian fusion that's won the
chain A-list fans from LA to Tokyo –
the black cod in miso, the wagyu beef,
the sashimi with jalapenos, not to mention its blissful cocktails. While both
London outposts now boast one Michelin star, the David Collins-designed
Nobu Berkeley has a more youthful
vibe than its older, calmer sibling Nobu
London (19 Old Park Lane; 020 7447
4747), or perhaps that's just a higher
incidence of plastic surgery? Diners congregate in the downstairs bar,
where drinks are served by Amazonian
waitresses; upstairs, there's seating for
200, as well as a separate *hibachi* table
and sushi bar. It should be desper-
ately glamorous, but at times the bare
wooden tables, Euro-lounge music and
raucous crowd apparently desperate to
be noticed, make it seem more like an
upmarket canteen. Still, judging by the
number of flashy cars parked outside,
the capital's bright young things aren't
going to let the decibel level get in the
way of a good time.

Food 8, Service 7, Atmosphere 7

La Petite Maison *(top)*
53 Brook's Mews, Mayfair, W1
Tel: 020 7495 4774
www.lpmlondon.co.uk
Open: noon–3pm, 6–11pm Mon–Fri;
12.30–3.30pm, 6–11pm (10pm Sun)
Sat/Sun
French £55

You might wonder how the market-fresh, seasonal delights of Niçoise cuisine would translate to Bond Street, but success is manifest in the animated, sunny dining room hidden in Mayfair's backstreets. A mini-me of the original LPM in – yes – Nice, much loved by the great, the good, the gourmands and the frightfully rich (take heed), the chefs come ready trained in the Niçois style of southern French and Ligurian cooking (less of the French fuss, more of the Italian simplicity) – deep-fried courgette flowers, *passaladière* (onion tart with anchovies), gratin potatoes. But two words elevate this place from good to great – roast chicken. That is, the *poulet de Bresse*, served whole, for sharing, with a chunk of bread soaked in its delicious juices, and a fat slab of foie gras: bred in Bresse, it's so rich, complex, tender, and popular that few make it out of the country. Call ahead to pre-order, because everyone else seems to know how good it is, and they do run out. That, mixed with a thorough inspection of its French rosés and, in summer, dining alfresco in its tranquil terrace, will surely bring an Azur glint to the jaded Londoner's eye.

Food 8, Service 7, Atmosphere 7

Petersham Nurseries *(bottom)*
Off Petersham Road,
Richmond, TW10
Tel: 020 8605 3627
www.petershamnurseries.com
Open: noon–2.30pm Weds–Sun
European £56

Of course it's about the destination and not the journey, otherwise why bother going in the first place? But it's true to say that the trip to Petersham Nurseries – up a hedgerow-lined track along the river and through a series of vintage greenhouses – is thoroughly delightful. Parachuting in, however, would still deliver a memorable meal, also housed in one of the greenhouses. Celebrity chef and author Skye Gyngell attracts so many foodie pilgrims, there's usually a waiting list (reservation is essential; no dinner) – her talent lies in delicately combining flavours (salt cod and purple basil, say; raw artichokes and mint; panna cotta and roasted rhubarb) in a brief but beautifully crafted (if pricey) menu (a set menu has been introduced Weds–Fri). Whatever you're paying for, it's not for the food miles: sourcing is taken so seriously, whatever can be grown at the nurseries is, by Lucy Gray, daughter of River Café's late Rose Gray; other ingredients come from some of Britain's finest smallholdings. If you can't wait, the Teahouse (read: quaint old shed) serves up, without reservation, home-made soups, cakes and sandwiches on naturally leavened breads. You'll be grateful to walk it all off.

Food 8, Service 8, Atmosphere 8

Pizza East *(top)*
Tea Building, 56 Shoreditch High Street, E1
Tel: 020 7729 1888
www.pizzaeast.com
Open: noon–midnight (1am Thurs, 2am Fri); 10am–2am Sat; 10am–midnight Sun
Italian/American   £30

To call it Pizza Express for hipsters would be harsh but there's no denying that Pizza East, from Nick Jones' Soho House group, is aimed at the mass market. It's a vast 170-cover operation that opened in 2009 in Shoreditch's Tea Building, yup, a former tea warehouse (so lots of space, exposed concrete and industrial piping, now scrubbed up and flatteringly low-lit) that last saw action as the raucously hip T Bar. The social buzz lives on – or rather it follows Jones wherever he goes, not least since Pizza East is just next door to his hugely successful Shoreditch House. The pizzas are LA-inspired, baked in a wood-fired oven with a crunchy 10-inch base, with a dozen toppings on offer from simple buffalo mozzarella, tomato and basil to more gutsy veal meatballs with prosciutto, cream and sage; the menu is bulked out with smaller plates such as calamari, whole artichoke or chicken livers; main courses include lasagne, baked fish, and a very fashionable roast chicken for two with rosemary potatoes. In the basement is the Concrete bar (open Thurs–Sat), a basic, Berlin-style space with refectory tables and benches, racks of shots, and room to dance – the party express.

Food 6, Service 7, Atmosphere 9

Polpo *(bottom)*
41 Beak Street, Soho, W1
Tel: 020 7734 4479
www.polpo.co.uk
Open: noon–3pm (4pm Sat), 5.30–11pm Mon–Sat; noon–4pm Sun
Italian   £30

Annoyingly, the folk behind Polpo (Russell Norman, ex-operations director at Caprice Holdings, and Tom Oldroyd, ex-Bocca di Lupo chef) have got it so right with this no-frills, Venetian-style tapas bar (or bacaro) – with bar-dining, sharing plates, and authenticity and democracy over ostentation and ego – that getting a table can involve a two-hour wait at the bar (there's no booking for dinner). Though that in itself is genius. Why does everybody rate Polpo so highly? Probably because they drank much more (Italian) wine than intended while waiting for their table. The lightheadedness lends an easy joy to the cosy 18th-century townhouse where Canaletto once lived and painted, now transformed into a neighbourhood institution (white-gloss subway tiles, exposed brickwork, manila menus doubling as tablemats) with a relaxed, downtown New York vibe. Its numerous regulars have even changed their feeding routine to arrive before 7 or after 9 to get their hands on the excellent *cicchetti* (tiny plates of meat, fish and cheese), crostini and saucers of regional Italian specialities (a visit is incomplete without the *polpette*, or meatballs). Norman's best idea is yet to come: a tiny second outpost, Spuntino (61 Rupert Street) to catch the spillover.

Food 8, Service 7, Atmosphere 9

109

 St John *(left)*
26 St John Street,
Clerkenwell, EC1
Tel: 020 7251 0848
www.stjohnrestaurant.com
Open: noon (1pm Sun)–3pm, 6–11pm.
Closed Sat lunch and Sun dinner.
British **£48**

Fergus Henderson's stark, white and eternally modern former smokehouse of a restaurant, opened in 1994, has not only won a Michelin star (in 2009) and become a gastro landmark, but has since inspired an entire movement. Henderson is an advocate of 'nose-to-tail eating' – using the bits of animal that most folk leave behind – and his extraordinarily austere style of modern British cooking manages to conjure winning flavours from even the most obscure body parts. If you suddenly feel the urge to eat pig's spleen, rook chicks or bone marrow salad, this is the place for you (and even if you don't, there's less outré fare on offer). Evidently, more and more have learnt to stomach the offal – enough for Henderson to open, in 2003, St John Bread

and Wine in Spitalfields (94 Commercial Street, E1; 020 7247 8724), a bustling diffusion branch popular with adventurous suits and local creatives (Tracey Emin is a regular). It offers a daily line-up of (marginally) less unconventional dishes, often requiring translation from diligent staff in chefs' whites. A third has just opened at St John Hotel (see Sleep). And the imitators are countless.

Food 9, Service 7, Atmosphere 6

 Scott's *(middle)*
20 Mount Street, Mayfair, W1
Tel: 020 7495 7309
www.scotts-restaurant.com
Open: daily, noon–10.30pm (10pm Sun)
Fish/Seafood **£50**

Once the most glamorous oyster bar in town – Ian Fleming reputedly had his first Martini shaken not stirred here – Scotts was opened by a passionate Scottish fishmonger in 1860, and was talk of the town for the next 100

years. Until, that is, the IRA bombed it in 1975, killing one and heralding the start of its dark decades when only curmudgeonly old buffers went there. A buyout in 2006 by owners of The Ivy, Caprice Holdings, has sand-blasted the barnacles off this London institution, commissioning art works from YBAs Tracey Emin, Gary Hume and Michael Landy, and inviting Future Systems to design a 'crustacean display' (one for the CV, surely) which forms the centrepiece of its island oyster bar (a useful device for spying on the likes of Elton John, Jack Nicholson and Damien Hirst). But Scott's doesn't need to name-drop – its fresh, fresh fish does the talking (almost): there's an ample choice of native oysters as well as a simple, people-pleasing menu of exquisite fish, meat and game. Liveried doormen, white-coated barmen and a perfect Mayfair postcode, plus the low-cal oyster option, has proved it irresistible to the Names.

Food 7, Service 9, Atmosphere 8

■ **Sketch:**   *(right)*
■ **Gallery and Glade**
9 Conduit Street, Mayfair, W1
Tel: 020 7659 4500
www.sketch.uk.com
Gallery open: 7–11pm Mon–Weds;
7pm–1am Thurs–Sat
Glade open: 1–6pm Fri/Sat
Eclectic   **£65 /£35**

When this extraordinary, Grade II-listed gastro-complex opened in 2002, it was the Michelin-starred, £125-a-head Lecture Room and Library that captured the headlines. But you can eat incredibly well at Sketch for far less. At night, the downstairs Gallery – a contemporary art space by day – becomes one of the hippest brasseries in town, its white modernity softened with faux Louis-something chairs and a continuous 360-degree wall projection. The inventive menu (from French superchef and co-owner Pierre Gagnaire) ranges from neo-comfort food (Lobster bisque with three-colour basmati rice and horseradish cream) to expectation-defying genius (bubble-gum ice cream with lemon egg Wurtz

111

and orange-blossom marshmallow). Everyone from supermodels to septuagenarians eats here (the charismatic owner Mourad Mazouz says he hates his customers to be predictable) and it invariably makes for a fun time, if for some, style trumps substance. At midnight, the tables are lowered, the loungey tunes cranked up, and the party kicks off. For food that's both simpler and cheaper (posh club sandwiches, sashimi, cheese plates), check out Glade, a dining room by day, members' club by night – although the jury's still out on its modernist-meets-sylvan décor.

Food 8, Service 7, Atmosphere 9

Tom's Kitchen *(top)*
27 Cale Street, Chelsea, SW3
Tel: 020 7349 0202
www.tomskitchen.co.uk
Open: 8–11am, noon–3.30pm,
6–11pm Mon–Fri; 10am–4pm,
6–11pm Sat/Sun
European **£38**

Tom Aikens' eponymous fine-dining restaurant is one of the shining lights of contemporary cheffy cooking (nearby at 43 Elystan Street; 020 7584 2003). His attempts at more relaxed eating have been varied (his chippie bombed), but Tom's Kitchen, a chic, marble- and oak-dressed spot on a village green off the King's Road, is thriving, serving homely favourites like fish pie and macaroni cheese (with optional black truffle), alongside well-sourced meat dishes served simply with salads, classic sauces and decadent truffle chips with parmesan. But this is the brooding perfectionist's version of

comfort food, so never expect the ordinary, and there's more fois gras than you'd expect from a brasserie-style dining room, but, hey, this is Chelsea (the prices reflect this). So do the customers, a mix of upper-class oldies up from the country, splashy young royals and their crew, and bankers en famille (book ahead for weekend brunches, or anaesthetise the hunger at the upstairs bar). In summer 2010, Aikens opened Tom's Kitchen at Somerset House, featuring the same menu (The Strand, WC2; 020 7845 4646). The success of Tom's Kitchen's is a sign of the times.

Food 7, Service 7, Atmosphere 7

Viet Grill *(bottom)*
58 Kingsland Road, Hackney, E2
Tel: 020 7739 6686
www.vietgrill.co.uk
Open: noon–3pm, 5.30–11pm
(11.30pm Fri/Sat) Mon–Sat; noon–
10.30pm Sun
Vietnamese **£35**

Hackney's Kingsland Road is to Vietnamese food what Brick Lane is to curry. The Vietnamese settled here after fleeing in 1975, opening an array of restaurants and cafés. Most serve decent enough grub (try Que Viet at 102, Viet Hoa at 74 or Song Que at 134), although, thanks to strip lighting and plastic furniture, can be severely lacking in atmosphere. For the best food – and certainly the most lively ambience – head for Viet Grill, the big sis of the also excellent Cay Tre (301 Old Street, EC1; 020 7729 8662). Food is authentic, fragrant and delicious, with Indochine beef (like sweetly aromatic carpaccio) and a brilliant version of

the classic Vietnamese noodle soup *pho* (pronounced like the French 'feu'). A new wine list from The Guardian's wine columnist Malcolm Gluck has only increased their lead. And despite a fancy refurb, in 'French colonial' style, the sweet, black-clad Vietnamese staff still harbour none of the grandeur of your average Eat entry. It's a good – and not all that prodigal – idea to sample several of the dishes (takeaway also available), though a bowl of *pho* perfectly lines the stomach before burrowing deep into the East End in search of an all-night happening.

Food 8, Service 8, Atmosphere 7

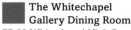

The Whitechapel *(left)*
Gallery Dining Room
77-82 Whitechapel High Street, E1
Tel: 020 7522 7896
www.whitechapelgallery.org/dine
Open: noon–2.30pm Tues–Sun;
6–11pm Weds–Sat
Modern British £40

Founded in 1901 to bring art to the East End, the Grade II-listed Whitechapel Gallery (see Culture) reopened in spring 2009 following a two-year, £13.5 million facelift that doubled its size and brought with it a handsome, pale oak restaurant in its old oak-floored library. The chef is Maria Elia – ex of the well-regarded Delfina Studio Café in Bermondsey. The menu is compact (with an excellent value three-course set lunch at £23), the ingredients British and seasonal, the descriptions fashionably terse, and the cooking spot-on in dishes such as pan-fried sea trout with buttered Jersey Royals, samphire and Scottish mussel broth. You could grumble that the seating is a mite cheek by jowl – they've crammed in 40 covers where 30 would have done – but better to revel in the arty canteen ambience. The service is sweetly efficient despite the waiters' struggles to swing a cat between tables. It's arguably at its best during the day when you can still hear yourself think rather than on weekend evenings when you might long for the peace of the old library.

Food 7, Service 7, Atmosphere 7

eat...

Viajante *(middle)*

Patriot Square,
Bethnal Green, E2
Tel: 020 7871 0461
www.viajante.co.uk
Open: daily, noon–2pm, 7–11pm

Eclectic £70

No-one knew what to expect from
Nuno Mendes' new project. The one-
time marine biologist, El Bulli graduate
and serious guy kinda bombed at Bac-
chus, to re-emerge with a pop-up supper club, The Loft, in his own apartment
in deepest Dalston – an underground
foodie hot ticket. But Viajante exceeds
expectations: the small but airy dining
room has a kitchen so open, you're
almost sitting in it. Forget everything
you've seen of bawling chefs in sweaty
kitchens – Mendes' team works with the
quiet control of a laboratory, with pre-
cision-arrangement using tweezers, or
razoring the perfect piece of coriander
to dress the plate. Food is colourful, surprising and exquisitely beautiful. Dishes
have names like Spring Garden, Thai
Explosion II and dark chocolate and
water, and are often the sort of unique

combinations (skate wing, yeast and
cauliflower – it works, honest) that have
made Heston Blumenthal a household
name. The wine-pairing is good value,
and favours lesser known European
wine-producers like Austria and Portugal, while service has a newness to it; an
ease and confidence that one doesn't
readily associate with establishments
that only offer six, nine and 12-course
tasting menus. Possessed of a lightness
that's sensual and feminine, this is the
fine-dining of the future.

Food 9, Service 10, Atmosphere 6

The Wolseley *(right)*

160 Piccadilly, Mayfair, W1
Tel: 020 7499 6996
www.thewolseley.com
Open: daily, 7am (8am Sat/Sun)–midnight (11pm Sun)

European £46

Everyone says it: the Wolseley has sto-
len The Ivy's crown as the top place
in London to see and be seen. And
it's true that no meal here is complete

115

without an amuse-bouche of star-spotting. The glittering restaurant – open from breakfast to dinner since 2003 – is the creation of Christopher Corbin and Jeremy King, the original owners of The Ivy and Le Caprice, and many of their former regulars have followed. The pair is big on the personal approach and you'll usually find one or the other working the room. There's a menu of 101 crowd-pleasing continental favourites (from oysters with chorizo to Wiener schnitzel); and the magnificent, Grade II-listed space (built in 1921 as a luxury car showroom for Wolseley Motors) has been remodelled to look like a mittel-European grand café. Peak times in the restaurant tend to get booked up, but there's also a separate tearoom and bar, and the café menu is served from 7am until midnight; if you can't get a table for lunch or dinner, pop in for their excellent afternoon tea instead. The amuse-bouches wil be no less in evidence.

Food 8, Service 7, Atmosphere 9

Yauatcha *(top)*
15 Broadwick Street, Soho, W1
Tel: 020 7494 8888
www.yauatcha.com
Open: noon–11.30pm Mon–Sat;
noon–10.30pm Sun

Tearoom: daily, 9am–11pm (10.30pm Sun)
Chinese £41

There's no missing this stunningly modern Chinese teahouse/restaurant (originally the brainchild of restaurateur Alan Yau – he sold it along with Hakkasan early 2008 but the name has stuck). At night, the opaque glass walls glow blue out of the darkness, drawing in diners like a moth trap. Occupying the lower floors of Richard Rogers' glass and steel building on the corner of Berwick Street, Yauatcha is high concept in every sense, from Christian Liaigre's minimalist interior (a sparse white tearoom on the ground floor – which brews 50 varieties of chai and serves exquisite European cakes resembling Lilliputian hats – and the atmospheric basement dining room with a star-spangled ceiling and fishtank bar) through to the staff uniforms – very Crouching Tiger... The food, too, has a concept – namely that you can eat dim sum from morning to night (traditionally they are only served at lunchtime). And what dim sum; compared with nearby Chinatown, the food here is both vibrant and surprising, and, unsurprisingly, has now been awarded a Michelin star; the cocktail- and wine list is equally original with both sparkling and chilled reds. It just goes to show it pays to rip up the rulebook.

Food 8, Service 7, Atmosphere 8

the best of the rest...

the classics...

Aubergine A foodie's favourite, serving brave French food in a pretty, cosy setting (11 Park Walk, Chelsea, SW10; 020 7352 3449; www.atozrestaurants/auberginechelsea)

Boisdale Eccentrically charming institution with live jazz, Cuban cigar humidor and terrace, and a gourmet Scottish menu (15 Eccleston Street, Belgravia, SW1; 020 7730 6922; www.boisdale.co.uk)

La Famiglia Family Maccioni have been serving classic pastas, fish and meats at the ever-popular Tuscan trattoria since 1976 (7 Langton Street, Chelsea, SW10; 020 7351 0761; www.lafamiglia.co.uk)

Racine Classic Knightsbridge bistro returns to form, thanks to owner Henry Harris's own return (239 Brompton Road SW3; 020 7584 4477; www.racine-restaurant.com)

Sophie's Steakhouse Inspired by a Brooklyn steakhouse, Sophie Mogford's lively no-bookings joint excels in casual Steak Frites (Covent Garden: 29 Wellington Street, WC2; 020 7836 8836; Chelsea: 311 Fulham Road, SW10; 020 7352 0088; www.sophiessteakhouse.com)

ethnic...

Hakkasan Chinese food's answer to Nobu serving Michelin-starred dim sum for lunch, subtle yet inventive dishes by night (8 Hanway Place, Fitzrovia, W1; 020 7927 7000; www.hakkasan.com)

Momo Mourad Mazouz's Maghrebi-influenced cuisine serves couscous dishes and tagines in a gorgeous orient excess setting (25 Heddon Street, Mayfair, W1 Tel: 020 7434 4040; www.momoresto.com)

Sake No Hana With new chef Daisuke Hayashi, an easier menu and a lighter bill, Alan Yau's Japanese dining room is on the ascendant (23 St James's Street, Mayfair, SW1; 020 7925 898; www.sakenohana.com)

the fine-dining that survived...

Alain Ducasse at the Dorchester With three Michelin stars plus some 16 others in his career, the Frenchman is one of the world's best chefs; with a tasting menu at £115, he's also up there in price (Park Lane, W1; 020 7629 8866; www.alainducasse-dorchester.com)

Le Caprice A modern European menu perennially served to socialites and lovers in this dark Art Deco dining room (Arlington House, Arlington Street, SW1; 020 7629 2239; www.lecaprice.co.uk)

Chez Bruce Bruce Poole's Michelin-starred French/Mediterranean food easily puts Wandsworth on the culinary map (2 Bellevue Road, SW17; 020 8672 0114; www.chezbruce.co.uk)

Le Gavroche Opened in 1967 by the Roux brothers, it is now under Michel Roux Junior with two Michelin stars (43 Upper Brook Street, Mayfair, W1; 020 7408 0881; www.le-gavroche.co.uk)

Gordon Ramsay at Royal Hospital Road Ramsay's flagship with a French menu and three Michelin stars. Good luck getting a table (68 Royal Hospital Road, Chelsea, SW3; 020 7352 4441; www.gordonramsay.com/royalhospitalroad)

Pétrus Gordon Ramsay's revenge restaurant opened summer 2010 to trump Marcus Wareing; haute cuisine, vintage vin and Ramsay's big new idea – the chef's table, or eating in the kitchen (1 Kinnerton Street, Knightsbridge, SW1; 020 7592 1609; www.gordonramsay.com/petrus)

the new wave...

Arbutus Well-priced, well-loved set menus of Michelin-starred European peasant food (63-64 Frith Street, Soho, W1; 020 7734 4545; www.arbutusrestaurant.co.uk)

Bocca di Lupo Prodigy chef Jacob Kenedy nails the formula du jour with bar eating, great-value small sharing plates, and robust, regional Italian food (12 Archer Street, Soho, W1; 020 7734 2223; www.boccadilupo.com)

Heston Blumenthal at the Mandarin Oriental From December 2010, one of Britain's most creative chefs finally opens his first restaurant outside his home village of Bray, Berkshire, with a twisted British menu (66 Knightsbridge, SW1; 020 7235 2000; www.mandarinoriental.com/london/dining)

Quo Vadis Fino and Barrafina's Sam and Eddie Hart stepped in to save this Soho institution in 2008, now serving modern British food (26 Dean Street London W1; 020 7437 9585; www.quovadissoho.co.uk)

Wild Honey The boys from Arbutus' second restaurant that won a Michelin star in 2008 for its considered European inventions (12 St George Street, Mayfair, W1; 020 7758 9160; www.wildhoneyrestaurant.co.uk)

sceney...

Dean Street Townhouse All-day dining for media mavens, with a retro British bent – roasts, pies, and amusingly, a very serious 'mince and boiled potatoes' (69 Dean Street, W1; 020 7434 1775; www.deanstreettownhouse.com)

The Ivy An institution since 1917, its

waiting list and attendant paparazzi are almost as famed as its modern Brit–Euro food (1–5 West Street, Covent Garden, WC2; 020 7836 4751; www.the-ivy.co.uk)

Pollen Street Set to be the Italian answer to the Wolseley, from one of the partners behind private members' club Maddox (5 Pollen Street, Mayfair, W1; 020 7856 9844; www.pollenst.com)

Randall & Aubin The party person's pit-stop: no-reservations seafood joint perfect for langoustines with chips and garlic butter, champagne and loud music (16 Brewer St, W1F; 020 7287 4447; www.randallandaubin.com)

Redhook Jonathan Downey's resurrection Mark II (cf Giant Robot, see Snack) – a US-inspired steak and seafood restaurant (89 Turnmill Street, Clerkenwell, EC1; 020 7065 6800)

Zuma Glamorous, gastronomic Japanese restaurant and cocktail bar loved by bankers and their WAGs (5 Raphael Street, Knightsbridge, SW7; 020 7584 1010; www.zumarestaurant.com)

eat...

Mark's Bar

drink (bars)...

What makes a good bar? In his autobiography My Last Breath, legendary Spanish film director Luis Buñuel offered the following prescription: 'The bar... is an exercise in solitude. Above all else, it must be quiet, dark, very comfortable – and, contrary to modern mores, have no music of any kind, no matter how faint. In sum there should be no more than a dozen tables, and a clientele that doesn't like to talk.' It is quite possible that the entire 609 square miles of Greater London doesn't contain a single bar that would have met with Buñuel's exacting standards – an indictment, perhaps, of his misanthropy, but also of the reality of lifestyle in a modern megalopolis. On peak nights (Thursdays, Fridays and Saturdays), people, people and more people making vast amounts of noise form a compulsory accompaniment to your drink. On other nights it would have been the modern menace of piped-in music and attention-seeking décor that would have irritated the surrealist Spaniard. But he's dead, so who cares what he thinks...

In the opinion of lots of other people, London's bar scene took off from a standing start in the 1990s. Back then, it was all about the Met Bar and the Atlantic, two paparazzi-patrolled institutions that set the glam tone and signalled New Britain's aspirations of upward mobility – to get ruinously drunk (a British constant, impervious to fashions), not on warm pints down the local but instead on caipirinhas and cosmopolitans made with gold-labelled, quadruple-distilled premium spirits, preferably within hazy eyesight of a Z-list celebrity. The 'style' bars that spread virus-like throughout the capital have of late moved on from that design showroom/minimalist, exposed-piping thing to something much more interesting and playful. With a conveniently cheap aesthetic of furniture from Ebay, fleamarkets and even salvaged from the streets (very fashionable), London's new wave of style bars (Callooh Callay, Barts, Barrio North and Central, Shunt) are proudly rough round the edges. It's telling that the Buddha Bar, opened in 2008, went bust – anything 'done' (like the Met Bar, for example) is considered a little naff these days.

Meanwhile, in a move away from Britain's alcopop shame and dropping grands on tables, connoisseurship and chin-stroking in specialist and single-spirit bars has suddenly become our new favourite waste of time. There's The Rake and The Old Brewery for beer, Bar Pepito for sherry, Vinoteca for wine, The Artesian for rum. Perhaps the slow movement has arrived: London's thinking bars have re-

121

turned to the uncut corners of yesteryear – 69 Colebrooke Row insists on seating you before you order and drink their pitch-perfect Martinis, Nick Strangeway at Mark's Bar has tirelessly composed an epic menu of 'Early British Libations', while Lounge Bohemia only allows drinkers with appointments to ensure their complex craftsmanship is duly appreciated. Much more thought is going into the art of inebriation, allowing for a more dignified take on working your way from left to right through a bar.

We have had to restrain ourselves somewhat to avoid an east-heavy review section, but it's true to say that Hoxton, Shoreditch, and increasingly Dalston are monopolising the market of merriment. Some new arrivals to the East End were easy to dodge, being of the commercial variety out to appeal to the growing hordes of bridge and tunnellers. Some of the more underground variety won't hang around long enough to be here when we hit the shelves (yes, the panacea that is the pop-up shop has reached the drinking scene). The most exciting developments are the Dalston dive bars – those late-night boogie basements infiltrating old supermarkets/video stores/kebab shops and filled to bursting with the 'alternative scene' (loitering musicians, artists and the fashionably unemployed).

If bar-hopping time is limited, then Soho and Mayfair should constitute your primary zone of investigation. Soho's vibe is informal, populist and often raucous, especially on Friday nights when local workers celebrate the end of the week and their inalienable right to drink 10 pints as quickly as possible and collapse of 'exhaustion'. Mayfair offers more distinguished (and expensive) drinking opportunities. The perennial splendours of Claridge's form a backdrop against which money (new and old) mingles with celebrities across the alphabetical spectrum; Dukes Bar is equally civilized, provided the de-civilizing effects of alcohol are discounted. For nothing, we have proved to ourselves, can deter a Londoner's thirst.

Dalston Dives

Once upon a time, not so long ago, a hip night out used to be all about Hoxton and Old Street, but then the corporate chains caught on, tidying away the East End's real character, bringing in their own identikit branding instead. In a bid for freedom (and lower rents), the cool kids retreated north to Dalston. With scuzzy streets, pound shops and social housing, Dalston is not about to win any prizes for prettiness. But if you're well-versed in the aesthetic of East Berlin, which makes a virtue of the rundown, the raw and the downright rat-infested, it has potential. And so, groups of friends (or, as they call them around these parts, collectives) started opening their own anything–goes, cheap-as-chips hotspots, promoting them via Facebook, and making up their own rules. Some of them were not intended to last, and didn't, but some of them, resonating with the boho vibe of a close-knit community, have become neighbourhood institutions and more (cf Dalston Superstore, see Party).

Often dark and low-ceilinged, always loud, and normally heaving with a preponderance of skinny jeans and 1990s haircuts (even on weekdays), Dalston's dive bars embody the seedy glamour of the area. **The Alibi** (91 Kingsland Road, E8; 020 7249 2733 thealibilondon.co.uk), launched by the underground clubbing collective Real Gold as a location for their parties, is a relative, and welcome, newcomer. **Visions Video** (588 Kingsland Road, E8) was there in the 1980s, when it actually was a video shop. But though some of the original decor remains, this DIY basement sweatbox has become a favourite spot for a late-night dance of the electronic variety. At the equally sweaty **Vogue Fabrics** (and yes, once a clothier), there's a real sense that you've stumbled upon a squat party – not least because of the honesty bar where you serve yourself drinks, and the – shall we say? – slightly bohemian loos (66 Stoke Newington Road, N16; on Facebook). It's not all so down at heel though. With its quirky Victorian aesthetic of moustachioed artworks and bowler-hat chandeliers, the former pop-up **Moustache Bar** has settled into a permanent basement home at the top of the strip (58 Stoke Newington Road, N16; on Facebook), while 'establishment' dives include the **A10 Russian Bar**, a late-night drinking den where you can sample kitsch communist décor and Russian drinking habits (267 Kingsland Road, E8; 07809 425905; on Facebook), and the friendly **Dalston Jazz Café** (4 Bradbury Street, N16), which doesn't, as you may have guessed, actually play jazz, and feels like it's been around for as long as its battered retro furnishings.

Dalston dive bars can be cliquey (though it helps if you're gay or profoundly fashionable in a fleamarket way), smug and full of hideous egomaniacs, and of course, it's all been done before (like, the Lower East Side in the 1980s – one day it will work its way to Wigan), but if you want a taste of the edge, this is where it is. Or was – to find the very latest, aim for the biggest clusters of skinny jeans and drag queens smoking on the pavement at the top of Kingsland Road from 11pm onwards. They will no doubt lead you to the dive bar du jour.

drink...

69 Colebrooke Row *(left)*

69 Colebrooke Row,
Islington, N1
Tel: 07540 528593
www.69colebrookerow.com
Open: daily, 5pm–midnight (1am
Thurs; 2am Fri/Sat)

Chichi Islington has long been crying out for a neighbourhood bar that befits its well-heeled residents. What they may not realize, however, is that they've actually had one for some time. Tucked away off the main drag, with little in the way of exterior signage, 69 Colebrooke Row is a delightfully intimate, wilfully under-the-radar Martini bar that has, quite rightly, become a firm favourite among those in the know. Since summer 2009, it has turned a small corner of N1 into a heaving, breathing slice of the good life – or La Dolce Vita to be precise, since it's very much styled on the glamorous 1950s excesses of Fellini's film. The brainchild of The Charles Lamb's landlady Camille Hobby-Limon (see Pubs) and cocktail maestro Tony Conigliaro (winner of International Bartender of the Year 2009), it's an object lesson in giving people what they want; from being greeted and seated by the charismatic hostess Kim Ireland, to the arrival of a glorious cocktail in your hands (recommended is the Serafin, which combines tequila with poire liqueur and ginger beer). You'll realise then why this is the bar with no name or sign.

Barrio North *(bottom)*

45 Essex Road, Islington, N1
Tel: 020 7688 2882
www.barrionorth.com

Open: 5pm–midnight Tues/Weds/ Sun; 5pm–1am Thurs; 5pm–2am Fri/ Sat:

Barrio (Spanish for 'neighbourhood') is so-called because it's pitched as a neighbourhood bar. But if you came from Harlem (or you're just really worldly), you'd know that 'barrio' also refers to a Hispanic ghetto. Which is excellent news, because it gives Barrio a great excuse for some sizzling Latino music and fun décor. Of course, Barrio doesn't really look like a ghetto – it looks much cleaner, richer and happier, with reclaimed allsorts creating a kaleidoscopic décor of mismatched tiles, flower garlands, and even a stripped-out vintage caravan, which the owners bought from eBay. And like any self-respecting ghetto, there's eye-catching graffiti, while the barmen, well-versed in all things Latino, mix a mean Mojito. Weekdays see an influx of older, after-work crowds thirsty for cocktails, while on the weekends it's the turn of younger revellers, who descend to knock back shots of cachaça and enjoy DJs spinning latin-infused house. And there's more tequilas, Caipirinhas, late-night DJs and ghetto-chic décor at its new sister bar, Barrio Central, opened in 2010 in Soho (6 Poland St, W1; 020 3230 1002 www.barriocentral.com). Low socio-economic status is, like, sooo exotic!

Barts *(right)*

87 Sloane Avenue, Chelsea, SW3
Tel: 020 7581 3355
www.barts-london.com
Open: daily, 6pm–12.30am (1.30am Fri/Sat; 11pm Sun)

A secret knock won't get you in, and there's no concealed button near the entrance, so if you want to gain entry to Barts, you're going to have to hope that you pass muster with the person whose eyes appear to size you up from behind a sliding hatch on this bar's main door. It's all part of the fun, of course. Styled as a Prohibition-era speakeasy, you'll find inside this shoe-box-sized venue a wholly surprising riot of quirky spectacle – from rambling décor (think mounted deer heads and Marcel Duchamp-style Mona Lisa prints) to the dress-up box that allows more adventurous visitors to really party like it's 1929. Cocktails range from well-made classics (Mojitos, Moscow Mules) to the potent – and secret – signature drink, the Park Avenue. And this being a favourite haunt of the Sloane set (unsurprisingly, given that behind Barts is royal pal Charlie Gilkes of Maggie's, see Party), there's copious amounts of bubbly on offer. The door policy may be a gimmick, but if planning a weekend visit, do make a reservation, otherwise it could be an embarrassing case of that hatch slamming in your face.

....

Benugo Bar & Kitchen @ BFI *(top)*

2166 Belvedere Rd,
South Bank, SE1
Tel: 020 7401 9000
www.benugo.com
Open: 9am–11pm Mon–Sat; 10am–10.30pm Sun

In Hollywood, the movie moguls mooch around Chateau Marmont, that absurd pseudo-gothic castle complete with pool, jungle garden and monogrammed doggie bowls. In London, matters are (appropriately) rather more low-budget – for face time and free WiFi, film folk bring their first drafts and showreels here. But the first hurdle is finding the right Benugo. Amateurs and tourists get no further than Benugo's perfectly passable riverside option, but the insider's bar is on the east side, past the BFI's three screens. Industry activity is clearly divided between the zones: treatment and script brainstorms in the dark, cosy lounge bar featuring swirly, stripy Designers' Guild sofas, and high-powered schmoozing in the whitewashed, glass-fronted restaurant that opens out into Pompidou-esque architecture. Ably serviced by the Warner bros (no, not those ones – Ben and Hugo Warner; see Serpentine Bar & Garden, see Snack), the slickly run bar offers cocktails made with pride and posh spirits, a restaurant-calibre wine list, imported speciality beers, British organic cider and gourmet snacks (Maris Piper chips, charcuterie, Neal's Yard cheese boards). Rather like 'Le Chat', business loosens up considerably after dark, with pianists at the white baby grand, DJ parties, and inevitable indiscretions.

....

Bistrotheque *(bottom)*

23–27 Wadeson Street,
Hackney, E2
Tel: 020 8983 7900
www.bistrotheque.com
Open: daily, 6.30–10.30pm (11pm (Fri/Sat); 11am–4pm Sat/Sun

Playing hard to get has become a highly developed tactic in the East End: art galleries, bars and restaurants try hard to avoid looking like they're, well, trying too hard. Based on appearances alone, scene-makers Pablo Flack and David Waddington's Bistrotheque has perfected this art. Located in a converted clothing factory on an unprepossessing Hackney side-street filled with identical industrial buildings, Bistrotheque – with impressive self-confidence – eschews any exterior decoration that might distinguish it from anonymity (from Cambridge Heath Road, it's the first entrance on the left – a discreet concrete courtyard). Upstairs, you'll find a whitewashed brasserie – the best and still most fashionable in a now-fashionable area – and downstairs, a comfortable bar with a nicely spare colour scheme (mostly black) and not-too-loud music. Given its far-flung location, the crowd is 'genuine' New East End – fashion types, artists or those connected to the local gallery scene (such as on the parallel road, Vyner Street; see Culture), and a generous camp of gays, to whom Bistrotheque's girly cocktail menu may well be targeted. The scene is completed with regular outré cabaret and tranny comedy in the 'Play Room' where, amusingly, not trying hard goes out the window.

Once the preserve of the proletariat and impoverished students, ten-pin bowling is enjoying something of a moment in London. In the underground car park of the Tavistock Hotel is an authentic (and massive) 1950s Americana playpen: eight bowling lanes imported from the States, curvy red pleather diner booths (for chewing on 'Kingpin burgers', hotdogs and cheesecakes), a mass of kitsch 1950s carpet, and a horseshoe-shaped bar made from the old bowling lanes of New York's legendary Lucky Lanes. For those disinterested in strikes and spares, there are also an old jukebox, witty arcade machines, two karaoke booths, pool tables, a film screening room and a dance floor (on weekends, a clubby atmosphere brings live music, queues and crowds). Cocktails are quick and cheap; beer is on tap and draft. This is no Disney interpretation – purposefully more seedy than its boutique neighbour, All Star Lanes (Victoria House, Bloomsbury Place; 020 7025 2676), the Bloomsbury has captured what late-night bowling should be all about, so much so that it's become a spiritual home for tattooed and quiffed rockabillies. The Big Lebowksi dudes are altogether harder to spot among us all.

■ **Bloomsbury** *(top)*
Bowling Lanes
Tavistock Hotel,
Bedford Way, WC1
Tel: 020 7183 1979
www.bloomsburybowling.com
Open: daily, 1pm–midnight (3am Fri/Sat)

■ **Callooh Callay** *(bottom)*
65 Rivington Street,
Hoxton, EC2
Tel: 020 7739 4781
www.calloohcallaybar.com
Open: daily, 5.30pm (6pm Sat)–11pm (1am Fri/Sat)

'O frabjous day! Callooh Callay!'

Named after an exclamation of celebration in the twisted tongue of Lewis Carroll, the latest addition to Hoxton's sceniest drag follows the playful, warped world of Carroll right through to its surreal furnishings (bathtub for two, anyone?) and mischievous cocktail menu (Afternoon Twee). Okay, so allow for literary licence (or confusion) when the reference segues into CS Lewis – to walk into the more decorative backrooms (ie, Narnia), you have to step through a Victorian wardrobe, but you'll be charmed into forgiveness. At the helm is ex-Lounge Lover manager Richard Wynne, so think alchemic mixology – culminating in the Mad Hatter's Punch served up for groups in a gramophone – and whimsical design, with mixy-matchy neo-Victorian furniture, and, in the loos, floor-to-ceiling mosaics of old cassettes (Bros, DIY chart recordings, Three Blind Mice…). Things to discuss in the ladies, sharing cocktails and Alice in Wonderland… If it's starting to sound like a hen's paradise, fear not – it's unmarked save two neon C's (so Chanel, sweetie!), and even then, veils and L-plates are banned on the door. Brillig.

Claridge's Bar *(top)*
Brook Street, Mayfair, W1
Tel: 020 7629 8860
www.claridges.co.uk
Open: daily, noon–1am (midnight Sun)

There are, of course, people whose engines only run on champagne. And of those, there are many who insist on only drinking it at Claridge's – otherwise, frankly, why bother? For the elegant Art Deco-style Claridge's Bar (and its darker little sister, The Fumoir, a gorgeous 1930s-themed, Lalique-panelled speakeasy) of arguably London's top hotel are considered by many to be matchless as bastions of refinement. And after the recent, sublimely modern facelift courtesy of designer darling David Collins, Claridge's lead has moved up a gear. So now, in addition to the hotel's straightforward plutocratic regulars, the occasional film/pop/art star pops in to take a break, no doubt, from the tedium of their palatial suites. However, if you are not put off by such facts, and have unlimited means, then an afternoon or evening or a life even spent here is an extremely pleasant way of fuelling the economy – perhaps with a dollop of beluga caviar, an expertly mixed cocktail or maybe some of their rarest vintage champagne. Or all of the above.

Dick's Bar *(bottom)*
at El Camino
25–27 Brewer Street, Soho, W1
Tel: 020 7734 7711
www.elcamino.co.uk
Open: 6pm–3am Tues–Sat

Asking directions for Dick's Bar in amongst Soho's seedy sex shops might seem like something of a stitch-up. Especially when, technically, there is no Dick's Bar, and certainly no signage for it. The cosy, 48-cover basement lounge, officially called The Baja Room, at new Mexican cantina El Camino is so-called because it's helmed by Dick Bradsell, widely acknowledged to be king of cocktails and all-round industry Gandalf – wherever he works ends up being called Dick's bar ('If you want nice drinks, you need me making them'). The Mexican theme continues(ish) downstairs, with a menu of ambrosial Margaritas, Daiquiris and Batidas (actually a Brazilian blend with cachaça, fruit and sweetened condensed milk – it probably boosts voluptuousness), and as long as the ingredients are stocked, you can order off-menu. You could invite an invention (previously by Bradsell, the Bramble and the Vodka Espresso), though, he warns, that's the fastest way to get a bad drink. No, this is an after-work joint for local industry insiders (for whom work finishes at midnight) who know to stick with perfectly crafted cocktails, and that the best secret party is hidden in the arse-end of Soho. NB: Entry only through day membership, gained by asking nicely at Elcaminolondon@ gmail.com or by eating at El Camino

Dukes Hotel Bar *(top)*
35 St James's Place,
Mayfair, SW1
Tel: 020 7491 4840
www.dukeshotel.co.uk
Open: daily, 2pm (noon Sat/Sun)–11pm

For the last word in elegant liquid suicide, head far away from the herd and down to Dukes Hotel, a charming old-school establishment, tucked away in its own courtyard off St James's. There, amid the traditional wood-panelled and tastefully decorated surroundings of its bar, you will find Alessandro, head barman and mixer of reputedly the best Martinis in London. At your pleasure Alessandro will wheel out his Martini trolley to your table, prepare his paraphernalia and ask

you, 'Gin or vodka, Sir/Madam?' The answer is academic, for either path is a route to swift and sure inebriation. Ernest Hemingway, recalling the effect of his first two Martinis, claimed, 'They made me civilized'. If being civilized equates to being oblivious to the hideousness of one's fellow man, then one must concur. After a couple of Dukes Hotel Martinis (such is the imposed limit), the typically odd Mayfair crowd that frequents the bar – at once wealthy, tawdry and slightly disreputable – fades into the background, the conservatively patterned wallpaper and tasteful old-school prints blur, and one is left only semi-conscious, clutching a large bill and in urgent need of paracetamol.

Favela Chic *(bottom)*
91–93 Great Eastern Street,
Hoxton, EC2
Tel: 020 7613 4228
www.favelachic.com
Open: 6pm–1am Tues–Thurs; 6pm–2am Fri/Sat

Styled on the Rio slums, there is the ready accusation that the Hoxton trendoids have romanticized poverty at its most rudely commercial. But just as only Jewish people can tell Jewish jokes, the driving force behind this bar/restaurant/club is the Brazilian dynamo Rosanne Mazzer who first created a tiny Favela Chic in 1995 in Paris. It's now a big deal both there and here. Set in the high-ceilinged former bank on the Old Street golden triangle, and artistically scuffed with peeling paint and stuffed with reclaimed 'brazila-brac', it's the antithesis of that passé pricey gloss. Fizzing with kooky carni-

drink...

val spirit, a grown-up French/Brazilian menu satisfies the stomach, affordable cachaça cocktails stoke the spirit (NB: no draught beer), while the knowing DJs spin the main bar into a dance floor (even the spellbound staff dance on the bar). Latin sounds and laidback-ness predominate (as such, it's tasty bait for homesick young South Americans) – things hot up from Thursdays with live music, fiestas and heatwaves. People grumble about surly security and the suspect hold on entry before 9pm (after which it costs £5; £10 after 11pm), though it is circumventable by reserving a restaurant table. Maybe they're just trying to recreate the iniquities of the favelas.

Lounge Bohemia *(top)*
1E Great Eastern Street,
Hoxton, EC2
Tel: 07720 707000
www.loungebohemia.com
Open: 6pm–midnight Mon–Sat;
6–11pm Sun. Reservations only.

Hoxtonites like to think they're bohemian, so it's fitting that this intimate bunker bar pays homage to the original Bohemia. Invisibly tucked between a kebab shop and a newsagent, it was opened in 2007 by Czech 'molecular mixologist' Paul Tvaroh who has achieved a seamlessly understated, communist theme – from the newspaper-ed walls to the miserably greige 1960s furniture to the menus fashioned from classic Czech novels. The egalitarian commie vibe stops short of the door policy: no suits, no groups over 10, no standing, and no one without an appointment. You see, the cocktails are made with such complex craftsman-

ship that they'd be wasted on boozers and brawlers. Made with Tvaroh's own range of infused vodka (and quite possibly a chemistry set), the inexpensive inventions include 'Tea for Two' (Earl Grey iced tea with Becherovka, lemon vodka, and honey and peach liqueurs) served in a 1960s patterned teapot, and Lab Test, six shots of those infusions, served in a test tube rack. Also popular are the hard-to-find Czech lagers and traditional Czech canapés; less so is the waiting staff, variously thought to have a sardonic sense of humour or none at all. Perhaps it's for keeping the crowds at bay.

Mark's Bar *(bottom)*
HIX Soho, 66-70 Brewer Street,
Soho, W1
Tel: 020 7292 3518
www.hixsoho.co.uk
Open: daily, noon–midnight (11pm Sun)

Follow artists Tim Noble and Sue Webster's neon sign (a louche red hand pointing downwards) to Mark's Bar, the clubby basement hangout at chef Mark Hix's Soho hotspot (see Eat). With its long zinc-topped bar, Chesterfield sofas, bar billiards and New Yorky tin panels, the look alone makes it the kind of place most blokes would like to spend their entire lives in. But then there is Nick Strangeway, essentially an artist in alcohol, who has devised London's most original drinks menu. Forget such conceits as tartinis and tropipolitans: this incredibly researched selection recalls British history, with, say, Lamb's Wool – a 1648 recipe of warm ale, apple purée and spices, or Criterion Milk Punch – an aged, clarified concoction of rum, brandy, pineapple, spice and milk (choosing can be strenuous so ask for recommendations), and of course, there's HIX's 150-strong wine cellar, plus interesting ales, bitters and stouts. What's more, you can order HIX's à la carte food menu here, and because of licence requirements, eating is obligatory (a couple of oysters will suffice, or Twiglets even) – because of its easy ambience, many choose to eat here and not upstairs. You could well be following Noble and Webster down in person.

The Old Brewery *(top)*
Old Royal Naval College,
King William Walk, Greenwich, SE10
Tel: 020 3327 1280
www.oldbrewerygreenwich.com
Open: 11am–11pm Mon–Sat; noon–10.30pm Sun

We counted 52 different artisanal thirst-quenchers on the menu of Greenwich's new microbrewery, opened in spring 2010, including Trappist ales, Belgian Lambic varieties and even an unusual yet exquisite smoked number. The Old Brewery is a temple to the amber nectar – and not just because of the excellent salty bar snacks, or the calming, low-lit décor of exposed brickwork and glass (a must, seemingly, if you want to concentrate on your ale). But first, let's clear up this confusion of whether it's a new or old brewery. Right: beer has been brewed on this site since Henry VI's time, though it had stood empty for 20 years before the much-admired Greenwich-based Meantime Brewery (Fergus Henderson is a fan) came and installed beautiful copper-clad vats and the like for more merry ale-making, as overseen by Meantime's founder and award-winning brewmaster Alistair Hook. Old thus became new. Overlooking the Thames, this destination venue (with a café, restaurant and museum, and plenty of site-specific brews) already sees a regular flow of gastro-tourists. The Old Brewery will no doubt be around for a very long time. Again.

The Rake *(bottom)*
14 Winchester Walk, Borough Market, SE1
Tel: 020 7407 0557
Open: noon–11pm Mon–Fri; 10am–11pm Sat

You wouldn't want to perform star-jumps inside this Borough Market institution. It's so small, holding just 40 folk at 13ft by 7ft, that there's barely enough room for a simple bar, and all are in clear and present danger of knocking over someone's beer. Which would be a tragedy, because each of the 130-odd varieties available here (which includes 10 or so daily-changing draughts) has been hand-selected by owners Mike Hill and Richard Dinwoodie. As the men behind the gourmet beer importers Utobeer (the company also has a stall at Borough), they have scoured the globe for the best microbrews. And rather than swanky décor, they let their top-notch product do the talking. An outdoor area adds a little more breathing room – especially nice on a sunny day – but save the Saturday sessions for the beer buffs: when the market is in full flow, it can get claustrophobic. No, best come early in the week with a professed beer-phobe – if they can't find a single beer that they like here, then they win.

drink...

Roxy Bar and Screen *(left)*
128–132 Borough High Street,
London Bridge, SE1
Tel: 020 7407 4057
www.roxybarandscreen.com
Open: 5pm–1am (midnight Mon,
1.30am Fri) Mon–Fri; 1pm–2.30am
Sat; 1pm–midnight Sun

Turn up expecting beret-wearing Truffaut fanatics and you might be disappointed. Film buff Philip Wood's The Roxy is London's first cine-bar. Unlike the concept, which sounds as pretentious as a German expressionist film convention, there are few airs and graces here. Red velvet drapes line the walls while a hotchpotch of seating for 120 (weathered Chesterfields, bistro tables and chairs) are scattered in front of a professional cinema set-up with a 4m screen. Surely the best part of a film is immediately afterwards, discussing its merits over a fine glass of wine, unusual bottled beer or even a custom cocktail – at The Roxy, you needn't even leave your seat. Arrive early to bagsy those sofas – an informal vibe means no tickets, no seat numbers and a low, sometimes zero, charge for its imaginative programme (Sun–Weds) spanning recent releases, cult classics, non-commercial shorts and documentaries, plus live sports. Tempting gastropub-style dishes (roasts, pies, risottos, posh burgers) are mostly sourced from nearby Borough Market and on weekends, VJs use the screens to nourish revellers aesthetically. The velvet, the low light, the collective experience – it's actually rather Lynchian.

St Pancras Champagne Bar *(bottom)*
St Pancras International, Pancras
Road, NW1
Tel: 020 7923 5453
www.searcys.co.uk/stpancrasgrand
Open: 10am–11pm, Mon–Thurs;
7am–11pm Fri/Sat; 8am–11pm Sun

What better excuse for fizz than finding a bar that serves it for breakfast? None of London's champagne bars can match St Pancras' on its opening hours, its magnificent backdrop of soaring glass-and-iron arches, and the glamour of seeing sleek, high-speed trains slink away to Paris while sipping on a glass of perfectly chilled bubbly. It also claims (misleadingly) to be Europe's longest champagne bar, at 96m, though the actual serving bar is a central glass cube, while the long bit, running parallel to the Eurostar track, seats 110 (plus ample standing room) at polished wood banquettes offering sweeping views of the terminal. The bar, overseen by knowledgeable champagne sommeliers, boasts over 70 bins, ranging from affordable glasses (some 20 different types are available) to vintage Krug bottles stashed in a nearby safe, while a sophisticated all-day menu includes champagne breakfasts (for example, salmon and eggs), afternoon tea with a glass of Pommery, and – of course – oysters and caviar. Given that it's trackside, the ambient temperature is 'seasonal' – ie, bitter in winter. To compensate, there are heated leather seats, adjustable fan heaters, blankets on demand and the good old-fashioned romance of champagnes and trains. Toot toot!

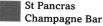

drink...

Village East *(top)*
171 Bermondsey Street, SE1
Tel: 020 7357 6082
www.villageeast.co.uk
Open: noon–11.30pm Mon–Thurs;
noon–1.30am Fri; 11am–1.30am Sat;
11am–11pm Sun

Here's proof, if it's needed, that Shoreditch (or New York, for that matter) doesn't hold the monopoly on Manhattan-style warehouse-conversion design bars. Local duo Clive Watson and Adam White (the boys behind The Garrison gastropub, also in Bermondsey) have created a buzzing venue that ticks all the right hipster boxes almost as soon as you enter the glass-fronted warehouse. The correct combination of polished steel, exposed brickwork and retro designer furniture (all picked up by White in fleamarkets and antiques fairs) puts its media-type clientele in the loft apartment of their dreams, while the drinks menu includes enough intelligent takes on old classics to keep even the biggest cocktail addict in raptures (for example, the vanilla and ginger Mojito, and Tuscan Mule, brimming with rum, Tuace liqueur and raspberry purée). And there's an excellent cheffy brasserie menu – served in either the canteen or a more formal dining room – it's no surprise that the well-turned out locals arrive early and stay late. Then again, it is a little closer than the Lower East Side.

Vinopolis *(bottom)*
8 Stoney Street,
Borough Market, SE1
Tel: 020 7940 8333
www.vinopolis.co.uk
Wine Wharf open: 6–10pm Mon–Weds; noon–11pm Thurs–Sat
Brew Wharf open: noon–11pm Mon–Sat
Bar Blue open: daily, noon (5pm Mon–Weds)–11pm (4pm Sun)

Few have tried to combine drinking and education in one go, but Vinopolis has made a business of it. Catering for the ever-widening wine market, Vinopolis offers a range of wine tours for those keen to progress beyond the 'I'll have the Liebfraumilch please' stage of affairs. Frankly, there are better things to do with wine than tasting it – such as drinking the stuff, which you can do in Wine Wharf, Brew Wharf or Bar Blue – the three drinking establishments housed within Vinopolis' expansive two-acre complex under the dramatic bare-brick arches of a Victorian railway viaduct. For those eager to bypass wine completely, Brew Wharf is lubricated by its own microbrewery, proudly featuring 'Hoptimum' as well as all sorts of imported world beers, while Bar Blue is an upmarket wine/cocktail bar. Best, however, to head to Wine Wharf where you'll find over 300 different wines, ports, sherries, sparklies, desert wines and – brace yourselves – wine cocktails (all complete with tasting notes). And if you manage a glass of each, you can award yourself a diploma in intoxication.

Vinoteca *(bottom)*
7 St John Street, Smithfield, EC1
Tel: 020 7253 8786
www.vinoteca.co.uk
Open: noon–11pm Mon–Sat

To cosmopolitan types such as ourselves, there's something fundamentally naff about the notion of a wine bar. Perhaps it's the vision it inspires of 1980s yuppies quaffing a liquid lunch, or the thought of sharing a venue with a raucous hen party fiending for Chardonnay. One visit to Vinoteca, however, will pleasurably expel this prejudice. Gone is any pretence or outmoded stuffiness, and in its place is a warm, welcoming paean to the vinotecas and enotecas of Spain and Italy. Though the décor is laidback and rustic, it's also a venue that as polished in its offering as its chattering Clerkenwell patrons. Oenophile owners Brett Woonton, Charlie Young and Elena Ares have sourced the finest wines from across Europe and beyond, focusing on distinctive but affordable cuvées, while the delicious tapas-style menu – cheeses with nobbly homemade oatcakes, cured meats, plus full roasts – is largely procured from foodie mecca Smithfield Market; tasting evenings (£10) and grape-matched dinners (£70) put to use some of their 280 different wines. And if you love the wine, you can even buy some from the instore shop. We take it all back about wine bars.

the best of the rest...

for cocktails...

Artesian at The Langham David Collins's stunning Chinese-goes-Deco space in this five-star grand hotel, with a fine line in fine rums (1c Portland Place, Oxford Circus, W1B; 020 7636 1000; www.langhamhotels.com; see Sleep)

Le Bar at Joel Robuchon Glamorous lounge bar of the Michelin-starred restaurant: red velvet curtains, black floors and petal-garnished cocktails (13 West Street, Covent Garden, WC2; 0871 971 4546; www.joel-robuchon.com; see Eat)

Blue Bar The five-star Berkeley Hotel's in-house bar painted Lutyens blue by David Collins; champagnes, whiskies and classic cocktails, plus tapas-style snacks (The Berkeley, Wilton Place, Knightsbridge, SW1; 020 7235 6000; www.the-berkeley.co.uk)

Loungelover Surreal, high-camp cocktail bar imaginatively adorned with taxidermy, curios and bric-a-brac (1 Whitby Street, Bethnal Green, E1; 020 7012 1234; www.lestroisgarcons.com)

Montgomery Place High-end neighbourhood bar harking back to the golden era of New York saloons: understated luxury, fine vintage wines, masterfully mixed cocktails (31 Kensington Park Road, W11; 020 7792 3921; www.montgomeryplace.co.uk)

Shochu Lounge From the creator of restaurants Zuma and Roka (which is upstairs) comes this impeccable if posy Japanese cocktail bar, serving – yup – shochu, vodka-like spirits infused with herbs and fruits (31 Charlotte Street, Fitzrovia, W1; 020 7580 6464; www.shochulounge.com)

Skylon Bar and Grill The Royal Festival Hall's grand flagship bar: a seasonally changing cocktail menu, a serious wine list and panoramic views of London (Level 3, Royal Festival Hall, South Bank Centre, Belvedere Road, SE1; 020 7654 7800; www.skylonrestaurant.co.uk)

Zuma Bar & Grill Japanese restaurant with lounge bar, sake and shochu cocktails for goodtime girls and boys (5 Raphael Street, Knightsbridge, SW7; 020 7584 1010; www.zumarestaurant.com)

the lo-fi and the low-key...

Bar Pepito Tiny and authentic Andalucian bodega specialising in sherry and the kind of snacks that should be eaten with it, under the same ownership as Camino (3 Varnishers Yard, The Regent Quarter, King's Cross, N1; 020 7841 7331; www.camino.uk.com/pepito)

Café Kick Jolly long-standing bar with babyfoot, live footy on telly and

drink...

143

tapas (43 Exmouth Market, Clerkenwell, EC1; 020 7837 8077; www.cafe-kick.co.uk) and its younger brother, **Bar Kick** (127 Shoreditch High Street, E1; 020 7739 8700)

The Coburg Bar The Connaught Hotel's intimate bar is the paragon of politesse. Expect five-star drinks at five-star prices, plus the invaluable hush of discretion (Carlos Place, Mayfair, W1; 020 7499 7070; www.the-connaught.co.uk; see Sleep)

Life Japanese 'concept' number with bar, restaurant and shop; understated, subtle and authentic, with Japanese beers, sushi and sake served at the requisite 98.4°F (2–4 Old Street, Clerkenwell, EC1; 020 7250 3737; www.life-oldst.com)

The Mahogany Bar A nightly knees-up (Mon–Fri) at Wilton's Music Hall's atmospheric wood-panelled bar; a thoroughly charming, and hidden, Victorian timewarp (Graces Alley, E1; 020 7702 9555; www.wiltons.org.uk)

Royal Court Theatre Café Bar A well-kept secret amongst thesps, the RCT's basement bar in the 19th-century 'pit' is modern, spacious and discreet (Sloane Square, SW1; 020 7565 5058; www.royalcourttheatre.com)

Trisha's Look away now if you like it lush: an unmarked, much-loved dive bar serving cheap, basic drinks, jazz and Soho bohemia to a loyal, characterful crowd (opposite the Pillars of Hercules; 57 Greek Street, Soho, W1; 020 7437 9536)

for a party...

Big Chill House From the dudes behind The Big Chill Festival is a DJ bar with live music, three floors and a smoking terrace (257 Pentonville Road, King's Cross, N1; 020 7427 2540); also the smaller Big Chill Bar off Brick Lane (Dray Walk, E1; 020 7392 9180; www.bigchill.net)

The Book Club The one-time Home Bar's new incarnation pitches itself as the thinking man's drinking hole, with talks, classes, workshops, and ping-pong, but it's the dance floor they come for (100 Leonard Street, Shoreditch, EC2; 020 7684 8618; www.wearetbc.com)

Cross Kings Kidult playground with cheap drinks, comedy, party bands and DJs; inclusive, up-for-it vibe in a friendly sitting room-style setting (126 York Way, King's Cross, N1; 020 7278 8318; www.thecrosskings.co.uk)

Dream Bags Jaguar Shoes Named after its previous incarnation of two old crappy shops, 'Jag Bags' has a Berlin vibe – bare, shabby and crawling with trendsters (34-36 Kingsland Road, E2; 020 7729 5830; www.jaguarshoes.com)

Green Carnation Three Oscar Wilde-inspired floors of pseudo-opulence (flocked wallpaper, gilt frames, wood-panelled walls) that can handle the spillage and scuzz of Soho's weekend traffic (5 Greek Street, W1, 020 8123 4267; www.greencarnationsoho.co.uk)

sceney...

Cecconi's Bar Take a seat at the marble island bar at this classic Italian restaurant for American cocktails served by gentlemanly white-tuxedoed waiters (5A Burlington Gardens, Mayfair, W1; 020 7434 1500; www.cecconis.co.uk; see Eat)

Concrete@Pizza East The industrial bunker bar of Nick can-do-no-wrong Jones' latest restaurant at the Tea Building; cocktails, decent wines and, inevitably, dancing, but only open Thurs–Sat (56 Shoreditch High Street, E1; 020 7729 1888; www.pizzaeast.com; see Eat)

E&O Bar A visual feast of minimal Japanese décor, elegant cocktails, dim sum bar food and a moneyed, starry crowd (14 Blenheim Crescent, Notting Hill, W11; 0871 971 6506; www.rickerrestaurants.com; see Eat)

Harvey Nichols Fifth Floor Bar Excellent anthropological opportunities (or the chance to show off how much you've bought) plus fine wines, cocktails and champagne (109 Knightsbridge, SW1; 020 7235 5250; www.harveynichols.com)

Nobu Berkeley Bar Glossy, David Collins-designed bar at Nobu Matsuhisa's Japanese fusion restaurant: sake cocktails, big bills and the socially ambitious (15 Berkeley Street, Mayfair, W1; 020 7290 9222; www.noburestaurants.com; see Eat)

Refuel Bar at Soho Hotel Exemplary hotel bar for media dahlings, with a fine wine list, fresh cocktails and a spirited (read: noisy) atmosphere; also a quieter drawing room (4 Richmond Mews, Soho, W1; 020 7559 3000; www.firmdale.com; see Sleep)

drink...

THE RT HON EARL KITCHENER OF KHARTOUM

GENTLEMEN

LAGER BEER
Heineken

The Prince of Wales

drink(pubs)...

It's often said that alcohol oils the wheels of society, and in Britain it's in pubs where this oiling happens. But the British pub is more than a mere purveyor of potation – it's the very heartbeat of the community. Pubs are such social institutions that all Britain's soap operas have one written into the plotlines (usually as the setting for scandals, showdowns and scurrilous gossiping). Every neighbourhood has a love-worn local – aka the old man's pub, after the demographic of its most thirsty regulars.

Pub culture even has its own vernacular – so if invited for a cheeky half (half a pint, and a euphemism for very many pints) down the old rub-a-dub-dub (pub), where after a few pig's ears (beers), the guv (landlord) might take to the old Joanna (piano) for a right old knees-up (fun), never turn it down. Beer is to Britain as wine is to France – where they have Bordeaux, Chablis, Chardonnay etc, we have bitter, stout, lager and ale. Some connoisseurs go to great lengths to seek out 'real ale' pubs (such as the White Horse and the Salisbury): these serve traditionally brewed, non-carbonated, unpasteurized 'live' beer, which, unlike the mass-produced stuff, continues to ferment and improve right up until you drink it. Note that if you find a palate-pleasing beverage, you may only find it in establishments owned by the same brewery – such as Youngs, Fullers, Harveys etc. Free houses (independently owned pubs) can sell any beer they like, though more and more pubs are controlled by the breweries or replaced by national chains such as All Bar One, Pitcher &

Piano, the Slug & Lettuce, and the cheapo Wetherspoons – fine if you want McDonalds homogeneity, not if you want soul.

While getting drunk is a favourite British pastime (with a current vogue for doing it on English or French cider; with ice to be totally cool), pub life is also about relaxing and diversion – many boozers have pool tables, fruities (fruit machines), pinball machines, dartboards and a tatty selection of games – chess, backgammon, cards etc. Pub quizzes are a friendly way of engaging the community (even though they are often taken scary-seriously by some Londoners), and there is always room for new recruits. London's smoking ban in 2007 has led to the (sociologically fascinating) rise and rise of the smoking terrace (where British strangers actually interact – or 'smirt', ie, flirt while smoking). And while the recently relaxed licensing laws were somewhat overhyped and we haven't indeed turned into a nation of 24-hour alco-zombies, the more music-orientated are taking advantage of calling 'Time, please!' an hour or two later, pitching themselves more as clubs than pubs (The Boogaloo, the Lock Tavern, the Old Queen's Head, The Rest is Noise). Usefully, Britain's DIY indie/folk wave is providing plenty of cheap gig material from young bands keen to take their music beyond their parents' garages. Other pubs prefer the traditional lock-in – where pints carry on being pulled till the (usually fabulously eccentric) landlord/lady decides the party's over.

Pub grub is no longer the pork scratchings/curled-up sandwiches/chicken-in-a-basket of days gone by – the London gastropub scene that started in the 1990s has become so ubiquitous since the smoking ban that our new entries seem ever more food-focused. Even the superchefs have nailed the gastropub, with Gordon Ramsay at the Narrow and the Warrington, and Angela Hartnett at the York & Albany, and sometimes beer is matched to food as sommeliers would for wine. But inevitably, with ubiquity (not least since shifting food has become the pelican's way of warding off closure), the term 'gastropub' is starting to devalue. While many genuine gastropubs (the Eagle, the Anchor & Hope, the Duke of Cambridge) attract punters on the merits of their restaurant-quality cuisine alone, the many new pretenders have made it something of a dirty word in the industry – it's often no longer a valid indicator of quality. Since a new term is needed (especially when, in 2010, the Michelin inspectors awarded their first ever star to a London pub, the Harwood Arms), we propose 'restro-pub' – the Harwood is certainly more this than that.

Thankfully, the classic pubs are remarkably resilient to change – 'Website? What's that?' – and like great oaks, many stand for centuries and centuries (see the Holly Bush and Ye Olde Mitre). In summer, people brave the Great British Weather to drink in beer gardens, and in winter, tables around open fires are highly prized. And of course, there's always the great tradition of the pub-crawl – where you drink a pint in each pub until very well oiled indeed.

When a Pub is Not a Pub

Pubs serving champagne (the Fox & Anchor), pubs hosting jumble sales (the Old Queen's Head), pubs sending waiters to take your reservation at the door (The Harwood Arms), pubs with a bourbon collection that would defeat Jim Morrison (The Lexington) – a new breed of pub is not looking much like a pub at all. At the same time, pub land is in trouble, with around 40 closing down a week in Britain. The two facts are not unconnected – the pub landlord is going all out to stay alive, and many aren't. While the purists may balk at such frivolities, the fact is that, in such insolvent times, savvy licensees are harnessing that unique DNA of the welcoming British pub – that invites people to sit around all day without judgement – and add the good qualities of all those other forms of hospitality (the bar, the café, the restaurant, the club) that can never quite reach the pub's spirit of relaxation and role as community cornerstone. (That said, pub DNA is not indestructible, and, naming no names, pubs can go too far in introducing non-pub conceits.)

And so we are seeing speciality pubs, pubs resembling European cafés with Jing tea and WiFi, and, yes, the restro-pub. People with tightened purse-strings are more likely to eat in a pub than a restaurant because it feels more prudent. Even though of course it's not, if one has spent all night in the boozer, as opposed to a couple of hours in a restaurant – specifically because a pub is so much more welcoming. Similarly, the point of the pub is that it's a casual drop-in place – although booking at pubs is on the rise, pubs still invite spontaneity, and so lunch or dinner down the local doesn't seem much of an upheaval. It's an idea the club pubs are capitalising on too – why go to an expensive and attitudinal nightclub in town when your friendly neighbourhood pub is putting on DJs and pulling cheap pints? The progressive pub is looking outwards and bringing in, packing a tutti-frutti programme of old pub (Sunday roasts, pub quizzes, comedy nights) and new (fancy-dress parties, spoken word, film screenings). The hedonist is happy.

149

The Anchor & Hope *(top)*
36 The Cut, Waterloo, SE1
Tel: 020 7928 9898
Open: 5–11pm Mon; 11am–11pm
Tues–Sat; 12.30–5pm Sun

After a takeover and makeover in 2003 by The Eagle's Michael Belben (think simple scrubbed wood floors, red-painted walls, farmhouse furniture), The Anchor & Hope no longer looks like the kind of joint where meat might be raffled and men might meet their ends. Now it's a gastropub serving robust British dishes cooked by former St John chefs – many say it is London's finest and many have modelled their own pubs on it; in 2007 it was awarded a Michelin Bib Gourmand for 'good food at moderate prices'. The only possible objection is its no-booking policy (except Sundays' set lunch), which can mean a long, long wait in the admittedly agreeable tavern-style bar. But it is worth the wait, so start with a sherry – there's a proper selection, not the rubbish you serve to mad Auntie Joan at Christmas (plus plenty of gastropub-worthy wines and beers) – and sample the tapas-style nibbles at the bar. It's best to come with company, as many of the roasts on the twice-daily changing menu are to share (including the legendary slow-cooked duck) – if, that is, you can be trusted only to eat your fair share, after one too many sherries on an empty stomach.

The Boogaloo *(middle)*
312 Archway Road,
Highgate, N6
Tel: 020 8340 2928
www.theboogaloo.co.uk

Open: 6pm–midnight (1am Thurs, 2am Fri) Mon–Fri; 2pm–2am Sat; 2–10.30pm Sun

Anyone who's anyone has played an acoustic gig here. The jukebox has every song you'd ever want to listen to and none that you wouldn't. It's Shane McGowan's 'office'. The Boogaloo is already close to achieving the founders' ambition of becoming one of the greatest rock'n'roll bars of all time (and all that comes with that). Located unprepossessingly on a main road within sight of Archway's 'Suicide Bridge', this pub, since throwing open its cheery red doors in 2002, has become a mecca for music lovers, musicians, groupies and wannabes – and is where the volatile (now ex) lovers Pete Doherty and Kate Moss famously duetted. If you're feeling knowledgeable enough, the Tuesday evening music quiz is fiendishly hard and pits the geekiest musos against the music-makers, plus there are literary readings, poetry slams and club nights. Hungry? Shut up and have another Guinness: the Irish landlord – Gerry O'Boyle of Filthy McNasty's infamy – knows how to pull a proper pint.

The Canton Arms *(bottom)*
177 South Lambeth Road,
Stockwell, SW8
Tel: 020 7582 8710
www.cantonarms.com
Open: 5–11pm Mon; 11am–11pm
Tues–Sat; 11am–10.30pm Sun

Let them eat foie gras! Who would have thought this French delicacy would be embraced in the borough of Lambeth, but times they are a-

drink…

changin'. The Canton Arms, under the ownership of ex-Eagle/Great Queen Street chef Trish Hilferty, proudly proffers the already notorious foie gras toasties as part of its bar menu alongside haggis toasties and scotch pies. The irony is that The Canton Arms sees itself as a boozer for The Common Man in spite of its highfalutin' gourmet snack. Having reopened in February 2010 after merely a lick of paint to its old self, it claims to be 'a pub with a dining room' rather than a gastro, and indeed the original regulars still cling to the bar area, nursing their remarkably inexpensive pints of real ale. Meanwhile, the gastro pilgrims have to queue, just like at The Anchor & Hope, though it has already shaken off the Anchor & Hope-lite tag and developed its own identity based upon an excellently priced, creative yet traditional, daily-changing menu. There's even an array of newspapers, glossies, fiction from trashy paperbacks to Shakespeare, and WiFi access to boot. Don't underestimate Saarf London, eh?

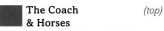

The Coach & Horses *(top)*

26 Ray Street, Clerkenwell, EC1
Tel: 020 7278 8990
www.thecoachandhorses.com
Open: noon–11pm Mon–Fri; 6–11pm Sat; 1–5.30pm Sun. Closed weekends in July and August.

Listen closely enough and you can still hear the horses galloping past the 1855-established Coach & Horses. Or so legend has it. Belief may depend on how much has been imbibed, but there is no escaping history here. This back-street hostelry lies on the River Fleet which linked Victorian Hampstead and The City, and was next to Clerkenwell's bear-baiting arena of Hockley-in-the-Hole. In 2003, the pub and its heritage were rescued by Giles and Colette Webster, who dismantled the hideous 1970s refit, returning it to former glories. The now celebrated kitchen, under Henry Herbert of BBC2's Great British Menu, serves modern British nosh (regularly sourced from the underrated wilds of London including blackberries from Hampstead Heath and mushrooms from Epping Forest), including an oft-exalted scotch egg. Mrs Webster has handpicked an impressive wine list, and keeps a fine selection of cask ales and over 30 malts and whiskies, though guests are equally welcome for a cuppa and a natter (there's also a lovely beer garden). But, beware the ghosts in residence – an old man in the beer cellar and a black cat on the second floor are familiar though benign presences, say the Websters. Brrr!

The Cow *(bottom)*

89 Westbourne Park Road, Notting Hill, W2
Tel: 020 7221 0021
www.thecowlondon.co.uk
Open: daily, noon–11pm (10.30pm Sun)

You might expect The Cow to be named after a particularly meat-heavy menu – and it's true that The Cow's draw first and foremost is its excellent gastropub fare (albeit for seafood and not steaks). However, the name comes not from an animal, but a human – it's how the locals used to refer to the pub's original landlady. Now the land-

lord is one Tom Conran, son of uber-restaurateur Sir Terence Conran and is unlikely to attract such abuse: this small pub, authentically styled on old Irish pubs – scruffy cream walls, wooden pub furniture and ironic lino floors – is still attracting Notting Hill's finest, with a smattering of celeb regulars for that extra head-turning factor. With Tom's foodie pedigree (he also has his own deli/café nearby, Tom's Deli), there's due praise for a menu that's subtly Celtic in theme – think modern Irish without the 'Oirishness'; Guinness and oysters are a favourite. Stick with the theme with Irish and Scottish whiskies, and weekly guest ales, or shell out for champagnes and a respectable wine list. If you can't bear the scrum at the bar, head upstairs to the dining room, although peace doesn't come cheap. It's not a reason to hurl farmyard insults.

The Dove *(top)*
24–28 Broadway Market,
Hackney, E8
Tel: 020 7275 7617
www.dovepubs.com
Open: daily, noon–11pm (1am Fri/Sat)

Broadway Market, nestled between London Fields and Hackney's canals, is the current address of choice for East End hipsters, and The Dove, a free house with a prodigious selection of Belgian beers, is their New Best Friend. Here, the liquid equivalent of the latest haircut is The Dove's wonderful cherry beer, but there's also a decent wine list, British and Belgian ciders and, to go with the territory, organic options (some say the staff have a rude 'tude, which, again, could be put down to the

smug postcode). The menu features hearty Flemish stews, Leffe-battered fish and chips, and free-range sausages and burgers; book ahead for its crowd-pleasing Sunday roasts or join the long queue. There's a bohemian mittel-European feel to the décor (candle-strewn chequered tablecloths and a jumble of dark wooden chairs and benches), but in layout, The Dove is classic English – all higgledy-piggledy with various alcoves for lounging in comfort, and a roaring fire in winter, beer garden in summer. Its sister pub, The Dovetail in Clerkenwell (9 Jerusalem Passage; 020 7490 7321) is equally charming, though maybe after working through the pubs' selection of over 100 Belgian beers, anything would be.

The Eagle *(bottom)*
159 Farringdon Road,
Clerkenwell, EC1
Tel: 020 7837 1353
Open: noon–11pm Mon–Sat; noon–5pm Sun

It's easy to forget that BE (Before the Eagle), pub grub was microwaved from frozen. Founded in 1991 by the still-hands-on Michael Belben (also of The Anchor & Hope; see separate entry) and chef David Eyre (of The Eyre Brothers), The Eagle pioneered the gastropub revolution. Serving up honest, high-quality dishes (think robust Mediterranean), real ale and decent wine in a pub with polish, its influence was such that Belben and Eyre call it 'the pub stud farm', after so many followed suit. But there's more to it than gastronomy: having opened during a recession, the prophetic partners kept it modest: no side dishes, no tablecloths, no reservations ('We're a pub!'), no menus. Daily dishes were chalked up on the blackboard, and orders placed at the bar. Little has changed since then (not least the farmhouse-style décor, due a spruce – though booking is now permitted for groups of six or more earlybirds, at 12.30pm or 6.30pm) and its relevance endures. It's sometimes standing room only, always atmospheric (noisy) and service can be slapdash. It has attracted such fine chefs to its tiny kitchen – Sam & Sam Clarke (who met here; see Moro, Eat), Margot Henderson (see La Rochelle; Snack), the incumbent Ed Mottershaw – that in 2009, Eyre released The Eagle Cookbook: Recipes from the Original Gastropub. So a chef stud farm too.

 Fox & Anchor *(top)*
115 Charterhouse Street, Farringdon, EC1
Tel: 020 7250 1300
www.foxandanchor.com
Open: daily, 8am–11pm (1am Fri; midnight Sat)

There has been a public house on this spot for at least 110 years, but while the façade may date from such a time, an intervention of sorts in November 2007 has lent a modern twist to its Dickensian origins. Firstly, like an old coaching inn, six bedrooms are available upstairs. But these are no straw-bale mattresses with oily blankets – refurbished by Malmaison, there are claw-footed baths, kingsize beds and Bose sound systems (plan ahead – they book up months in advance). On the pub floor, there's real ale (six of them, on a changing rota),

but you'll also spy men wooing women over bottles of champagne (the snug nooks make for perfect date material). There's a meat-heavy menu as there always would have been, thanks to its proximity to Smithfield, but there's also locally sourced oysters, steak tartare and goose-fat chips, as orchestrated by veteran Malmaison/Hotel du Vin chef John Woodward. However, there's plenty of room at the inn for students and market traders (with outrageously early opening hours, unobtrusive sport screens, and man-sized English breakfasts), as well as city boys and girls. Like it says itself: it's 'hops and chops, cuvées and duvets' at this 21st-century inn.

The George & Dragon *(bottom)*
2 Hackney Road, Shoreditch, E2
Tel: 020 7012 1100
Open: daily, 6pm–midnight

This grubby old Victorian boozer has become the coolest drinkery in Shoreditch since its kitsch gay makeover by part-time queen and East End linchpin Richard 'Richardette' Battye, who, as an employee, liked the place so much he bought it. In fact, The George is now such an institution that the Institute of Contemporary Arts (see Culture) recreated it as a live arts installation – right down to Battye's late great-grandmother's antiques, heart-shaped lights and vintage cowboy ephemera that adorned its fag-cured walls. Tranny DJs (including Battye) spin unashamedly trashy pop to a crowd that is gay, straight or somewhere in between; all sport the local dress code of thrift chic and studied

drink...

cool. Raid your dressing-up box or just admire the exhibitionism as the scene hags overflow onto the pavement (be sure to hide your pashmina, though, or face their withering looks). The George doesn't bother with the practicalities of food (the peckish should forage in Kingsland Road's Vietnamese noodle bars; see Eat) – the pub comprises just one small room, unless you count the White Cubicle art gallery: yes, located in the ladies'.

The Golden Heart *(top)*

110 Commercial Street, Spitalfields, E1
Tel: 020 7247 2158
Open: daily, 11am–midnight (10.30pm Sun)

The Golden Heart is an exemplary East End boozer – rough and ready, classic pub drinks (no highfalutin' quadruple distilling here), and, crucially, run by an eccentric landlady – namely local celebrity Sandra Esquilant who's pulled its pints for over 30 years. Her celebrity status has been hard-earned by being the golden-hearted publican to Spitalfields' seriously arty residents – among them, Tracey Emin, Gillian Wearing and Gilbert & George; Esquilant was recently voted one of the art world's 100 most influential people. Fame has not gone to Sandra's rather elegant head, however, and she clearly rules the roost. If she doesn't like the cut of your jib, you'll be asked to vacate the premises (there's even a paparazzi ban); if she does like you, she'll give you that maternal heart, and maybe a bottle of plonk on the house. A loyal community of Spitalfields' barrow boys, City slickers, hipsters and

that art pack variously refer to her as family, a force of nature, and a best friend. Look out for the framed photos of Ms Emin, the occasional piece of donated Brit Art, and of course, wayward drunken artists.

The Harwood Arms *(bottom)*

27 Walham Grove, Fulham, SW6
Tel: 020 7386 1847
www.harwoodarms.com
Open: daily, noon (5pm Mon)–11pm (midnight Fri/Sat)

The Michelin pub is an oxymoron in London no more. As the city's first ever pub to secure a Michelin star (in January 2010), The Harwood has changed the pub landscape forever. Masterminded by Brett Graham of The Ledbury, Mike Robinson of the Pot Kiln country pub in Berkshire and Edwin Vaux of the Vaux Brewery dynasty, the refurbishment of this Fulham mainstay in 2008 coupled an informal, countryside feel with cosmopolitan décor and an ever-changing, Michelin-quality (though good-value) British menu. Devised by (ex-Ledbury) head chef Stephen Williams, it features first-of-the-season produce and game shot by Robinson himself (which speaks volumes about the Harwood's socio-economic status). Post-Michelin, the pub is now 90% dining, booking is mandatory, and non-diners will feel marginalised at feeding time – gone is the community cornerstone for all classes (unless Chelsea's playing, when the Harwood has little choice), and, in its place, a deluxe shelter for Euro-Sloanes and Michelin migrants.

drink...

Harwood Arms Mark II is expected in 2011 in another yummy mummy enclave, and no doubt its imitators will follow with their first-flush produce and personally shot game. And perhaps more stars.

 The Holly Bush *(left)*
22 Holly Mount,
Hampstead, NW3
Tel: 020 7435 2892
www.fullers.co.uk
Open: daily, noon–11pm (10.30pm Sun)

On a cold winter's evening, there are few better places to nurse a pint of real ale than fireside at The Grade II-listed Holly Bush. This cosy, traditional pub is nestled in the heart of a most picturesque, and expensive, part of London, but when it opened in 1807, Hampstead was home to the working classes. Then, in Victorian times, the middle classes, evidently taking to the Holly Bush, instigated some kind of social and gender apartheid, dispatching the working class to the tavern bar, and ladies (to 'protect their dignity') to the Coffee Room – as much is writ in the antique window etching. Nowadays its warren of dark, woody rooms is less about social segregation, more about conjuring a vintage atmosphere. In fact, happily, about the only modernization (and one hopes that remains the way, now under the ownership of Fullers) is its acclaimed menu, offering their take on, say, pie (with rabbit and tarragon), egg and cress sandwiches (with duck egg), and surf'n'turf (fillet steak and lobster sausage). Which probably does rather alienate the labourers.

 The Jerusalem *(middle)*
Tavern
55 Britton Street,
Clerkenwell, EC1
Tel: 020 7490 4281

www.stpetersbrewery.co.uk/london
Open: 11am–11pm Mon–Fri

With its old-fashioned murky green bottles of beer and topsy-turvy layout, this is the kind of olde-worlde pub you might find down Harry Potter's Daigon Alley. The building was once a merchant's house and an artisan's workshop, and, prior to this 1720 incarnation, the Jerusalem tavern occupied various other sites since the 14th century (it was named after The Priory of St John of Jerusalem, and it is said that from here, the Knights of St John left to fight the Crusades). However, the estimable St Peter's Brewery of Suffolk only arrived relatively recently, in 1996, and has made jolly fine work disguising it, with sage-coloured walls, wall-mounted ale barrels at the bar, and a charmingly chipped fireplace. Perch in one of its many creaky nooks and crannies to sample its unusual brews, all from St Peter's – if curious about what a pint tasted like a thou-sand years ago, try the King Cnut ale, a surprisingly delicious blend of barley, nettles and juniper; for more modern pleasures, try the lemon and ginger ale, the spiced ale and the organic bitter; there's also solid lunchtime sustenance. In summer, bag one of the outdoor tables, but don't leave it till the weekend when the old man puts its feet up and shuts up shop.

The Lexington (right)
96 Pentonville Road,
Islington, N1
Tel: 020 7837 5371
www.thelexington.co.uk
Open: daily, noon–2am (4am Fri/Sat, midnight Sun)

As everyone knows, bourbon is the tipple of choice for any self-respecting rock god – and few spots in London can compete with The Lexington's 50-odd selection of sour mash whiskeys. Indeed, music runs through the very

veins of this buzzing baroque-styled pub-cum-lounge bar. There's lo-fi live music upstairs (with programming from the likes of White Heat and Club Fandango, and gigs most nights) and a regular clientele who, while sprawling effetely on mismatched sofas, clearly try very hard to look as if they are, or at least should be, in a band. Rocker/owner Stacey Thomas has an unrivalled vision in creating shabby chic music bars – especially in this part of town. Also the brains behind the nearby Buffalo Bar (see Party/live music), since re-opening this venue in early 2009, she has transformed what was a distinctly average nightspot in the more down-at-heel end of Islington into the epicentre of the capital's indie elite. Rough Trade Records host Mondays' pop quiz, there's rock'n'roll bingo every Tuesday, and it's the perfect Sunday afternoon spot to get elegantly wasted – you might even catch a super-hot band in the process.

The Norfolk Arms *(top)*

28 Leigh Street,
King's Cross, WC1
Tel: 020 7388 3937
www.norfolkarms.co.uk
Open: daily, 11am–11pm (10.30pm Sun)

The Norfolk Arms is proof that good things come in threes. Michael Kittos, the brains behind one of London's first and finest gastropubs The Peasant in Farringdon, and its Regent's Park offshoot The Queens Head & Artichoke, opened Number Three, The Norfolk, in 2006, as a tapas pub, revolutionising the old man's lair with utter disregard for its King's Cross roots, and, evidently, the ghosts of the Victorian Gin Palace which originally occupied the site. This Iberian gastro delight now resembles an admittedly incongruous corner of España: Serrano hams dress the window, succulent salamis dangle behind the bar and The Virgin Mary watches over you as you sup a glass of La Gitana Manzanilla (made by grapes fermented by the sea) in the Norfolk's bright bleached interior. The extensive, carefully sourced Spanish/Mediterranean menu caters for carnivores and herbivores alike, largely a bunch of happy locals and refined types from nearby Bloomsbury. The pub was once divided into three – one room for gentlemen, one for ladies, one for gin collection; now the unholy trinity is Muro Blanco, Manchego and Manzanilla. Reasons to be cheerful...

The Old Queen's Head *(bottom)*

44 Essex Road, Islington, N1
Tel: 020 7354 9993
www.theoldqueenshead.com
Open: daily, noon–midnight (1am Thurs, 2am Fri/Sat)

And so it came to pass that when late drinking licences were issued, pubs became clubs. With ex-Fabric founding partner Steve Blonde taking over the helm in 2006, The Old Queen's Head was evidently in well-connected hands: its almost nightly musical line-up far exceeds pub status (recently, Jack Peñate, The Kooks and Andrew Weatherall; expect a weekend cover charge). That's not to say it's too big for the unsigned and the unplugged – or the uninhibited, as a cool crowd equipped with concept haircuts, fashion-over-flattery

jeans and all the right moves piles into its party room upstairs. No space? A warm welcome awaits downstairs: slouchy leather sofas, reindeer chandeliers and a 17th-century log fire. Its menu rightly puts drinking first, and food first equal – cocktails, wine and champagne (beer goes without saying) to wash down topside burgers, fish and hand-cut chips and Tom's pies from Devon, plus sharing plates and all-day Sunday roasts. But more equal are its frequent all-day benders (including The Sunday Social). Still no space? Book a table, or check out the riotous growing family: The Westbury, in Kilburn, Paradise by Way of Kensal Rise, and Queen Boadicea, in Clerkenwell.

The Prince of Wales *(top)*
38 Old Town, Clapham, SW4
Tel: 020 7622 3530
Open: daily, 4pm (1pm Sat/Sun)–
midnight, (1am Fri/Sat, 11pm Sun)

Eschew Clapham's bland high street populated with Oakley sunglasses and Fat Face, and make for the quaint Old Town and its jolly local pub, The Prince of Wales (clue: it's the white-painted corner pub with blue neon POW POW POW on the walls). A true original, it's jam-packed with ephemera and car-boot junk – taxidermy, toys, artificial limbs even, much of which is strung from the ceiling. Unlike other self-consciously 'eccentric' pubs, the POW is more an authentic monument to the work of a lifelong hoarder – a time-capsule filled with stuff that marks the passage of time. It's also a favourite of local fashion doyenne Vivienne Westwood, and is probably considered just too inscrutable for the Clapham clones. The music veers towards the indie end of the spectrum and is not so loud that you can't chat design with Dame Westwood. There's no food (though you can now order in excellent wood-fired pizza from Oregano) – just drinks (and real ale), kitsch and chat, and a great big soul.

drink…

■ The Punch Bowl   *(middle)*
41 Farm Street, Mayfair, W1
Tel: 020 7493 6841
www.punchbowllondon.com
Open: daily, noon–11pm (5pm Sun)

Would you Adam and Eve it! The God-father of Mockney, Guy Ritchie, continues to preside over The Punchbowl, the second oldest pub in Mayfair. Renovated in spring 2008 by Mr and Mrs Madonna alongside club moguls Piers Adams, Nick House and contemporary court jester Guy Pelly, the Punchbowl has been attracting celeb-spotters ever since (despite a ban on photography). The Punchbowl quickly gained notoriety with its raucous lock-ins attracting the royal princes and Hollywood glitterati, from De Niro to Al Pacino, leading to a paparazzi frenzy, opprobrium from the neighbours and never-ending tabloid coverage. But below the surface, the pub grub overseen by two Gordon Ramsay disciples (bangers'n'mash, fish'n'chips) is exquisite, if over-priced.

The working-class regulars are testament to the quality of the pub as a traditional boozer (with real ale and everything) and the 18th-century décor, wooden interior and portrait of Winston Churchill sit easily in the old-school ambience. In response to litigious locals and a 2009 licence review, two bouncers now police intake, misbehaviour and noise (the Irish music from house band The Punchbowl is notorious). Rumour has it there are to be two Punchbowls stateside (New Yoik and LA, of course). Rule Britannia, innit.

■ The White Horse   *(right)*
1 Parson's Green, SW6
Tel: 020 7736 2115
www.whitehorsesw6.com
Open: daily, 9.30am–11.30pm (midnight Thurs–Sat)

The White Horse is as much about the beer as its ridiculously stereotyped Sloane crowd. Brays of 'Oh, look Annabelle, there's Annabelle' resound

165

from the rugby-shirted scrum amid discussions of upcoming hols to Val d'Isère. However, if you can look past all this, to the grand Victorian pub's welcoming interior, with deep Chesterfield sofas, mahogany bar, beamed roof and flagstone floors, plus a roaring fire in winter, daily summer barbeques (weather permitting; check the website) and the option to meander onto Parson's Green to mull your pint in the sunshine, then The White Horse has undeniable charms. What's more, The White Horse is a 'beer pub' – what pub isn't, you might ask? Perhaps one without beer festivals, beerfood pairing in its large dining room, up to 14 cask and draught beers, over 135 varieties of bottled beers, six of the seven Trappist monasteries' beers currently available, and, deservedly, a platinum Beautiful Beer award. For that, there's a rival tribe in town: the

bearded beer tourist, who in their specs and cagoules, present an amusing foil to the yah majority at what is snarkily referred to as The Sloaney Pony.

Ye Olde Mitre *(top)*
1 Ely Court, Farringdon, EC1
Tel: 020 7405 4751
Open: 11am–11pm Mon–Fri

There are few secrets left in London. Perhaps it takes the protection of a private road – Ely Court is one such gated lane, built in 1772 to keep Londoners out of the pretty pocket of land around Ely Palace, the Bishops of Ely's London residence (technically, though, it's not London but Cambridgeshire but that's another story). Now the lane simply serves to distance London's roar when visiting Ye Olde Mitre. And it really is old, first opening here in 1546 to quench the palace's servants. With antique beer barrels for outside seating, a beamed roof and a tasteful amount of artefacts, this quaint wooden warren is a step back in time: no music, no TV, just dominos and cribbage and real ales (such is its commitment to the stuff, it opens on one weekend a year, for the Great British Beer Festival); food is vintage tavern tucker – pork pies, scotch eggs and its renowned toasties. Look out for the diamond dealers from nearby Hatton Gardens who come for a quiet pint. Amusingly, the crims are also in on the secret: because it's not London, the police can't arrest them there. Brings a whole new meaning to the lock-in.

the best of the rest...

restro-pubs...

The Cadogan Arms This Sloanes' stalwart was expertly resurrected in 2009 by the unstoppable Martin brothers (see The Botanist; Snack): real ales, modern European food and their signature polish (298 King's Road, Chelsea, SW3; 020 7352 6500; www.thecadoganarmschelsea.com)

The Duke of Cambridge For those who find eating an ethical minefield: Britain's only certified organic gastropub, opened in 1998, is 'obsessed' with having a tiny carbon footprint (30 St Peter's Street, Islington, N1; 020 7359 3066; www.dukeorganic.co.uk)

Great Queen Street Tom Norrington-Davies's lauded nose-to-tail food in a tarted-up old boozer; unpretentious, popular, noisy – hardly surprising that it's the lil sis of The Anchor & Hope (32 Great Queen Street, Covent Garden, WC2; 020 7242 0622)

The Peasant Opened in 1993 on Clerkenwell's golden mile for food, this early gastropub, now under the Wright brothers, is still cooking up seriously good, British-focused fare (240 St John Street, EC1; 020 7336 7726; www.thepeasant.co.uk)

The Thomas Cubitt Named after Belgravia's master builder, superlative standards continue with modern British cuisine, an excellent wine list and a handsome setting. Book upstairs to avoid the braying crowds (44 Elizabeth Street, SW1; 020 7730 6060; www.thethomascubitt.co.uk)

The Warrington Gastro-ed by Gordon Ramsay Holdings, the food is standout, the drinks list diligent, the décor sympathetic to the original Warrington Hotel (93 Warrington Crescent, Maida Vale, W9; 020 7592 7960; www.gordonramsay.com).

party pubs...

Dogstar As London's original rave pub, this three-floor Brixton institution is still 'somewhere to end up at' thanks to its very late licence and urban vibes – hip hop, drum'n'bass, dubstep etc (389 Coldharbour Lane, SW9; 020 7733 7515; www.antic-ltd.com/dogstar)

The Lock Tavern DJ Jon Carter's perennially popular and packed play-pen puts on the big-name parties Weds–Sun – especially Sunday: its warm-up roast is a major draw (35 Chalk Farm Road, Camden, NW1; 020 7482 7163; www.lock-tavern. co.uk)

The New Rose When pubs need bouncers, you know where it's heading. Opened in 2009 with DJs, real ales, and pizzas and burgers, this place handles a crowd in elegance (84-86 Essex Road, Islington, N1; 020 7226 1082; www.newrose.co.uk)

The Old Blue Last As Vice Magazine's hedonistic HQ (erm, vice den), OBL puts on live music and DJs six days a week; tattoos, fashionably bad dye jobs and a high tolerance for hordes are requisites (39 Great Eastern Street, Hoxton, EC2; 020 7739 7033; www.theoldbluelast.com)

The Rest is Noise The latest off-shoot from 580 Ltd (the rowdy Lock Tavern/Amersham Arms gang) with the same ingredients: late licence, trendsters, live bands and decent grub and love of Sunday lunches (442 Brixton Road, SW9; 020 7346 8521; www.therestisnoisebrixton.com)

Star of Bethnal Green Party-hardy Rob Star (of Mulletover raves) went vaguely overground in 2008 with the Star's renowned club nights (including DJ Hannah Holland's Batty Bass), gigs and a karaoke room (359 Bethnal Green Road, E2; 020 7729 0167; www. starofbethnalgreen.com)

real ale pubs...

The Carpenter's Arms Nowt sinister now about this one-time gangster pub owned by the Kray brothers, just a preponderance of Belgian and British beers, and world specialities (73 Cheshire Street, Bethnal Green, E2; 020 7739 6342; www.carpentersarmsfreehouse.com)

The Draft House Le Café Anglais owner Charlie McVeigh's 'beer boutique', opened in 2009, offers 17 ales on tap, over 50 bottled, and variously served in third-, half- and full pints, as they should (Clapham: 94 Northcote Road, SW11; 020 7924 1814; Battersea: 74 Battersea Bridge Road, SW11; 020 7228 6482; and next in Tower Bridge; www.drafthouse.co.uk)

Royal Oak Trad old pub that's cosy, friendly and unspoilt by time; under the ownership of Lewes brewery Harveys, so expect its real ales, seasonals and British cask ciders (44 Tabard Street, Borough, SE1; 020 7357 7173)

The Salisbury Romantic Victorian pub with hand-etched windows, delicate mirrors and gilt-framed booths, serving exquisitely silky cask ale; winner of a Beautiful Beer Platinum award but touristy (90 St Martin's Lane, Covent Garden, WC2; 020 7836 5863)

The Wenlock Arms This charming if tatty East End boozer has the old Joanna, the resident dogs and the pickled eggs, but also – as a real ale free house – seasonal ales, knowledgeable cellar 'elves' and plenty of awards (26 Wenlock Road, N1; 020 7608 3406; www.wenlock-arms.co.uk)

The Charles Lamb Camille Hobby-Limon's prettily restored free house with guest ales (they take requests), Californian micro-brews and St Peter's Organic ale, plus Mascha the dog (16 Elia Street, Islington, N1; 020 7837 5040; www.thecharleslambpub.com)

sceney pubs...

The Clarendon This new cocktail lounge-cum-gastropub, decorated in now-ubiquitous eclectica (vintage lampshades, zebra skins, butterflies) is the go-to for Holland Park gossip (123a Clarendon Road, W11; 020 7229 1500; www.theclarendonlondon.com)

The Commercial Tavern Grand old pub on two floors, trippily decked out with Deco touches, peely paint, cups and saucers and Polaroid photos, and over-run with scene- and City slaves alike (142 Commercial Street, Spital-fields, E1; 020 7247 1888)

The Elgin A boho-chic refit to this Notting Hill stronghold is keeping the locals in a manner to which they are accustomed, plus the perks of locally brewed ales, over 20 gins and posh-ish British food (96 Ladbroke Grove, W11; 020 7229 5663; www.geronimo-inns.co.uk/theelgin)

The Endurance Soho veterans (here, good-time media, fashion and film posers and the odd Soho soak) are well-trained in, umm, enduring the crush of popularity of this hip, knowing pub (90 Berwick Street, W1; 020 7437 2944; www.thetemperance.co.uk/endurance)

The Hawley Arms Those naughty indie-rockers, the 'Camden Caners' (Noel Fielding, Amy Winehouse, Johnny Borrell), have largely returned to their second home after a fire razed it in 2008 (2 Castlehaven Road, NW1; 020 7428 5979; www.thehawleyarms.co.uk)

The Nelson's Head Being hard to find in Hackney is exactly the draw – look for the Tudor-style exterior festooned in hanging baskets for a quirky, fashiony local filled with amusing trinkets (32 Horatio Street, E2; 020 7729 5595; www.nelsonshead.com)

The Swan & Edgar Sister to vintage gin palace Bourne & Hollingsworth, this miniature 'design pub' features secondhand books for a bar, Scrabble tiles in the loos and The Financial Times for wallpaper (43 Linhope Street, Marylebone, NW1; 020 7724 6268)

drnk...

snack...

Forget the lipstick index. In times of economic strife, Londoners are seemingly seeking solace in the affordable luxury of cake. The list of London's fashionable new bakeries is as big as our appetite – be it for The Hummingbird Bakery's pastel-coloured cupcakes with profuse buttercream icing, or Pop Bakery's cake balls on sticks (perfect sponge orbs with colourful icing), or Cocomaya's sticky toffee cakes resembling roses, or – anytime – the macaroons of Ladurée and Pierre Hermé... This is, without question, what you call comfort-eating.

But you only need to watch one episode of Eastenders, the BBC's cockney soap running since 1985 (and do, for educational purposes), to know that, whenever trouble knocks, Brits put the kettle on. It's invariably always time for tea: tea is Britain's national drink, and has been since the Industrial Revolution when it was recognized as a cheap, warming tonic for the workforces. So silly are the Brits about tea that it is often prescribed in hot weather as a refreshing beverage, and how we drink it has always divided the classes. So Milk in First (MIF) or 'not our cup of tea' has become snob-speak to describe common folk whose tea-making methods are deemed déclassé.

Not that coffee is without snobbery – but here, Londoners are currently going mad for how it's done down under. London's caffeine scene has been revolutionised by the Antipodeans, who have brought with them their 'flat whites' (ie, strong espressos served in small cups with textured milk), along with their infectious enthusiasm for serious coffee, their mellow surfer-dude baristas, and good taste in music. Not only has it changed the physical landscape, with new cafés such as Lantana, Kaffeine, Flat White and lil sis Milk Bar – all founded and run by Aussies and Kiwis, but even the cookie-cutter chains are now imitating them.

Meanwhile, that other great British institution, afternoon tea, is the ritual of high society, a tradition attributed to Anna, 7th Duchess of Bedford, who, in 1840, caved in to her afternoon hunger pangs and demanded a tray of tea, bread and butter in her room at 4pm. It was soon served at the grandest hotels, such as Claridge's, The Ritz and Brown's, where the bourgeoisie (and arrivistes) still to this day take tea with finger sandwiches, scones and cake. It's more popular than ever (we've even added its own section in our Best of the Rest), appearing on any self-respecting all-day menu – perhaps it's because the ceremony is so serene, and besides, no doubt offering mouthwatering cakes when the four o'clock dip hits is a nice little earner.

'The other half' traditionally feasts at the Great British 'greasy spoon' – greasy for its full-fat full English breakfasts of bacon, eggs, bangers and fried bread (washed down with a nice cuppa, of course). Much of their charm is in their resolutely old-fashioned furnishings, community spirit and cheap prices – a sadly vanishing virtue in London. The most authentic is Bethnal Green's cockney caff E Pellicci, still with its original 1940s décor. Yet more idiosyncratic are the 13 Grade II-listed Victorian cabmen's shelters. These green-painted wooden sheds (no larger than a horse and cart, in accordance with an 1875 bylaw) are dotted around the capital – for example, in Kensington Park Road, Northumberland Avenue, Temple Place and Hanover Square. Today they provide food (sometimes even à la carte), non-alcoholic drinks and a resting spot for London's black cab drivers. Or anyone who asks nicely.

The Mexican Revolution

London might seem like an unlikely destination for good Mexican food, and, until recently, that was undeniably the case. But London's new crop of Mexican restaurants banish memories of the low-rent Tex-Mex – a bastardised mix of Mexican and American that often translated as grizzly, gristly chilli, flabby fajitas and nachos smothered in insipid, sweaty cheese and watery sour cream. With the emphasis very much on burritos and tacos, the new-wave Mexicans have returned to Mexico for inspiration to deliver affordable food that is light, fun, fresh and delicious, and not just something to mindlessly soak up lime-garnished bottles of beer or endless shots of cheap tequila.

London's new Mexicans come in all shapes and sizes, from **Daddy Donkey**'s lunchtime-only 'burro-mobile' parked in Leather Lane Market, Clerkenwell (www.daddydonkey.co.uk), to the rapidly expanding **Wahaca**, fronted by the telegenic poster girl for Mexican food, Thomasina Miers, which now has three branches across London (see separate entry). Notting Hill has its own Mexican parallelogram with the pioneering **Taqueria**, with its own corn tortilla machine, sustainable fish and free-range eggs, chicken and pork (139 Westbourne Grove, W11; 020 7229 4734 www.taqueria.co.uk), Tom Conran's successful if pricey sanitisation of street food at **Crazy Homies** (125 Westbourne Park Road, W2; 020 7727 6771 www.crazyhomieslondon.co.uk), **Santo**, London's only Mexican-owned Mexican (299 Portobello Road, W10; 020 8968 4590 www.santovillage.com) and from the erstwhile bad boy of the Conran dynasty, son Ned and wife Sage's **El Camino** (272 Portobello Road, W10), with a late-night licence and wicked cocktails, and now a second Soho branch (see Dick's Bar, Bars). Head east, and Shoreditch has the hip Jaliscan-inspired cantina and late-night bar **Green & Red** (51 Bethnal Green Road, E1; 020 7749 9670 www.greenred.co.uk).

Then there are the flashily branded takeaway joints, Benitos Hat, Tortilla and Chilango, all jostling for taco and burrito supremacy. But you know that London's Mexican love-in is being taken seriously when **Chipotle**, a behemoth with 950 branches across North America and a cult following, have just set up shop in the West End (114 Charing Cross Road, WC2; 020 7836 8491 www.chipotle.co.uk), the first of many, apparently. Even Mexican tequila stands a chance of being drinkable nowadays, now with more aged, and smooth, varieties available, and with the likes of Patrón being pitched as being as prestigious as Grey Goose, Tanqueray and Stoli, is actually intended for sipping, not shotting.

Albion *(top)*

2–4 Boundary Street,
Shoreditch E2
Tel: 020 7729 1051
www.albioncaff.co.uk
Open: daily, 8am–midnight

Conran does caff! In a sign of the times, uber-restaurateur Terence Conran has stepped down to join the small movement. Albion is the ground-floor 'caff'– his words – of the Boundary Project, which also includes a micro-hotel (see Sleep) and restaurant (see Eat). Hailing the simple pleasures of British nostalgia, Albion (geddit?) is all plump Brown Betty teapots with knitted cosies, Tate & Lyle Golden Syrup tins as cutlery pots, tractor seats for stools, and, just like your trad greasy spoon, a no-booking policy. But Albion is by no means low-rent, thanks to clean Conran lines and the patronage of the Shoreditcherati (ad execs from nearby Mother, upstarts exploiting the free WiFi, architects filling the communal oak tables with warehouse conversion plans, as this indeed was). Generous, comforting classics (pie, fish and chips, Welsh rarebit, apple and cinnamon crumble) mostly come in under a tenner, plus there are English ales, a decent wine list and cocktails, and a deli selling the likes of Daylesford Organic, Neal's Yard Dairy and Barton Court, Terence Conran's country home. Its onsite bakery even has a Twitter feed (@albionsoven) announcing fresh batches. Trust Conran to improve on the past.

Aubaine *(middle)*

260–262 Brompton Road, South Kensington, SW3
Tel: 020 7052 0100 www.aubaine.co.uk
Open: 8am–10.30pm Mon–Sat; 9am–10pm Sun

Hailed as one of Tatler's Top 10 social restaurants, le tout South Kensington gathers at this chichi bakery-cum-restaurant at weekends, drawn as much by the French bonhomie as by the cuisine (such is the demand that a second branch in Mayfair has opened: 4 Heddon Street, W1; 020 7440 2510). An airy, contemporary space, the restaurant has a feminine feel thanks to the country-style white chairs, Venetian mirrors and a vintage dresser adorned with fresh flowers. To them, there's truth in the meaning of Aubaine ('godsend'): with bakers, pâtissiers and imported French flour and butter onsite, Aubaine was founded to combat the founder's pining for pain français. Aubaine prides itself on its breads, gateaux and savoury food in equal measure: stop for a coffee and a croissant at breakfast, a soup or tartine (open sandwich) at lunch, seasonal cakes for tea, or à la carte for lunch or evening. Don't be taken aback if your waiter addresses you in French – so many of the locals are from across La Manche that they often innocently assume customers speak the language.

Balans *(bottom)*

60 Old Compton Street,
Soho, W1
Tel: 020 7439 2183
www.balans.co.uk
Open: daily, 8am–5am (6am Fri/Sat, 2am Sun)

snack...

If Old Compton Street is Soho's gay parade, Balans – buzzy, clubby, queeny – is its Gossip Central. Dishing up bear-sized portions of trusty British, French, Italian and Asian staples through much of the night (steaks, burgers, roasts, grilled fish, Thai curries and all-day breakfasts – the perfect post-clubbing replenishment), Balans has served succour to many a spurned lover, and with its lethal cocktails and happy hour, has seen a scandal or two in its time. Not that you need to be part of the queen scene: Balans offers some of the finest anthropological moments in London (Balans' branches in Kensington, Earls Court, Westfield and Chiswick are all plain Janes to Soho's saucy Suzy; there's also Balans Café, at 34 Old Compton Street, but this is the epicentre). If it's late, get a booth at the back for swapping tales of shamelessness – though eavesdropping will do too (we recommend swallowing the shock with one of their exemplary Cosmopolitans); by day, secure a table in the window and watch the world and his pretty boy go by.

Bar Boulud *(top)*
Mandarin Oriental Hyde Park, 66 Knightsbridge, SW1
Tel: 020 7201 3899
www.barboulud.com
Open: daily, 6.30pm–1am

If intimate with New York, you'll know that Lyonnais chef Daniel Boulud is a sensation there, with five restaurants and three Michelin stars (you'll also know to say 'boo*luu*'). So it was a coup that the Mandarin Oriental hotel brought his concept of pairing char-

cuterie and wine to London. There's little point for herbivores here – it would be regrettable not to order the sharing charcuterie boards, a tease of starters with beautifully tender house-made terrines, pâtés, fine hams and saucissons. More substantial bistro classics include coq au vin, steak frites and steamed mussels, plus there's Boulud's 'NY' burgers and an artisan sausage menu. And it would be remiss not to wash it all down with a Rhone or Burgundy (Lyon's surrounding wine regions), cheerfully recommended by sommelier David Vareille. If it's all sounding a bit formal, it's not meant to be – classy, yes, but cosy: a Adam Tihany-designed space with warm downlighters, low, curved ceilings and nutty tones. It tries hard to be casual, though that is rather at odds with the Mandarin Oriental's insistence of swooping waiters serving food in synchronicity – you can't help but feel ashamed when you drop your fork.

The Botanist *(bottom)*
7 Sloane Square, Chelsea SW1
Tel: 020 7730 0077
www.thebotanistonsloanesquare.com
Open: 8am–11.30pm Mon–Fri; 9am–11.30pm Sat/Sun

This is the epitome of pub reinvention. The profoundly unremarkable Royal Court Tavern was in 2008 re-imagined by two brothers that neighbours of dive pubs have come to be very grateful to: Tom and Ed Martin. This is the brothers' sixth such rescue (also The Gun, The Empress of India, The Prince Arthur...), and the first to eschew the gastropub in favour of a Paris-style

brasserie. Black leather and glass now dominate, with sliding doors separating the bar from the serene dining area that's bathed in light from its bay windows. Since it's named after the original Mr Sloane, Sir Hans, the 18th-century authority on natural sciences, the walls are adorned with his botanical sketches. The kitchen delivers top-notch Anglo-French nosh designed by Neil Cooper, of Chez Bruce vintage, from breakfast through dinner – ladies who lunch favour the seasonal salads whilst gentlemen feast on 35-day-old Aberdeen Angus rib-eye. There's also a pre-theatre menu for Royal Court thesps and an afternoon tea with Jing tea, Joseph Perrier champagne, or the house hot chocolate (in honour of Sir Hans's invention of milk chocolate – indeed). Thus making three very necessary fathers of invention.

Bumpkin *(top)*
209 Westbourne Park Road,
Notting Hill, W11
Tel: 020 7243 9818
www.bumpkinuk.com
Open: daily, 11am–11pm

Dogged cosmopolites regard trips to the countryside akin to being buried alive. Far better to get the only decent thing worth dislocating oneself for – farm produce – to come to London. And so there is Bumpkin, a romanticized ersatz of a country pub, serving up simple, trad food – think fine Toad in the Hole, ample Sunday roasts and fruit crumbles slathered in thick custards – cooked with seasonal fruit and veg from Secretts Farm near Guildford, sustainable British fish and organic

cheese (if a rather more opaque 'farm assured' meat provenance). Its three dining rooms, each with their own open kitchen, lie in ascending snob factor (this is after all from the folk behind Boujis, see Party) – on the ground floor is the pubbish brasserie (populated by young, blonde thoroughbreds), on the first floor, the restaurant (same menu, a generation older) and on the second floor, the private dining room (for avoiding the mere middle classes altogether). A second Bumpkin has opened in South Kensington, so the Boujis crowd must be pleased (102 Old Brompton Road, SW7; 020 7341 0802). An absence of village idiots cannot be guaranteed in either, however.

Claridge's *(bottom)*
Brook Street, Mayfair, W1
Tel: 020 7629 8860
www.claridges.co.uk
Open: daily, 7am (8am Sun)–10.30pm

Since the end of the 19th century, when taking afternoon tea became the done thing in British high society, the opulent surrounds of Claridge's Foyer and the more secluded Reading Room have done a roaring trade in the ritual (served 3–5.30pm). It is obvious why – just sitting in the high-ceilinged, chandelier-festooned Art Deco grandiosity makes you feel as starry as the many silver screen stars who have done the same over the years. A choice of over 30 teas including the Royal White Needles (a champagne among teas since the needles can only be picked at dawn on two days in the year) is served in elegant mint-and-white Bernardaud porcelain and accompanied by dainty

finger sandwiches, scones with clotted cream and (tea-flavoured) Marco Polo jelly, while nostalgic tunes are tinkled out of the grand pianoforte. Socialites, industrialists and A-listers congregate here for power-breakfasts, bruncheons, luncheons, afternoon tea and end-of-day meetings (any excuse, see?) for what is a less obvious and tourist-ridden indulgence than The Ritz (booking advised). The smart casual dress code is loosely adhered to and little fingers are kept erect at all times.

Daylesford Organic (top)
44B Pimlico Road, SW1
Tel: 020 7881 8060
www.daylesfordorganic.com
Open: 8am–7pm Mon–Sat; 10am–4pm Sun

Lifestyle envy is a highly profitable syndrome, as the folk behind Daylesford Organic (namely Lord and Lady Bamford of JCB riches) have realized. Their 4,500 square-foot lifestyle emporium is a gorgeous, blonde temple to all you need to buy for a life just like theirs – ie, super-chic, super-pricey eco-luxury. Straight from the organic fields of Daylesford's Gloucestershire farm are three floors of seasonal groceries, dairy goods and heritage breed meats (including Gloucester Old Spots and venison), plus artisan homewares, organic and biodynamic wines from the Bamford's Provence estate, and, crucially, the chance to taste the Bamford 'brand experience' at the café. It's too much for Belgravia's bourgeoisie to resist, as furs, cosmetic surgery and new teeth settle round the communal table for excellent salads, wild-caught fish, posh sandwiches, homemade

cakes and louder-than-necessary posturing. To compare and contrast the moneyed construct of Daylesford with the reality of British farming, visit on a Saturday morning when the Pimlico farmers' market is in full swing. Daylesford now also has a three-floor café/store in Notting Hill that includes a raw bar (208 Westbourne Grove, W11; 020 7313 8050) and a takeaway deli at Selfridges' Food Hall (see Shop).

Dehesa (bottom)
25 Ganton Street, Soho, W1
Tel: 020 7494 4170
www.dehesa.co.uk
Open: noon–3pm, 5pm–11pm Mon–Fri; noon–11pm Sat; noon–5pm Sun

Sod the slow food movement – sometimes life is just too short. This is the raison d'être of the Italian/Spanish charcuterie and tapas bar Dehesa, named after the Spanish woodlands where the black-footed Iberico pigs live (before becoming very fine ham). In one corner you'll find a stand-up charcuterie bar where Atkins diet-friendly sharing plates of freshly shaved *jamón* and Manchego cheese can be enjoyed on the hoof with a fortifying glass of prosecco – perfect for a mid-shop pit stop. Said savouries can also be enjoyed off the hoof, perched atop high wooden stools; also on the menu are very reasonably priced meat, fish and vegetable tapas, Spanish and Italian desserts, and well-chosen regional wines. No wonder queues form as soon as the local media offices close (no booking) – not always such fast food then. If oversubscribed, try your luck at its older sister restaurant Salt Yard (54 Goodge Street, Fitzrovia, W1;

snack...

020 7637 0657) – both are winners of a Michelin Bib Gourmand for 'good food at moderate prices', or book ahead for Dehesa's 12-seater private dining room. Quickly.

Electric Brasserie *(top)*

191 Portobello Road,
Notting Hill, W11
Tel: 020 7908 9696
www.electricbrasserie.com
Open: daily, 8am–midnight (1am Thurs–Sat, 11pm Sun)

For some years now the Electric has been the hub of the Notting Hill scene, and was established by one of London's major players, Nick Jones, the man behind Soho House in London and New York. At weekends it is rammed with fashionable locals and TV personalities whose swanky cocktails and sharp elbows jostle for space at the crowded bar (though the inner circle of this scene takes to The Electric's private members' club, Electric House, upstairs). However, face-time anywhere in the Electric's sleek urban interior – complete with zinc-topped bar, steel tables and lobster tanks – is good for status. The back restaurant is a little more secluded, and an upmarket US diner-esque menu of generously portioned breakfasts, casual bites (steak sandwiches, American-sized burgers, moules marinières, smoked duck salads) and à la carte dishes (that serve up those lobsters, plus prime steaks, caviar and oysters) is available all day. Next door, the Electric's playground continues with the historic cinema from which the Brasserie takes its name (see Culture).

Fernandez & Wells *(bottom)* Food & Wine Bar

43 Lexington Street, W1;
Tel: 020 7734 1546
www.fernandezandwells.com
Open: 11am–10pm Mon–Fri; noon–10pm Sat; 2–10pm Sun
Café 73 Beak Street,
W1; 020 7287 8124
Open: 7.30am–6pm Mon–Fri; 9am–6pm Sat; 9am–5pm Sun
Espresso Bar 16a St Anne's Court, W1; 020 7494 4242
Open: 8am (noon Sat)–6pm (8pm Tues; 10pm Weds–Sat) Mon–Sat

The opposite of the one-stop shop, Fernandez & Wells is the realised vision of food/wine/coffee aficionados Jorge Fernandez and Rick Wells, who wanted to bring outstanding farmers' market fare to Soho – in three small, separate parts. Because, of course, cakes aren't so appetizing when underneath a dangling *jamón*, and coffee just doesn't sit with fresh deli food. At the decidedly savoury Food & Wine Bar, bagsy one of the few tin stools at the slab of oak for a counter to sample a plate of 24-month-cured French Le Noir de Bigorre ham (not cheap at £18) or unpasteurised Manchego with Wells' well-chosen wines (also available by day are posh salads, sandwiches, soups and stews). The sweet/savoury Café offers fresh sandwiches (for example, Montgomery cheddar, red onion and leek), made with Poilâne bread, stone-baked baguettes or olive oil ciabattas, plus mountains of paella, lovely salads, plump pastries and Portuguese custard tarts. Meanwhile, the exemplary Espresso Bar is Fernandez' speciality, as Monmouth Coffee Company's ex-general manager (it also

43

Dorset Ham &
Montgomery's
Cheddar
Ciabatta
Toasted
with Piccalilli Sauce
£4·80

Roast Dorset
PORK
on a Rosemary &
Sea Salt
Foccacia
with Homemade Apple Sauce
£5·00

FERNANDEZ & WELLS

does the juicy sarnie spread for take-away). Order a 'stumpy' (like a Spanish *cortado*) and drink it at the counter – in true espresso bar style, it's standing room only.

space (all vaulted walls, exposed sandstone brickwork and Vitra furniture) serves as a calming antidote to abstract art and King's Road crowds. Even Nigella, a local, is occasionally spotted taking refuge.

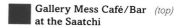

Gallery Mess Café/Bar *(top)* at the Saatchi

Duke of York's Headquarters, King's Road, SW3
Tel: 020 7730 8135
www.saatchi-gallery.co.uk
Open: daily, 10am–11.30pm (7pm Sun)

The Mess is as close as us lot will ever get to eating chez Nigella (Lawson) and Charles (Saatchi), the power couple behind domestic goddessery and British contemporary art. So-called for being, like the gallery (see Culture), within the Duke of York's Headquarters – the handsome Georgian institution that's previously housed the Territorial Army – the Mess is amply in keeping with the London trend for quality eateries in art galleries. Although it's not Nigella, but the respected 'food design' company, Rhubarb, at the helm, her casual culinary influence is evident. Legend has it that she's scoffed everything here, but then choice is mercifully limited: Spanish charcuterie, chic salads (eg Niçoise) and retro classics (bangers and mash, sundaes, crumbles and sponges), all delivered with utmost professionalism. There are also pastries for breakfast, all-day bar snacks and afternoon tea (2.30–6pm), as well as wines, champagnes, proseccos and pitchers of Pimm's (potentially dangerous when surrounded by artworks for sale). The high-ceilinged, whitewashed

Giant Robot *(bottom)*

45 Clerkenwell Road, EC1
Tel: 020 7065 6810
www.gntrbt.com
Open: daily, 10am–midnight (2am Thurs–Sat, 10pm Sun)

The rivals of Jonathan Downey, the man who built an empire on affability, must have rubbed their hands in schadenfreude when, in March 2010, JD's gleaming East Room members' club and Sosho nightclub burnt down. Not so fast! Two months later, he returned with this American diner/cocktail bar where once his own Match bar stood. Born of a boredom with careful, quiet dining and British revival food, Downey wanted to bring back social restaurants, where there's always room for one more, food is shared, and you can eat well, late (food is under Ollie Couillard of La Trompette and The Square). There's all-day mix'n'match saucers of fine cheeses, charcuterie and seafood; there are Italo-American meatballs served with mash, pasta or salad (and optionally wedged in a bun – the 'slider'), and for pud, there's the perfect metaphor of good-time food: a mountainous baked Alaska to share, flamed at your table. You can even share the staff meal for a fiver (5–7pm). Drinks are central: from the creator of cocktail club Milk & Honey comes killer cocktails (again, the DIY belli-

snack...

nis equal good-time) and Italian wine served in sociable carafes. It's just not giant, and definitely not robotic.

Inn The Park *(top)*
St James's Park, SW1
Tel: 020 7451 9999
www.innthepark.com
Open: 8am (9am Sat)–9pm to 11pm (depending on the weather) Mon–Sat; 9am–5pm Sun.

With its Scandinavian pod-like wooden structure, complete with turf roof (designed by the acclaimed Michael Hopkins), Inn the Park is something of an organism itself. Set within the sanctuary of the chocolate-box St James's Park and lake, in amongst the plucky ducks, the greedy pelicans and the coy moorhens, this is a place that adapts with the seasons. Thus, we cannot tell you what time it closes officially, because a wet and wintry Monday night is a different beast to a summer's Saturday when Inn the Park's Pimms-soaked barbeque is a-go. And it's a proudly British species – under the direction of gastropreneur Oliver Peyton (he of retro-luxe caterer Peyton & Byrne, at the National Gallery, The Wallace Collection and ICA; see Culture), sourcing is staunchly local and artisan – yes to organic beers and ciders, outright no to Coca-Cola. It's a complex creature: there is waiter service and à la carte dining (set menu only on weekends) in the Tom Dixon-designed chalet interior, a canteen for speed-diners and those preferring to dine alfresco on the decked lakeside terrace, and sandwiches and hampers for picnickers. Which, on beastly busy summer weekends, might be the best option.

J&A Café *(bottom)*
4 Sutton Lane, Clerkenwell, EC1
Tel: 020 7490 2992
www.jandacafe.com
Open: 8am–6pm, Mon–Fri; 10am–4pm Sat

Once frequented by the late, great Alexander McQueen (his design studio was around the corner), this homely little joint was established in 2008 by Dublin-born sisters Joanna and Aoife Ledwidge (hence the 'J' and the 'A'). Located in the cobbled backstreets of Clerkenwell, the café is popular with all sorts of fashionable types, not least since one of the sisters used to work for the designer Gareth Pugh, another regular. Not that this is reflected in meagre portions or miserly scrimping on the cream and butter (see the decidedly un-size-zero breakfast 'pancake mountain', served with either syrup, berries and cream, or scrambled eggs and crispy bacon). The fare is unpretentiously chic (for example, roast smoked trout salad, or couscous with roasted veg and goat's cheese), well-sourced (with the likes of Inverawe smoked salmon, Fentiman's old-fashioned softies, and Mighty Leaf's herbal teas), and reflective of the owners' Irish roots, with delights such as freshly baked soda bread and chocolate Guinness cake. With things getting boozy (champagne or Pimms) in time for afternoon tea, it's the authentic Irish craic.

■ **Ladurée** *(top)*
Door 1A, Harrods, 87–135
Brompton Road, Knightsbridge, SW1
Tel: 020 3155 0111
www.laduree.com
Open: 9am–10pm Mon–Sat; noon–
6pm Sun

Blinkering one's eyes from the tourist trap that is Harrods, make straight for the trademark pistachio and gilt doors of the celebrated Parisian tea salon Ladurée (founded in 1862 by French miller Louis Ladurée). The experience is rather like diving into an exquisite, and immaculate, jewellery box – there's the airy White Room downstairs, all serene white marble, candelabras and cake stands, the cosy Red Room with its rich, rust-coloured velvets and balcony overlooking a takeaway counter piled high with individual cakes (each a miniature work of art), and the Versace-esque Black Room, all in black and gold with Roman-style statues – a popular setting for evening dining. The all-day menu is perfectly serviceable (smoked salmon, caviar, club sandwiches etc), but it's really about sugar highs here – afternoon tea extravaganzas, giddying cream gateaux, and what Ladurée is best known for: macaroons. These delicate gerbets span the rainbow and an incredible variety of flavours – from white amber to dark chocolate – and have become quite the fashionable gift, not least because of their divine packaging. Admiring your takeout is an excellent blinkering device.

 snack...

■ **The Parlour** *(bottom)*
at Sketch
9 Conduit Street, Mayfair, W1
Tel: 0870 777 4488
www.sketch.uk.com
Open: 8am–2am Mon–Fri; 10am–2am
Sat. Members only after 9pm.

Food that's too pretty to eat – how convenient. The fashion crowd have been tottering into the delightful ground-floor tearoom of bon viveur Mourad Mazouz's multi-tasking and multi-million-pound Sketch since it opened in 2002. A dainty, buttoned-up salon for 50 is playfully decorated with furniture new and old, opulent fabrics, skull lampshades, and futuristic chandeliers resembling planetary constellations; doll-like waitresses are packaged in b Store frocks (see Shop), while menus and bills are delivered inside antique books. And on those menus? An expansive tea list (all the right single-estate loose leaves from Japan, China and India) conceived by Sketch's French superchef Pierre Gagnaire (see Eat), plus champagne, cocktails and a wine list of 30 bins. Oh and the food: a central patisserie counter boasts picturesque cakes, viennoiseries, and all you could need for a cream tea (served from 3pm), plus breakfast and all-day comfort food of the sushi/fancy salad/macaroni cheese variety. The main draw, however, is an invitation to one of the many fashion parties hosted here. Generating enough gossip to dine out on for weeks, it's no wonder the fash pack is off their food.

E Pellicci (top)

332 Bethnal Green Road, Bethnal Green, E2
Tel: 020 7739 4873
Open: 7am–4pm Mon–Sat

The Ivy, The Wolseley, Pellicci... three of London's most oversubscribed restaurants. The similarity ends there – Pellicci sits firmly, and proudly, at the silly-cheap end. It also trumps both on history, having been run by the Italian/cockney Pelliccis since 1900 ('E' stands for Elide, the original Pellicci matriarch). Team Pellicci now comprises Maria (or 'Mama'), who cooks fry-ups, meat and two veg, Italian pasta and stodgy puds ('worth a minor stroke,' complimented one customer), her adult children Anna and Nevio Junior and their cousin Tony. Sadly, in 2008, the affable octogenarian Nevio Senior, who'd dedicated over 50 years to the caff, passed away (to a hero's send-off and a Times obit), but predictably, Pellicci's exceptionally perky atmosphere and wisecracking soon returned. With your meal comes instant community, which has included the Kray brothers, the Eastenders cast and footballers (just ask to see Nevio Junior's autograph book), as well as cabbies, hipsters and pensioners (always addressed 'young lady/gentleman'). It's just as well there's no alcohol licence – the tiny Pellicci can't take much more buzz: zone out from the chatter and clatter by admiring its 1940s Grade II-listed Art Deco marquetry. No wonder all eyes are on Nevio Junior and Anna to further the family line.

Princi (bottom)

135 Wardour Street, Soho, W1
Tel: 020 7478 8888
www.princi.co.uk
Open: 7am–midnight Mon–Sat; 9am–10pm Sun

You'll hear Princi (pronounced 'prrrinchie') before you see it – or rather the Italian ex-pats that flock there, talking fortissimo outside. No wonder they're excited. Milan's Armani of bread, Rocco Princi, has opened his first international bakery with restaurateur Alan Yau (once of Hakkassan, Yauatcha and Wagamama). It's signature Princi: a stunning, elemental space (bronze-clad communal tables, rough-hewn granite standing tables, a wood-fired oven behind glass) serving a panoply of great-value sophisticated snacking. A Princi day typically starts with an (excellent) cappuccino and pastries, followed by a lunch of juicy salads, first-rate pizzas and pasta; after work, an aperitif at the bar, closing on drunken delights (tiramisu, glazed fruit tarts) and takeaway daily-baked organic bread for home. NB: because it's Italian, there are no rules – everything is available at any time (alcohol included, though hot food only from noon). There's no table service – the 'system' is that you choose and collect your food from the vast counter and then find a seat (good luck on Saturdays). For those not versed in the art of Italian queuing, be warned that it's each man for himself. We recommend flirting with waiters for preferential treatment. They're Italian, after all.

Rochelle Canteen *(top)*
Rochelle School,
Arnold Circus, Shoreditch, E2
Tel: 020 7729 5677
www.arnoldandhenderson.com
Open: 9–11am, noon–3pm Mon–Fri

London's art and fashion scene is a behind-closed-doors affair. Press the 'Canteen' buzzer just by the 'Boys' entrance to the former Victorian Rochelle School, however, and gain instant access. Initially a staff canteen to service the ex-school's working studios where London's style mafia – Giles, Katie Hilier, Luella – have variously worked (hence a weekday-only service), everyone is now welcome in the whitewashed ex-bike shed to feast on the nose-to-tail offerings from onsite caterers Arnold & Henderson. Yes, that's Henderson as in Margot Henderson, wife of Fergus of St John (see Eat), so there's a nostalgic, northern English influence on the daily-changing menu (posted online). Breakfast is so basic (and quiet), it just goes on the blackboard: maybe eggs on toast, porridge, granola. Lunch is much busier (read: scenier), with perfectly executed dishes such as oxtail stew, Lancashire hotpot and posset for pud, all at very reasonable prices (how else to lure the artists?). In summer, the communal tables are deployed onto the tranquil, grassed-over playground; for dinner, you can hire it all, as have their prestigious clients, Acne, Adidas, Aesop…etc. There's no licence, so bring your own and share it around to infiltrate one of London's coolest cliques.

Serpentine *(left)*
Bar & Garden
Serpentine Road,
Hyde Park, W2
Tel: 020 7706 8114
www.serpentinebarandkitchen.com
Open: daily, 8am–6pm (7pm April,
9pm May–August)

'Public space eating' implies rubbery canteen food for unsuspecting, easy come, easy go tourists. Patrick Gwynne's 1960s winged structure with the idyllic Serpentine lake for a backdrop has seen all that. Then in summer 2009, brothers Ben and Hugo Warner (aka benugo, the caterers reversing the fates of so many public-space eateries, among them the V&A, Natural History Museum and the BFI; see Drink) came along, bringing with them a wood-fired oven, a baby grand (do play if you really can), and locally sourced food and speciality British beers and ciders. Think nostalgia and doing things properly, albeit on a scale. With 300 covers inside and out (no booking, no table service, but then nothing is over £10), there's an all-day à la carte-lite menu (think British revival-lite – posh roasts, ham hock, potted shrimps, sticky puddings) served on floral Burleigh crockery at vintage wooden tables, plus pizza, afternoon tea, grab'n'go sarnies, hampers and breakfast. Unfortunately, you will not be alone in thinking how nice it would be to watch the sunset here with a glass of wine in high season.

Terroirs *(right)*
5 William IV Street,
Covent Garden, WC2
Tel: 020 7036 0660
www.terroirswinebar.com
Open: noon–11pm, Mon–Sat

If you know what 'terroir' means, then

snack…

you must come here directly – this is the place for you. If you don't, allow us to attempt an explanation: *les terroirs* are the specific characteristics – the micro-climate, the hand of the winemaker and the *je ne sais quoi* – that makes two wines (or coffees or teas) from the same area taste different. The three 'muscateers' behind Terroirs, Eric Narioo (whose wine importers Caves de Pyrène supply most the wine), chef Ed Wilson and wine connoisseur Oli Barker, are finely honed in such distinctions, and would like to share their passion – as well as showcase artisan fare that is free of additives and produced with sensitivity. As such, Terroirs is a Parisian-style tapas bar, opened in 2009, where organic or natural wines (ie, those produced not only without additives, but without machinery, since it is believed to damage the wine) are paired with reasonably priced small plates (variously French, Spanish, Italian and British) – hearty charcuterie, recherché cheeses, juicy panzanella, garlicky prawns *à la plancha*. Diners can do all that sharing business, and there are also some big plates, but it's really about the pure, evolving flavours of natural wine. Educate and inebriate.

....

Tierra Brindisa *(top)*
46 Broadwick Street, Soho, W1
Open: 020 7534 1690
www.tierrabrindisa.com
Open: noon–11pm. Closed Sundays.

In London, the name Brindisa is synonymous with Spanish tapas. It's a brand that, since 1988, has brought restaurant-quality Spanish produce to wide-eyed (-mouthed) Brits in the foodie dreamland of Borough food market. We had to wait until 2004 for its first tapas bar, Tapas Brindisa (18 Southwark Street, Borough, SE1; 020 7357 8880), but, undeterred, we crowded in and queued up to get our hands on its pitch-perfect Iberian classics such as Manchego cheese with quince jelly and the legendary acorn-fed pata negra ham. Now, finally, there is more room for its many fans (booking advised) in Tierra Brindisa (and also, Casa Brindisa in South Kensington, 7 Exhibition Road, SW7; 020 7590 0008), whose menu, essentially matching that of Tapas Brindisa, features bestsellers such as giant olives stuffed with orange and oregano, sizzling chilli prawns, and deep-fried goat's cheese with honey; an inviting list of Spanish wines, sherries and cava has been composed to work with the food. Needless to say, its towering reputation is undiminished here. All of which is highly conducive to making a toast, which, ironically, is what 'brindisa' actually means.

....

Villandry *(bottom)*
170 Great Portland Street, Marylebone, W1
Tel: 020 7631 3131
www.villandry.com
Restaurant open: noon–3.30pm, 6–10.30pm Mon–Sat; noon–3.30pm Sun
Bar open: 8am–11pm Mon–Sat

Named after France's Chateau de Villandry, it's true that Villandry is something of a castle to cuisine – all cream stone floors and tall, whitewashed walls, it's an emporium of gourmet delicacies from around the world. With three kitchens catering variously for those who want to enjoy their food slowly, fast

or offsite, there's a crisp, airy 100-seat restaurant with a daily-changing European-flavoured menu and an extensive, largely French wine list, frequented by discerning corpo-media types, there's a 50-seat all-day bar area that whips up lighter, less formal meals and sharing tapas with more wallet-friendly price tags to match, and a vast food hall, resembling a (glorified) old-fashioned food market, with its counters of charcuterie (bresaola, Bayonne and Iberico hams etc) and fine cheeses (e.g. handmade Roquefort and Neal's Yard), cakes, fresh bread baked onsite and three-course meals from its takeaway kitchen. Bespoke picnic hampers are also available, and there's even an outside catering service, should you have a castle-sized budget. In 2009, the smaller

Villandry Kitchen opened (95 High Holborn, WC1; 020 7242 4580), featuring an all-day café, bar and deli – the same three-tier class system.

....

Wahaca *(above)*
66 Chandos Place,
Covent Garden, WC2
Tel: 020 7240 1883
www.wahaca.co.uk
Open: daily, noon–11pm (10.30pm Sun)

Leaving no gaps along the spectrum of 'Mexican market eating' – from tortilla chips and guacamole to tapas sharing dishes, hearty soups and salads, and big dishes for big appetites – one senses the presence of ambition at Wahaca (named phonetically for fick people, after the fertile Mexican region Oaxaca). Step forward, winner of MasterChef 2005, Thomasina Miers, who in 2007 opened her cantina after working at Villandry and Petersham Nurseries. She's also on it environmentally – chicken and pork is free-range, beef is grass-fed, and all produce is seasonal and locally sourced (chillies from Devonshire, no less). The tequila – double-distilled from 100% blue agave, and in aged *reposado* and *añejo* varieties – actually stands a chance of being drinkable, while beer is Mexican and wine South American. To describe Wahaca as a Mexican Wagamama might be accurate in (sprawling) spatial terms, but is a disservice to the colour and buzz that lures large, young groups, and can push waiting time for a table up to an hour (no reservations) – tortilla chips time at the bar. Two new openings take the overspill, in Westfield Shopping Centre (Ariel Way, W12; 020 8749 4517) and Canary Wharf (40 Canada Square, E14; 020 7516 9145).

the best of the rest...

for afternoon tea...

Bea's of Bloomsbury Bea Vo's 10-cover girly tearoom (booking essential) is quality over quantity: Valrhona chocolate, Jing teas and all cakes, tarts and cookies baked in-house; also savouries and hot dishes (44 Theobald Road, WC1; 020 7242 8330; www.beasofbloomsbury.com)

Cocomaya Jewel-like artisan chocolates, exquisite cakes and afternoon teas more like edible theatre (booking essential) are available to just eight lucky ones in Serena Rees' petite salon (12 Connaught Street, Marble Arch, W2; 020 7706 2883; www.cocomaya.co.uk)

The Lanesborough Boasting Britain's first 'tea sommelier' and the gloriousness of a grand hotel, attention to detail includes gluten- and dairy-free options, as well as reckless indulgence (1 Lanesborough Place, Hyde Park Corner, SW1; 020 7259 5599; www.lanesborough.com)

The Orangery How more authentic than a royal palace? Kensington Palace's exquisite pillared glasshouse built for orange trees in 1761 now amply supplies the cucumber sandwiches, scones and champagne (Kensington Gardens, W8; 020 7376 0239; www.hrp.org.uk/kensingtonpalace)

The Wallace Under Oliver Peyton's stewardship, this Georgian conservatory attached to the Wallace Collection art gallery is an appositely grand setting for English- or Parisian-themed teas (Hertford House, Manchester Square, W1; 020 7563 9505; www.wallacecollection.org)

for bakery binges...

The Hummingbird Bakery Elevating the cupcake to art form (or is that fashion?), this teeny American-style bakery, first opened in 2004, is the metaphorical candy store to sweet tooths and socialites (Notting Hill: 133 Portobello Road, W11; 020 7229 6446. South Kensington: 47 Old Brompton

snack...

Road, SW7; 020 7584 0055. Soho: 155a Wardour Street, W1; 020 7434 3003; www.hummingbirdbakery.com)

Maison Bertaux   Defiantly French café established 1871 and landmark of Soho bohemia serving *café au lait* and full-fat patisseries, baked on the premises in shabby chic surroundings (28 Greek Street, W1; 020 7437 6007; www.maisonbertaux.com)

Maison Blanc   Michelin-starred French chef Raymond Blanc's salons de thé selling sandwiches gastronomiques made from *pain au levain* (a yeast-free loaf) and a glutton's paradise of tarts, gateaux and patisseries (Holland Park: 102 Holland Park Avenue, W11; 020 7221 2494. St John's Wood: 37 St John's Wood High Road, NW8; 020 7586 1982. Fulham: 303 Fulham Road, SW10; 020 7795 2663; www.maisonblanc.co.uk)

Midnite Cookies   Yup, late-night cookie heaven (triple chocolate, caramel pecan, peanut butter chip, made onsite with Belgian chocolate), plus milkshakes, brownies, ice cream and cookie dough shots (15 Exeter Street, Covent Garden, WC2; 020 7836 5131; www.midnitecookies.com)

Le Pain Quotidien   The Belgian organic bread specialist that does mean salads, eggs any way you like 'em and wickedly tasty chocolate spreads is itself spreading (West End: 72 Marylebone High Street, 18 Great Marlborough Street, Soho, and 48 The Market, Covent Garden Piazza, WC2. South Kensington: 15 Exhibition Road, SW7. Chelsea: 201 King's Road, SW3. Portobello: 81 Notting Hill Gate, W11.

Southbank: Royal Festival Hall, Belvedere Road, SE1; all enquiries 020 7486 6154; www.lepainquotidien.com)

Patisserie Valerie   Established in 1926 by the Belgian Madame Valerie in Soho, its reputation has hinged largely on its outrageous chocolate cakes covered with thick leaves of solid chocolate. Also serves scrummy savouries, pastries and gelaterie (West End: 105 Marylebone High Street, W1; 020 7935 6240 and 44 Old Compton Street, W1; 020 7437 3466. Holborn: 2 Sicilian Avenue, WC1; 020 7831 7744. Chelsea: Duke of York's Square, SW3; 020 7730 7094. Spitalfields: 37 Brushfield Street, E1; 020 7247 4906; www.patisserie-valerie.co.uk)

for coffee nuts...

Caffè Vergnano 1882   Italian chain reputed to make the best espresso in London (served with a small bitter chocolate and a glass of cold water to bring out the flavours); also wicked hot chocolate, sandwiches and cakes (2 New Street Square, Chancery Lane; 020 7936 3404. Southbank: Festival Terrace, Belvedere Road, SE1; 020 7921 9339. Leicester Square: 62 Charing Cross Road, WC2; 020 7240 3512; www.caffevergnano1882.co.uk)

Flat White   i.e. 'An Antipodean-style coffee served as a strong espresso in a small cup with textured milk' – opened in 2005, this tiny, grunge-chic café revolutionised London's coffee scene with Australia's artisan approach; also good, hearty snacks (17 Berwick Street, Soho, W1; 020 7734 0370)

Kaffeine More of the Aussie/Kiwi coffee education: skilled baristas crafting handsome flat whites, plus considered bites sourced from local markets – salads, filled focaccias, home-baked cakes (66 Great Titchfield Street, Fitzrovia, W1; 020 7580 6755; www.kaffeine.co.uk)

Lantana Tiny but mighty café, run by – yes, an Australian – is particular about coffee (using Monmouth beans, serving the hit flat white), and also food – ambitious salads, gourmet mains, down-under desserts (13 Charlotte Place, Fitzrovia, W1; 020 7637 3347; www.lantanacafe.co.uk)

Milk Bar Flat White's bigger, younger sister – same great 'flatties', awesome hot chocolates, chill, cheery baristas, and low-key eats – sandwiches, bagels, muffins and Antipodean sweet treats (3 Bateman Street, Soho, W1; 020 7287 4796)

Monmouth Coffee Company Much more than a café, Monmouth has been supplying its own roasts to London since 1978. Its two outposts (takeaway plus cosy seating) brew silken coffee to loyal regulars, plus simple snacks (27 Monmouth Street, Covent Garden, WC2; 020 7379 3516 and 2 Park Street, Borough Market, SE1; 020 7940 9960; www.monmouthcoffee.co.uk)

ice cream indulgence...

Freggo From the people behind Argentine steakhouse Gaucho comes quality ice cream in Dulce de leche, chocolate and real fruit flavours, served till 2am Fri/Sat (27 Swallow Street, Piccadilly, W1; 020 7287 9506; www.freggo.co.uk)

Gelato Mio The Willy Wonka of gelato, Carlo Del Mistro from Lake Como is expanding his empire and waistlines with fruity, nutty, chocolatey bliss. Plus the promise of special requests (Holland Park: 138 Holland Park Avenue, W11; 020 7727 4117. Notting Hill: 37 Pembridge Road, W11; 020 7727 0194. St John's Wood: 138 St. John's Wood High Street, NW8; 020 0011 3889; www.gelatomio.co.uk)

Gelupo From Bocca di Lupo's Jacob Kenedy comes superlative daily-made gelato, sorbets and granitas, plus Italian coffee and deli treats (7 Archer Street, Soho, W1; 020 7287 5555; www.gelupo.com)

Oddono's More Italian gelato, from Christian Oddono, and his grandmother's artisan recipes made with top ingredients including Valhrona chocolate, Sicilian pistachios and Madagascan vanilla (4 Bute Street, South Kensington; SW7 020 7052 0732, and takeaway counters in Selfridges and Food Inc at Whiteley's Bayswater; www.oddonos.com)

Scoop Proper Italian gelato in 24 flavours, mostly made with organic fruit and dairy products; also gluten- and sugar-free flavours (40 Shorts Gardens, Covent Garden, WC2; 020 7240 7086; www.scoopgelato.com)

for the right-on...

Canteen Quiet on décor, loud on philosophy: nationally sourced ingredients, using only meat from farms practising good animal husbandry, and fish from the south coast, for a modern take on traditional British recipes: pies, roasts, crumbles etc (Spitalfields: 2 Crispin Place, E1. Southbank: Royal Festival Hall, Belvedere Road, SE1. Marylebone: 55 Baker Street, W1; all enquiries 0845 686 1122; www.canteen.co.uk)

Leon Leon's opening in 2005 heralded a new era in fast food: healthy, locally and ethically sourced food – wholesome salads, hearty soups and cheeky cakes, in friendly, retro settings (West End: 35 Great Marlborough Street, W1; 020 7437 5280, 73 The Strand, WC2; 020 7240 3070 and 275 Regent Street, W1; 020 7495 1514. Spitalfields: 3 Crispin Place, E1; 020 7247 4369. Southbank: 7 Canvey Street, SE1; 020 7620 0035; www.leon-restaurants.co.uk)

Mildreds London's favourite veggie restaurant, established 1988, cooks with organic ingredients from small businesses, with gluten-free and vegan options and some organic wines for a lively, informal crowd; no reservations (45 Lexington Street, Soho, W1; 020 7494 1634; www.mildreds.co.uk)

Saf No animals were harmed in the making of this organic food. Saf is (oxymoron alert) a trendy vegan restaurant, serving nut-based cheese, most dishes cooked below 48°C (to preserve nutrients) and organic wines (152 Curtain Road, Hoxton, EC2; 020 7613 0007; www.safrestaurant.co.uk)

for something a little more substantial...

Babylon at The Roof Gardens With 1.5 acres of Richard Branson's surreal parkland (including oak trees, flamingos and ducks) 100 foot up, who cares about the prices (high)? (99 Kensington High Street; entrance on Derry Street, W8; 020 7368 3993; www.roof-gardens.virgin.com)

Bibendum Oyster Bar Housed in the glorious Art Deco Michelin House, Bibendum's seafood café serves all food cold (with the exception of its fresh soups), such as its signature seafood platter (81 Fulham Road, South Kensington, SW3; 020 7581 5817; www.bibendum.co.uk)

Konstam at the Prince Albert 'Urban' chef off the telly Oliver Rowe's popular ex-pub that tries very, very hard not to look like one, but more importantly, sources most its food from around London (2 Acton Street, WC1; 020 7833 5040; www.konstam.co.uk)

National Dining Rooms Views of Trafalgar Square (at a safe distance), National Gallery art and lots of grey hair, enjoyed over Oliver Peyton's excellent if expensive food; set menus available, and, downstairs, the cheaper National Café (The Sainsbury Wing, The National Gallery, Trafalgar Square, WC2; 020 7747 2525; www.thenationaldining-rooms.co.uk)

Nicole's Chic, sleek and expensive – just what you'd expect of a Bond Street pit stop in designer Nicole Farhi's basement; unfussy Mediterranean menu plus elegant afternoon tea (158 New Bond Street, W1; 020 7499 8408; www.nicolefarhi.com)

Portrait Restaurant Confusingly (though not really) right next door to the

National Gallery at the National Portrait Gallery, with a slap-up restaurant with the views and a basement café, both operated by Searcy's of the Gherkin's 40/30 glory (St Martin's Place, WC2; 020 7312 2465; www.npg.org.uk)

S&M Café The S&M Cafés (short for sausage and mash, what else?) offer greasy-spoon comfort food, with the grease excesses tidied away – posh bangers, full English breakfasts, and vintage British drinks (Notting Hill: 268 Portobello Road, W10; 020 8968 8898. Spitalfields: 48 Brushfield Street, E1; 020 7247 2252. Islington: 4–6 Essex Road, N1; 020 7359 5361; www.sandmcafe.co.uk)

Tom's Kitchen and Tom's Terrace Somerset House can't get enough of Tom Aikens, with two new outposts: the Kitchen replicates the original (see Eat) in a fine-art, fine-architecture setting; the Terrace (summer only) is alfresco (The Strand; 020 7845 4646; www.tomskitchen.co.uk)

for global grazing...

Comptoir Libanais Fresh, visually pleasing café/deli with good-value Middle Eastern favourites: falafels, houmous, baklava, moussaka, couscous tagines, plus teetotal mint tea, coffees and fresh juices (Marylebone: 65 Wigmore Street, W1, 020 7935 1110. Westfield: The Balcony, Westfield Shopping Centre, W12; 020 8811 2222; www.lecomptoir.co.uk)

The Diner Authentic US-style diners serving everything from burgers in bas-

kets to blueberry pancakes in comfy booths, plus cocktails and bottomless cups of cwarfee (Hoxton: 128 Curtain Road, EC2; 020 7729 4452. Soho: 18 Ganton Street, W1; 020 7287 8962. Camden: 2 Jamestown Road, NW1; 020 7485 5223. Islington: 21 Essex Road, N1; 020 7226 4533; www.goodlifediner.com)

Ottolenghi London loves Yotam Ottolenghi's café/deli (despite the cost), which pays tribute to both Tuscany (from where the Ottolenghi family originates) and Israel (where they emigrated to). Notting Hill: 63 Ledbury Road, W11; 020 7727 1121. Belgravia: 13 Motcomb Street, SW1; 020 7823 2707. Islington: 287 Upper Street, N1; 020 7288 1454. Kensington: 1 Holland Street, W8; 020 7937 0003)

The Real Greek Share mezedes (appetizers) before tucking in to your own *fagakia* (small dish) or *kirios piata* (main course) in a contemporary, animated environment (Hoxton: 14 Hoxton Market, N1; 020 7739 8212. Marylebone: 56 Paddington Street, W1; 020 7486 0466. Covent Garden: 60 Long Acre, WC2; 020 7240 2292. Bankside: Unit 1, Riverside House, 2a Southwark Bridge Road, SE1; 020 7620 0162. Westfield: Southern Terrace, Westfield Shopping Centre, Ariel Way; 020 8743 9168; www.therealgreek.com)

snack...

party...

Don't believe what they say about British reserve. After dark, decorum is safely tucked up and the wildcats come out to play: fetish is now fashionable, pool parties are making a splash (at Shoreditch House and Aquarium), and illegal drinking dens (knock thrice on the blue door next to the sex shop) is where the too-cool-for-school crowd like to hang.

But first a lesson in party politics, because you wouldn't want to get your Ermenegildo laughed out of the East End, or your grandma's marketwear (which might go down very nicely in Hackney) linger in purgatory in Mayfair. London's nightlife is geographically divided – nocturnal protocol is tribal. For example, Smithfield and Vauxhall are for partycore chemical kids up for some all-night dance music (Vauxhall is also home to a well-established gay village, as is Soho's Old Compton Street); Brixton is thumping with urban music – dubstep, grime, drum'n'bass. But the real rivalry is between the East and West Ends (where the West End is not west but central London). Exactly what gets you past the velvet rope 'up West' (suits, chinos, polo shirts) is what will get you kept out in the East, and vice versa (trainers, hoodies, old teeshirts).

So where to go? Your tastes will dictate what postcode you head for: if you like to pay for a table for the sake of space and privilege, can still appreciate, and afford, a fine champagne on the other side of the night, and like your surroundings to be of the shiny variety, then head directly to the West End (Mahiki, Whisky Mist, Luxx, DIU), where you'll find celebs, WAGs, bankers, rich Ruskis, debutantes on exeat, and those wayward young royals. It's a very particular world, one which the recession has done little to tame. Competitive bar spends can reach tens of thousands of pounds, no doubt due to the look-at-me sparklers, dancing girls and all-round acknowledgement of status and wealth that come to big spenders; club hostesses of the Rachel Uchitel (see Tiger Woods) variety can earn £250,000 a year cosseting their VIP guests. Entry is not a given, and there's rarely any walk-in trade at the weekend (when the West End can get ugly – flesh-flashing girls in gutters, barfing boys in disco shirts, police sirens screaming – the best nights for these clubs are weeknights, when the townies are safely on the other side of those bridges and tunnels). Dress up, call ahead for the (payable) guest list or reserve a table, or work it on the night with intimations of dropping thousands on a table (it's no doubt obvious, but these places are eye-wateringly expensive).

If, however, you're more into the Berlin/Brooklyn scene, you like a little vintage or unfathomable fashion, then you should head to Dalston or Bethnal Green (but not Hoxton which on a weekend is like Leicester Square), where you will find a quite a

sight – it's exhibitionism again, but of a very different variety. Here, money is practically irrelevant (everyone is skint) – no, the currency is creativity, experiment and shock, as all the club kids out-dress and out-alarm each other in outrageous DIY drama and drag. In fact, since the self-titled real queen of England, Jodie Harsh, proved that a big wig and a lot of make-up could create a celebrity, an entire species of (gay) girl-boys has been spawned – yes, sequins and full make-up on a man will help you get into Dalston Superstore or the Resistance Gallery.

Most likely, you belong to neither of these tribes – don't worry! There are plenty less appearance-obsessed, micro-managed nights out there (though even if neither scene talks to you, they are both sights to behold – as novelties if nothing else). London has plenty of unpretentious offerings – St Moritz for rockers, Proud Camden and Punk for cool fun, Madame Jojos for indie music and (watching) breakdancing, Maggie's for 1980s obsessives, Fabric for technophiles, Passing Clouds for partying with a conscience, etc. We've also introduced lots of new sections to direct you to your perfect night out – a more leisurely supper club perhaps, after-hours for non-stop hedonists, and, for a little fresh air, London's finest music festivals. And for those who wouldn't be seen dead in a club, we share the kind of word-of-mouth parties that it can take years – or a magic knock – for Londoners to uncover.

The Bathhouse *(left)*
7/8 Bishopsgate Churchyard,
The City, EC2
Tel: 020 7920 9207
www.thebathhousevenue.com
Open: noon–1am Thurs; noon–5am
Fri; 8pm–4am Sat. Bar open: noon–
midnight Mon–Weds

Like a Trojan horse in amongst the steel and glass City powerhouses is a tiny, rather random Victorian kiosk modelled on Jerusalem's Church of the Holy Sepulchre (think onion dome, turquoise tiles, decorative columns). It's underground in more ways than one: the kiosk is simply a tardis-like entrance, built in 1895 to conceal a subterranean Turkish bathhouse rumoured to be quite naughty (gay). Nowadays, the interior resembles a Victorian opium den – a sumptuous marble, gilt and red velvet affair echoing former gothic glories with erotica and skeleton portraits, a giant birdcage for a DJ booth, and candles, fruits and

flowers. Its club nights are equally un-City-ish, thrown by the resolutely Hoxton ex-333 manager, Tava O'Halloran: Thursdays' Boom Boom Club is a macabre 'gin-soaked' cabaret compèred by the graciously sordid Dusty Limits, Fridays' indie/electro night, Caligula, attracts East End clubkids competing in their own stock market of absurd drag, black lipstick and studied wreckedness, while Saturdays sees media dahlings and art tarts (the Shoreditch House set) pretend that it doesn't hurt a bit to dance to rock'n'roll, swing and blues in towering heels. You see, Uggs (and less so, trainers) are a recognised enemy of the Bathhouse.

....

Bethnal Green *(middle)*
Workingmen's Club
42 Pollard Row, E2
Tel: 020 7739 7170
www.workersplaytime.net
Open: 8pm–2am Thurs–Sat; 7pm–
midnight Sun (sometimes Mon–Weds;

opening hours vary frequently so please check listings before you go)

The BGWC is a members' club with a difference – money, power and good looks won't get you anywhere here. Since 1953, it's been a social club for real East Enders and until 2002 was a closed shop. However, faced with financial ruin, the committee opened the doors to local events producer Warren Dent, who let in non-members not of the workingmen variety, whose beer money has kept the club a-go-go. The 1970s interior is unchanged (mock teak panelling, swirling red carpets, leatherette chairs and laminate tables), and an authentic scuzz lingers. Members have their own private floor downstairs while Dent's delights take place upstairs – the BGWC has one of the most creative and fun party programmes in London. There's all kinds of 'oke, cabaret (from amateur show-offs to out-there performance artists), dance classes and, of course (it's a club

after all), live music, DJs and dancing. It's crawling with sharply dressed scenesters ('So ironic!' they squeal), though the charm (and cheap prices) of a workingmen's club lives on. And now with infamous guerrilla artist Banksy's Yellow Lines Flower Painter painted on its outside wall, the BGWC has been granted immortality.

Boujis *(right)*
43 Thurloe Street,
South Kensington, SW7
Tel: 020 7584 2000 www.boujis.com
Open: daily, 10pm–3am

Among certain circles (namely aristos, visiting A/B/C-list celebs and Eurotrash social climbers), Boujis is the best club in town – especially on Tuesdays. Others wouldn't stoop to sully their souls with something so status-obsessed, but that's just as well – it's a bijou 'boutique' club in sloaney South Kensington that can afford to be

selective about its clientele (and it is, in no uncertain terms), thanks to the frequency of champagne orders (vintage only, and available in bottles up to the 12-litre Balthazar). The official door policy is members and their guests only, but contamination is possible for the exceedingly beautiful (the aesthetically challenged should befriend a member in the queue, or pester A Small World associates). Inside this intimate basement club – champagne buckets, LED 'mood walls' and stiletto-spiked black pleather banquettes – impeccably groomed lovelies in designer slips-of-dresses dirty-dance to accessible cheese old and new and poppy R&B for their male counterparts – preppy, Blazer-ed and drooling. We couldn't possibly say that Paris Hilton has done as much for Prince William, but both are certainly regulars, drawn perhaps to its ban on photography and secret back exits.

Cable *(top)*
33a Bermondsey St Tunnel, SE1
Tel: 020 7403 7730
www.cable-london.com
Open: 10pm–6am Mon–Fri; 11pm–6am Sat; 5am–1pm Sun

For the meow-meow generation of middle-class white kids that come to Cable, the dance scene is certainly far from over. It's just gone back to its underground (or under-archway, in Cable's case) roots. In the late 1980s, these tunnels and caverns around London Bridge were home to the illegal raves that launched acid house. Retracing the steps of the scene, Cable opened in summer 2009, filling the void left by the closing of iconic

clubs such as Turnmills and The End. Bone-crunching beats whoosh through a beautifully raw maze of open-brick archways and tunnels to a thousand-capacity troop of eyeball-rolling, jaw-churning ravers, young and old alike. While there's a sense of familiarity for some older clubbers, the scene and music is fresh and without parody, with a welcome reminiscent vibe in the UV-lit chillout gallery upstairs where sweaty strangers hug and share loved-up chats on the tatty sofas. DJs come in the form of old-skool legends such as Goldie to modern tech-house hero, Boy 8-Bit, and the look is American Apparel hoodies, fluoro sunglasses, high-tops, and maybe the odd smiley face T-shirt: dress to sweat.

Cargo *(bottom)*
83 Rivington Street, Hoxton, EC2
Tel: 020 7749 7840
www.cargo-london.com
Open: daily, noon–1am (3am Fri/Sat)

Housed under three cavernous arches of a disused Victorian viaduct, Cargo is a lair for the Hoxton homie – he/she of concept haircut and Rough Trade vinyl obsession. As a one-stop shop, Cargo provides all they require – in arch one, the Street Food Café serves up global flavours in manageably small clubbers' portions, arch two is for lounging on leather benches, levering foreign bottled beer down necks and nodding just-so to bass-heavy beats, and arch three is for pogoing on one's rare Japanese trainers. All around is reassuringly hard-edged exposed brickwork and street art from, among others, Banksy. Like the food and beer, the music menu is an international mash-up – DJs and live bands play anything from dancehall and grime to Kiwi or Eskimo sounds (often with themed food to match) – anything, in fact, as long as it is cutting-edge, played on an impeccable, all-enveloping sound system. In summer, there's even an 'urban' barbecue in its fag garden. 'Is it is it wick-ed', as the homies say.

Dalston Superstore (top)
117 Kingsland High Street, E8
Tel: 020 7254 2273
www.facebook.com (search for Dalston Superstore)
Open: daily, noon–2am (some weekends till 4am or 6am)

It's a Scene – a Major Scene, arguably home to Britain's sceniest scene. The diamond in the rough of Dalston's dive bars (see Bars), this two-floored hotspot sees drag queens flirting with teddy boys, moustachioed dandies chewing toothpicks at the bar, and just about all the East End personalities being untouchably cool: DJ/artist Matthew Stone, DJ/fashion designers Pam Hogg and Gareth Pugh (yes, to be cool, you have to be able to DJ). Opened in summer 2009 by three of East London's hottest promoters – Dan Pope and Mikki Most of Trailer Trash and Dan Beaumont of Disco Bloodbath – this WiFi-enabled café-by-day/club-by-night draws inspiration from the hip hoods of Mitte and Williamsburg. But its cement walls splashed with neon graffiti and monthly-changing local art will be all but obscured at their notoriously wild weekend parties (the nights to name-drop are Horsemeat Disco and Homo Electric). Predictably, it's

very gay – it goes with the territory, but it's open to all. All, that is, that have 'it' – you either do or you don't, and the serious 'tude on the door is fascist in its discrimination. Tell them you're with the DJ.

Den & Centro (bottom)
18 West Central Street, Holborn, WC1
Tel: 020 7240 1083
www.thedenandcentro.com
Open: 10pm–3am Mon; midnight–6am Tues; 10pm–3am Weds; 10pm–6am Thurs–Sun

What's an anagram of 'Den'? Correct – The End superclub (RIP) faced its untimely end in 2009 when the developers came in to dig for property gold. But then the recession bit, so it seemed sensible to capitalize on the existing top-spec club design and epic sound system (soul-shaking speaker walls and everything). And so, in summer 2009, after a sensitive facelift to the End's black and chrome industrial design, plus new lasers and yoof-pleasing graffiti murals, the End became Den, and the legendary dance space lived on. With an 800 capacity in the Den, and 275 in the upstairs gig space Centro, it is still respected by trendbots, industry types and pro clubbers, who worship at its altar-like DJ booths. Programming is diverse, with regular indie, dubstep and electro nights (including London's cultish and long-running Popstarz – Fridays' perky, polysexual electropop night), superstar DJs exercising crowd mind-control, and after-parties for the likes of Grace Jones. Thanks to the kind of opening hours that wipe out next days, it's become a mop-up for

party...

disco diehards spilling out of shiny West End clubs. Take heed: not only did the End never end, but after midnight, nor does the queue.

....

 Fabric *(top)*
77a Charterhouse Street,
Farringdon, EC1
Tel: 020 7336 8898
www.fabriclondon.com
Open: 10pm–6am Fri,10pm–7am Sat

At Fabric, it's all about the beat. It used to be all about meat, when the building was once a meat cellar servicing Smithfield's meat market. With three dance floors, including a full-on warehouse rave den with a 'bodysonic' floor that pumps bass through the soles of your feet, and a constantly upgraded surround sound system, Fabric is for anyone into a runaway bpm. It is renowned for supporting new, underground DJs playing the latest breaks, drum'n'bass, house, techno and electro, and, to stay with the game, has introduced live music (electronic orchestras, rock bands, MCs, etc). But as a destination club, it lacks that vibe that only locals bring – this disparate 1,500-capacity crowd includes stag parties, bridge-and-tunnellers and tourists, happy to wait in Fabric's massive queues (it even sells queue-jumping rights with monthly membership and Ticketweb advance sales). There's some convergence around the unisex loos, where surprised strangers often slip into conversation, and there's some warmth in the chill-out areas. But Fabric – modern, cool and loud – is considered London's best dance club and, for that, not intended as cosy and cute. Nor indeed as a meat market.

 **Jamm** *(bottom)*
261 Brixton Road, SW9
Tel: 020 7274 5537
www.brixtonjamm.org
Open: 7pm–2am Thurs; 7pm–4am Fri/Sat; 5pm–1am Sun. Check listings for parties Mon-Weds (it's 'random')

Relax. There's no grim door purgatory, no pretensions and no dress code ('just wear clothes'). In an appealingly scruffy ex-Victorian pub is housed a cool Brixton warehouse vibe split between two capacious rooms – one for more hardcore clubbing, one for chilling on comfy sofas (though such obstacles don't seem to deter determined dancers) – plus, reputedly, London's largest smoking terrace. And with no official music policy, it's whatever goes, be it African drums and Peruvian flutes, or hip-hop, Detroit techno, grimy funk and raggalectro (this is Brixton, after all). Plenty of international DJs make this their London port of call, but you won't hear any chart music unless local Brixton boys Basement Jaxx or Alabama 3 happen to have a hit – both hold regular parties here. In fact, its roster of friends in high places has mushroomed since opening in 2005 (must be the new muso-pleasing Funktion One sound system and onsite recording studio and label). Hot Chip and Orbital also now have residencies, and it's fast becoming the venue of choice for Brixton Academy after-parties (recently, Massive Attack, Franz Ferdinand and Florence and the Machine). 'It's a magnet for music,' says Jamm's friendly founder-manager Jonathan Allen. A sticky jam, if you like.

....

party...

 Maggie's   *(left)*
329 Fulham Road, Chelsea,
SW10
Tel: 020 7352 8512
www.maggies-club.com
Open: 10.30pm–2.30am Weds/Thurs;
10.30pm–3.30am Fri/Sat

Fed up of trying hard to keep up with tryhard clubs? Perhaps it's time to embrace the decade that taste forgot. Named after the quintessential 1980s icon, Margaret Thatcher, this shamelessly silly club is a much-needed dose of humour on the stuffy Sloane scene. Opened in spring 2010 by old Etonian and royal chum Charlie Gilkes with Duncan Stirling (the duo behind Barts, see BARS), Maggie's is an 1980s onslaught of garish glitz and glam – from the splashy mural depicting caricatures of the era, including Timmy Mallet, the A-Team's Mr T and Mrs T herself, to Lycra-legginged, permed wig-wearing waitresses roller-skating between the giant Rubik's cube tables. Piña cola-

das, Slush Puppies and Babychams are served by shaker-throwing flair barmen dressed as Tom Cruise from Cocktail. There's no let-up even in the unisex loos, with Union Jack toilet seats, beano-lined cubicles and recordings of the Iron Lady's greatest speeches (NB: the music jumps the decades from 1am). While they've tried to avoid it becoming an unofficial Young Conservatives club (turning down Tory requests to host events here), it's inevitably blue, what with the founders' associations. And for that, Maggie's is rather elitist and expensive. So authentic.

....

Madame Jojos   *(middle)*
8–10 Brewer St, Soho, W1
Tel: 020 7734 3040
www.madamejojos.com
Open: 8pm–3am Tues/Thurs;
10.30pm–3am Weds; 10pm–3am Fri;
7pm–3am Sat; 9.30pm–3am Sun

It's a dilemma. What night to go-go to

the long-running and louche Madame Jojos? Pick a day, any day: there's the legendary deep funk Friday night that pulls in the coolest break-dancers (NB: amateur roly-polies inside the breakers' magic circle doesn't usually go down so well), tranny Kitsch Cabaret on Saturdays (a seated early-evening affair, served by the brittle Barbettes), White Heat's indie live band night every Tuesday, the high-camp, high-heeled Tranny Shack (essentially that) on Wednesdays, and all sorts of wildcards in the rest of the week. As well as a variety of ska, soul and disco nights, Madame Jojos has been known to put on some rockin' one-off live gigs with bands such as the Scissor Sisters, Kings of Leon and The Fratellis taking to the stage. Whenever you decide to visit this former strip club, you will come away feeling a little bit decadent and a little bit dirty – possibly something to do with the venue's retro trashy-chic décor of plush velvet booths, gilded balustrades and mirrored walls that still channels seedy Soho boudoirs.

....

Mahiki *(right)*
1 Dover St, Mayfair, W1
Tel: 020 7493 9529
www.mahiki.com
Open: 5.30pm–3.30am Mon–Fri;
7.30pm–3.30am Sat

You'd be forgiven for thinking the flashing lights emitting from Mahiki are from an electrified dance floor – no: it's the paparazzi, hoping to catch one of the young princes or their escorts spilling out. Mahiki is their club of choice possibly because it takes the pocket money of a prince to afford mixologist Papa Jules' lavish sharing cocktails served up in treasure chests, sailors' hats and other exotic whotnots, plus a new pan-Asian fusion menu by two ex-Nobu chefs. This tiki theme bar just about gets away with all the crazy coconuts because its holiday spirit (and super-strength cocktails) reminds its conservative posh-chav crowd of their rum-soaked holidays at Sandy Lane. The upper space is a wicker/bamboo-lined beach bar (think Hawaii Five-0, all palm fronds and exotic flowers); the lower bar is darker, glossier and home to the dance floor and cheesy pop. Often somewhere in there are those naughty princes, girls trying to pull them, and young hedge-funders and Gap Yah kids happy to mop up the left-overs (note that the clipboard bitches can afford to sieve out the unwashed masses, especially on its big nights Monday and Thursday). Why else would you need look-at-me cocktails? Aloha, sailor!

 Notting Hill *(top)* **Arts Club**
21 Notting Hill Gate, W11
Tel: 020 7460 4459
www.nottinghillartsclub.com
Open: 7pm (4pm Sat/Sun)–2am (1am Sun). Closed Mondays. (check listings)

To say that the NHAC's line-up is eclectic is understatement akin to 'the Bill Gates has savings'. All-encompass-ing might be more accurate, where 'arts' means anything from photogra-phy exhibitions to fanzine showcases to craft sessions to, yes, music. That's not to say that clubbers are required to come equipped with a crochet hook (that's provided) – music is its prime concern, and is yet more diverse – classical, country, flamenco, ska, gypsy, rock, and all in the least obvi-ous take. Long-running nights include DJ Seb Chew's Yoyo every Thursday (no tickets on the door, sign up via the website) and Rough Trade's free show-case afternoons every Saturday. In fact

the only things the NHAC doesn't do are open-mic nights ('we have stan-dards', they say) or anything that is clichéd or boring. With the emphasis on its cultural programme, the NHAC is a small, no-frills basement club that's mostly standing room only, and it can get hot and cramped. Organic bar snacks, champagne and 'fishbowl' sharing cocktails afford welcome com-fort to a loyal crowd, all enlightened in the NHAC's philosophy that 'a world created by artists is better than a world created by politicians'. Pseuds wel-come.

Passing Clouds *(bottom)*
1 Richmond Road, just behind 438 Kingsland Road, Dalston, E8
Tel: 07951 989897
www.facebook.com/passingclouds
Open: 7pm–1am Mon–Thurs; 8pm–3am Fri/Sat; 2pm–1am Sun

It's not a club, it's a revolution. And if you want to build a revolution, you have to throw great parties, say the people behind Passing Clouds. In the early days (mid-Noughties), the house-party vibe was such that people would wake up the next day on its engulfing sofas. Nowadays, matters are rather more ordered(ish) – they mean busi-ness with that revolution, but given that it's all about the independent con-science scene (yes, you can party con-scientiously), and that community is the order of the day, the make-yerself-at-home atmosphere endures. Housed in a handsome 19th-century ex-print-works down an alley by a disused rail-way line, the club is appropriately non-commercial and low-fi (read: cheap entry and drinks; scruffy antiques). Its

signature is live world music – gypsy, roots, afro-jazz – played out to both the downstairs dance floor and the more chill first floor, but its reputation is more that people go because it will be a wild, friendly party, not because they have any idea who's playing; Sundays see a local jam – to be kept in the loop, become their Facebook friend. It's a good look.

Proud Camden *(top)*
The Horse Hospital, Stables Market, Chalk Farm Road, NW1
Tel: 020 7482 3867
www.proudcamden.com
Open: daily, 11am–1.30am (2.30am Thurs–Sat, 12.30am Sun)

Camden should indeed be proud – this 10,000-square-foot, 200-year-old ex-horse hospital that once nursed nags injured from pulling canal barges is gallerist Alex Proud's unstoppable party space. Proud Camden started out as a photography gallery in the nearby Gin House, only to become better known for throwing riotous parties, seeing over 1,000 live-music acts. Eventually Alex Proud conceded, opening this vast new venue in 2008. By day, a gallery exhibiting moody shots of rock royalty (see Culture), by night, the volume is maxed, the dry ice pumped and the queue psyched, waiting to see the likes of Dizzee, Florence Welch and VV Brown perform, as well as regular sets from DJs Queens of Noize (who run Thursdays' cheeky Smash & Grab nights), Jodie Harsh and Kissy Sell Out. With interior design from Russell Sage Studio and Proud's wife, the craft queen Danielle Proud, the old stables have been converted into luxury play-

pens complete with, variously, Guitar Hero, karaoke, table football and pinball. A new restaurant, plus summer barbeques, a smoking terrace large enough for all Camden's show ponies and boys out to stud, and celeb spotting of the Mark Ronson/Geldof scions/Sadie Frost variety, makes for unbridled hedonism. Neigh.

Punk *(bottom)*
14 Soho Street, Soho, W1
Tel: 020 7734 4004
www.punksoho.co.uk
Open: 7pm (8pm Thurs; 5pm Fri)–3am Tues–Sat

Dispel all ideas of lawlessness and tartan Mohicans – after all, a true punk club might name itself after genitalia or queen-bashing, but never the P word. But actually, compared to your standard West End club, Punk at least understands anarchy, while its 'mash-up' music policy (electro, 80s, rock and a ban on townie R&B/funky house) is considerably easier on the ears than screaming. As such, it's one of the few central London clubs to lure hipsters (plus plenty of celebs), and repel the leery old git/gold-digger combo. It's not about competitive consumption here, but competitive singing (with the fortnightly Friday Rockaoke and monthly musicals night Musicalifragalistic) and dancing, at, say, Mondays' epic Anthem night (it does what it says on the tin) and Thursdays' fierce and filthy electro/disco showdown Your Mum's House. That Punk gets it is no doubt down to the founders' experience in good, honest hedonism, with party perennials The Social and Jerusalem also in their portfolio. They get

party…

the need for a bit of granny furniture (and lots of seats), with deep-buttoned armchairs, faux Louis XIV chaises longues and Chesterfields, which, thanks to its popularity, are rapidly getting the punk treatment.

held with Bizarre Magazine, featuring moshing to the latex-rubber DJ and freak-show performances. It's always original, often shocking and never mediocre, but be warned: mediocrity on the door may well feel the resistance.

Resistance Gallery *(top)*
265 Poyser Street,
Bethnal Green, E2
Tel: 07723 505641
www.resistancegallery.blogspot.com
Open: 8/9pm–2/3am Weds–Sat but always check listings first; sometimes open Mon–Weds

If the rest of London melts down into one big corporate mulch, the 'Res Gal' would surely be the last to yield. The creation of Garry Vanderhorne, Mexican Lucha Libre wrestler and firm friend to London's performance art scene, it is, as such, a flexible space to facilitate anything, so long as it's edgy (i.e., on the edges of boundaries, sanity and taste) and entertaining. It's a magnet for London's avant-garde community, unfussed by moneyed polish. Just as well: down a dark, Victorian alleyway, under the railway arches is a post-industrial corrugated shell, unmarked of course, with a basic bar, salvage-chic furniture and a lo-fi, anti-commercial vibe. Regular nights include Sink the Pink (Saturdays, monthly) – a straight-friendly gay disco/movement which 'celebrates the ridiculous', the, umm, bleeding edge, True Blood-inspired Fangtasia London (Fridays, monthly) where Vanderhorne, aka Vampire Sheriff of Area E2, whips up a gothic, fleshy fetish-fest for vampires and their human companions, and Bitchslap! (Fridays, monthly),

Supperclub *(bottom)*
12 Acklam Road,
Notting Hill, W10
Tel: 020 8964 6600
www.supperclub.com
Open: 7pm–3am (2am Weds/Thurs)
Weds–Sat

'No shoes on the bed' is the only familiar note of convention as Supperclub throws out all the rules. The concept has been imported bed-by-bed into Notting Hill's bender bastion (previously 12 Acklam Road, Neighbourhood and Subterranea) from Amsterdam, where, in 1992, a group of artists wanted to showcase their art in an old warehouse. Lacking furniture, they brought in their own mattresses, inventing a bed-based dining/clubbing craze that's spread to LA, San Fran, Istanbul and Singapore. The look has been compared to a mental ward: two floors of white day-bed banquettes surround a dance floor, while UV lights, the odd Panton chair, and white everything give off a comfy space-pod vibe. With performance art as a backdrop, a four-course, party-friendly meal (£45 excl drinks, incl entry), such as carpaccio, gazpacho and sashimi, is served on bed-trays – though it's not really about the food: the lounging-and-picking encourages some very un-British socialising. Then the food is cleared and the intercontinental house pumped up. The ice may get broken long before

you do, though will you be ready for the tongue-in-cheek 'light bondage' encouraged at the monthly Whippet? A rather more gentle 'Love Brunch' is on monthly Saturday mornings.

St Moritz (top)
161 Wardour Street, Soho, W1
Tel: 020 7734 3324
Open: 10pm–3.30am Weds–Sat

Spending the evening in St Moritz couldn't sound more misleading – it's not exclusive and it's nowhere near a mountain. There are some Swiss connections – it is run by two charming Swiss patriarchs, who have been known to entertain diners in their adjoining fondue restaurant with alpine horns, bells and an accordion (no yodelling, unfortunately). No such sounds down in the cave basement – St Moritz is a 'rawk' club, respected equally by rockerati (from Motörhead to the Kings of Leon) and the, uh, rockletariat – bikers, mods, indie kids. Gaz's Rockin' Blues, on Thursdays, run by ska-nut Gaz Mayall, is still going strong after over 30 years with blues, rockabilly and ska plus live bands; the road-blockingly popular Friday nights (indie rock) and Saturday nights (1980s' glam rock) are almost as long-running. This vintage club resembles the cellar of a Swiss chalet and its quaint alpine décor and intimate size make for an atomic atmosphere. What's not to like? Well, with all that air guitar action and rock-hopping, it gets pretty hot, and its primitive acoustics often induce tinnitus. But with resolutely cheap prices, you won't be needing a Swiss bank account.

Whisky Mist (bottom)
Hilton Hotel, 35 Hertford St, Mayfair, W1
Tel: 020 7208 4067
www.whiskymist.com
Open: 10.30pm–3am Tues–Sun

Psychologists studying the social behaviour of the wealthy (and nubile wannabes) should really spend more time at Whisky Mist. From Mahiki's Piers Adam and Nick House is a multi-sensory fetishisation of filthy lucre and all its associations. The décor is themed on that posh pursuit of hunting (a stuffed stag here, crystal antlers there). The resident DJs (playing pneumatic pop, electro and hip hop) and floor team all hail from St Tro, cuing 'Were you there?' conversation. In anticipation on every table are giant Moet buckets, and with every big order, leotard-clad dancers gyrate until those attention-seeking sparklers fizzle out, ensuring that all around can imagine your bar spend ('People are like children,' says the manager, 'when one sees it, they all order it'). Likewise, the Tree of Life sharing cocktail comes in a child-height goblet, and if ordered with Cristal (£1,200), is poured in public. It's been known for Wills and Harry, Paris and Jay-Z to all be present (Sundays and Tuesdays are the biggies), with men-civvies (an older, Euro/Russian/Arab crowd) trying to compete by dropping £10,000 (so yes, it's expensive). The problem is, the psychologists are unlikely to pass muster on the door.

the best of the rest...

commercial clubs...

East Village Big-name DJs, serious sound system and an up-fer-it crowd in this small-ish two-floor club (89 Great Eastern Street, Hoxton, EC2; 020 7739 5173; www.eastvillageclub. com)

Ministry of Sound Opened in 1991, this institution is one of London's longest serving superclubs where sound and dance music comes first (103 Gaunt Street, Southwark, SE1; 0870 060 0010; www.ministryofsound.com)

Plan B B is for Brixton so it's urban music, plus a spasm-inducing, bass-heavy Funktion One sound system, cosied-up industrial interior and the odd superstar DJ (418 Brixton Road, SW9; 020 7737 7372; www.plan-brixton.co.uk)

table clubs...

Chinawhite Notorious celeb haunt of the early Noughties, the club has modernised its sumptuous oriental theme in a slick new venue including a pan-Asian restaurant, winning back its popularity with the posers (4 Winsley Street, Fitzrovia, W1; 020 7290 0580; www.chinawhite.com)

DIU Open since spring 2010, it's currently winning the shiny competition with a twinkly-lit ceiling, gimmicky motion detector security beams, and black and gold scheme; housey playlist (12 Greek Street, Soho, W1; 020 7025 7844; www.diulondon.com)

Embassy For footballers, soap stars and Big Brother contestants, Embassy is your mecca (29 Old Burlington Street, Mayfair, W1; 020 7851 0956; www.embassylondon.com)

Kanaloa Club Trop in the City using Mahiki's tried-and-tested formula (tiki bamboo, fruity sharing cocktails, cash), plus debauched bankers and, the antidote, special treats for girls (18 Lime Office Court, Hill House, Shoe Lane, EC4; 020 7842 0620; www.kanaloa-club.com)

Luxx Anyone who gets to strut down the central neon-underlit catwalk is guaranteed an instant rush of self-love. Sleek black box opened in spring 2010, with R&B ban plus all-important LED light system (3 New Burlington Street, Mayfair, W1; 020 7297 2893; www.luxx-london.com)

Movida Shiny West End club set in bare-brick vaults with the requisite leather banquettes, commercial R&B and housey pop, and Cristal served with sparklers (8 Argyll Street, Oxford Circus, W1; 020 7734 5776; www.movida-club.com)

gay...

BarCode Cruise bar/club with butch design and butch boys warming up to house DJs. In the homo strongholds of Soho (3 Archer Street, W1; 020 7734 3342) and Vauxhall (Arch 69, Albert Embankment, SE11; 020 7582 4180; www.bar-code.co.uk)

Candy This ones for lezzies – three fun floors with Ibiza-style DJs and dance floor, karaoke, a pool table and erotic dancers Thurs–Sat (4 Carlisle Street, Soho, W1; 020 7287 5041; www.candybarsoho.com)

Heaven Shirts off for London's first gay superclub, opened in 1979 with a 1,625 capacity. Now under G-A-Y management, it's commercial pop over deep house (Under the Arches, Villiers Street, WC2; 020 7930 2020; www.heavennightclub-london.com)

The Joiners Arms Insidery, East End after-party vibe for the George & Dragon crowd (see Pubs); muscle Marys, spikey queens and fag hags, plus sweat, club scum and karaoke (116 Hackney Road, E2; www.myspace.com/joinersarms)

The Royal Vauxhall Tavern Legendary hangout for Vauxhall's gay village: a grand Victorian pub with gay bingo, gay love, and Saturdays' cultish Duckie cabaret (372 Kennington Lane, SE11; 020 7820 1222; www.rvt.org.uk)

sex clubs...

Hoist London's totally unironic answer to the Blue Oyster Bar – a fetish club for boys into leather, straps, rubber and worse (www.thehoist.co.uk)

Killing Kittens Pitched as a network for the sexual elite and seemingly styled on Eyes Wide Shut, entry to parties held at private residences is for successful, good-looking yet masked single girls and couples; only girls can initiate (www.killingkittens.com)

Rubber Ball Proudly pervy annual masked ball hosted by fetish mag Skin Two for the BDSM scene with a strict, rubbery dress code (www.rubberball.skintwo.co.uk)

Subversion More tacky than Torture Garden, but fetish is fetish; monthly (usually the first Saturday), with dance and dungeon action, dominated by Mistress Absolute, usually at Hub (2 Goulston Street, E1; www.clubsubversion.com)

Torture Garden Notorious-turned-fashionable monthly-ish fetish feast with cages, latex, spanking and tonguing; for gimps, dominatrices, slaves, and exhibitionists all round (www.tortuegarden.com)

after hours...

Aquarium Weekend escapism (albeit townie) with an in-club pool and hot tub, open till 11am on Saturday and Sunday mornings with minimal house and electro DJs (256 Old Street, EC1; 020 7253 3558; www.clubaquarium.co.uk)

Egg For boy racers and pedal-to-the-metal partiers: three dance rooms plus a garden (the place for sunrise) open till 10am on Saturdays, a meek 6am on Sundays, and noon on Mondays (200 York Way, King's Cross, N7; 020 7609 8364; www.egglondon.net)

Fire For 'energy' that just won't sleep, head to Vauxhall's most naughty; Fire, a voracious gay club, promises a dance-music workout till 3pm on Mondays; with lasers, dry ice and the odd stretcher (South Lambeth Road, SW8; 020 7582 9890; www.myspace.com/firelondon)

party...

can't sleep?

Beat sleep with **Bar Italia's** espressos, paninis and Latin liveliness (alcohol 11am–11pm; 22 Frith Street, Soho, W1; 020 7437 4520), join the off-duty chefs at **Vingt Quatre**, a very posh greasy spoon with a 24-hour alcohol licence (325 Fulham Road, SW10; 020 7376 7224), buy salt beef bagels just to laugh at the cool kids all drunk and not cool anymore at **Brick Lane Beigel Bake** (159 Brick Lane, E1; 020 7729 0616), and indulge in home-cooked Turkish food, at **Somine** (alcohol 11.30am–2am; 131 Kingsland High Street, E8; 020 7254 7384). If craving a pint after a 'hard night's work', muck in with the Smithfield Meat Market workers with a full, meat-heavy English breakfast at **The Hope & Sir Loin** – geddit? (94 Cowcross Street, EC1; 020 7250 1442) or **The Cock Tavern** (East Poultry Avenue, EC1; 020 7248 2918), both open from 6am, weekdays only. Failing that, take in the casino air at the West End's 24-hour casinos (see separate entry).

parties for those who wouldn't be seen dead in a club...

Aphrodisiacs No, not for swingers or fetishists, but discerning, avant-garde partiers who like a bit of themed dress-up, disco nu and old, and underground house (www.aphrodisiacslondon.com)

La Belle Epoque The scene of fin de siècle Paris from promoters Bourne & Hollingsworth: absinthe, acrobats, corsets and can-cans, green fairies and filthy winks (www.belleepoqueparty.com)

Blitz Bourne & Hollingsworth's impeccably set-dressed wartime-themed party with Land Girls and Victory rolls, tweeds and twiddled 'taches, and the sexual charge of sailors returning to port (www.theblitzparty.com)

Bugged Out! 'All-night mutant techno parties' and bank-holiday belters held in car parks, warehouses and clubs for hardcore clubkidz (www.buggedout.net)

Girlcore Yup, riotous and fashiony DJ-led parties that flip the usual male dominance of clubdom ('it's not a man-hating thing, it's a girl-loving thing'); boys are welcome but powerless (www.myspace.com/girlcorerules)

ETA These so-called 'raaaarves' – late-nighters for dressy dahlings of West London – raise the bar from four-packs of Export in a field, with a posh bar, big-name guest DJs and dress-up themes (www.estimatedtimeofarrival.com)

Jezebel Loft Party Jade Jagger's monthly late-night party for West London lovelies held in a loft studio with a premium bar, fancy sound and lighting, and house music and disco (77 Scrubs Lane, NW10; see Facebook or email info@eazybailey.com)

Last Tuesday Society Retro masked balls featuring edgy DJs, live bands, kooky dating games, erotic life-drawing and peacocks – of the human variety (www.thelasttuesdaysociety.org)

Mulletover Rob Star, master of deep,

tech-tinged house throws secret, often themed parties in abandoned warehouses, outdoors, or his own party pub, The Star of Bethnal Green (see Pubs) for the East End scene (www.mullet-over.co.uk)

Prohibition Flapper gowns and beads, silk dressing gowns and pipes – Bourne & Hollingsworth's Roaring Twenties-themed night in a secret location with Charleston dancing, gambling and guffawing (www.prohibition1920s.com)

SS Atlantica The Bourne & Hollingsworth boys hark back to the decadence of 1930s booze cruises aboard ocean liners (but not really): dinner suits, furs and silks, plus silent films, period games and a casino (www.ssatlantica.com)

The Underground Rebel Bingo Club Proper bingo followed by proper hedonism usually involving silly get-up and defacing others with bingo pens in a secret location; see website even just for the hilarious story of how it started (www.rebelbingo.com)

supper clubs for slower nights...

The Brickhouse The East End does cabaret, meaning, invariably, trannies – plus comedy, acoustic music and, oh, men in make-up. Expect a suitably raucous atmosphere, and less from the food (152C Brick Lane, E1; 020 7247 0005; www.thebrickhouse.co.uk)

The Pigalle Club Styled like a 1940s Chicago gangster joint, the Mean Fiddler's Vince Power is growing old gracefully with this dinner/dance club featuring big bands, jazz soloists and swing (215 Piccadilly, W1; 0800 988 5470; www.vpmg.net/pigalle)

Proud Cabaret Gallerist Alex Proud expands into the City with old jazz, chanteuses and cabaret, all served with supper in a 1920s speakeasy-style purple velvet dining room (1 Mark Lane, EC3; www.proudcabaret.com; 020 7283 1940)

Festivals

No camping, showers in your hotel room and, finally the chance for mass misbehaviour in a London park

Camden Crawl Camden has an awful lot of music venues at its disposal (the Roundhouse, the Dublin Castle, Barfly, Jazz Café, KOKO, etc) plus an indie scene ready to party, so it makes sense to bring in some 200 acts (previously New Young Pony Club, Teenage Fanclub, The Drums) to play over the first weekend in May (full ticket £57; www.thecamdencrawl.com)

Field Day A one-day alliance between London's coolest party promoters Eat Your Own Ears, Adventures In The Beetroot Field and Bugged Out! The out-there line-up won't feature international names, but there will be heroes of the hip East End; usually the last Saturday in June (£33.33; Victoria Park, E3; www.fielddayfestivals.com)

Land of Kings If you want to mainline Dalston's emerging arts scene, then buy your wristband for £15 and access some 50-odd gigs, cabaret acts and other experimental curiosities; one long Friday night in April (www.landofkings.co.uk)

Lovebox Weekender The boys behind Groove Armada have been running this annual three-day blinder since 2003, with DJ sets (eg, Norman Jay, Gilles Peterson, Mr Scruff), and live music (previously Grace Jones, Dizzee, Antony Hegarty) in 10 venues over 40 acres in Victoria Park, E3, in the 3rd weekend in July (full ticket £99; www.loveboxlondon.com)

Stag & Dagger One night in May, 20 venues, 100-odd acts – it's the Vice-backed Shoreditch crawl showcasing independent music and the kind of gigs you won't hear at the more commercial festies (£20; www.stag-and-dagger.com)

Wireless London's most commercial festival, a three-dayer in Hyde Park, W2, previously seeing Daft Punk, Jay-Z and Kasabian on the main stage; also artist signings, carnival rides and an acoustic band stand and lots of people, usually the first weekend in July (full ticket £110; www.wireless-festival.co.uk)

....

Live Music

Since every teenager in the country suddenly saw starting a band as their fast track into adulthood, venues large and small have seen to it that creative angst gets an audience. Our favourites, below, are of the more intimate, soulful variety where performers are within ogling distance.

Barfly
49 Chalk Farm Road,
Camden, NW1
Tel: 020 7424 0800
www.barflyclub.com
Open: daily, 3pm–1am (3am Fri/Sat)

Not one known for throwing around the niceties, Noel Gallagher said of Barfly, 'Ten years ahead of anybody's time.' No doubt it's just a thinly veiled self-compliment – seeing as Barfly plucked Oasis from obscurity way back when – but, all the same, nurturing new talent has been Barfly's speciality since 1996, and as such, puts over 1,000 bands on their stage each year (with live music daily), and not without some kind of Midas touch. Pedigree rock bands (Blur, Stereophonics, The Strokes) all cut their teeth on its small, dingy stage. That they've since opened heaps of branches nationwide (including at the University of London Union, Malet Street, WC1; 020 7664 2000) is proof that polish and pretensions are not requisites for rocking live music. Expect talent scouts to be lurking in the standing-room-only space (arrive early for a good view), alongside other musicians and musos, all sporting scruffiness and prog-rock hair and affecting couldn't-care-less cool. Sticking around in the downstairs pub after the gig to buy the band a beer is as good a start as any to a night of rock'n'roll mayhem.

....

Jazz Café
5 Parkway, Camden, NW1
Tel: 020 7485 6834
www.jazzcafe.co.uk
Open: daily, 7–11pm (3am Fri/Sat)

It doesn't just play jazz, and it's not really a café – the Jazz Café is so much more, and for that it's a live-music institution. Black music is a speciality but not a necessity – a huge, brave range is guaranteed, from gospel choirs and drum'n'bass collectives, to beat box and world music (buffs, be warned, however, of its regular hen-night-style after-parties on weekends, 'I love the 80s/90s' and 'Hairbrush Heroes'). Big and breaking stars alike take to its stage, though if it's the likes of De La Soul, Courtney Pine and Baaba Maal – exemplary Jazz Café guests – be sure to book in advance. The sedentary (for it does attract an older crowd) can dine in the candlelit gallery restaurant overlooking the stage, but committed music lovers know that there's most space for bouncing around to the right of the stage (they also know that the food can underwhelm). With its industrial, Blue Note-esque neon/steel décor and laid-back dress code, the vibe here is modern, upbeat and unaffected. There's no need to hear a pin drop during performances, and in fact some artists are so relaxed, they have been known to invite their famous musician friends from the audience to jam with them.

The Luminaire
311 High Road, Kilburn, NW6
020 7372 7123
www.theluminaire.co.uk
Open: daily, 7.30pm–midnight (1am Thurs, 2am Fri/Sat)

With friendliness written into its mission statement, 'Lumi's' commitment to putting on first-class gigs with a happy, well-mannered attitude towards bands, sound engineers and punters has reaped its rewards. Since opening in 2005 under the co-ownership of Irish publican John Donnelly and Scottish music obsessive and ex-band manager Andy Inglis, the venue's forward-thinking music policy and high-spec equipment has seen it become a music-lover's lair, presenting a line-up that ranges from futuristic-electro Japanese carnivals (quite) to blues heroes, as well as bands du jour such as Au Revoir Simone, Babyshambles and Bat for Lashes – and that's just the As and Bs. OK, so it is in Kilburn – but lower rents mean reasonably priced drinks. Plush red curtains lining the back of the stage, flickering candles and cared-for toilets give this venue a slightly more dignified feel than most (note that the management are very uppity about silence in session). Dignified, that is, until the mad moshing starts.

Ronnie Scott's
47 Frith Street, Soho, W1
Tel: 020 7439 0747
www.ronniescotts.co.uk
Open: daily, 6pm–3am (midnight Sun)

Such a national treasure is Ronnie Scott's that two entire books have endeavoured to tell its story. The potted version is thus: it was opened in 1959 by one Ronnie Scott (plus fellow musicians Pete King and Leo Green) – Scott was largely credited with importing modern jazz to Britain and in 1981 was awarded the OBE for services to jazz. He died in 1996, and in 2005, King sold it to theatre impresariette Sally Greene, who brought in Hotel Costes' designer Jacques Garcia for a £2 million facelift. Thankfully, however, when the lights are down, it looks exactly the same (think 1950s Soho – warm, dark, rich, red, and lined with black-and-white photos of all the musicians who have played here: Dizzy, Miles, Ella, etc). She's also brought in a decent menu, and opened a members' club upstairs (here, think unrestrained Hotel Costes – all luxe lounge bar). But when the old jazz cats are smoking up the smoothest tunes, there's nowhere else to be but in the magic and romance of the main room; ideal for conversationally challenged dates. Booking advised.

the best of the rest…
jazz and blues…

606 Club   The jazz players' jazz club – Steve Rubie's authentic, no-frills subterranean space running since 1976 (90 Lots Road, Chelsea, SW10; 020 7352 5953; www.606club.co.uk)

Boisdale   Quietly eccentric, loudly posh Belgravian institution, serving Scottish gastronomy, Cuban cigars and live jazz from the Boisdale Blue Rhythm Band (15 Eccleston Street, SW1; 020 7730 6922; www.boisdale. co.uk)

Charlotte Street Blues   Three American-themed and -sized floors with reputedly quantity-over-quality food, julep cocktails and bourbon, plus live blues, swing, soul and gospel (74 Charlotte Street, Fitzrovia, W1; 020 7580 0113; www.charlottestblues.com)

The Blues Kitchen   Camden's youthful take on New Orleans with live rhythm and blues daily, American food and bourbon cocktails from The Old Queen's Head's Steve Blonde (see Pubs; 111 Camden High Street, NW1; 020 7387 5277; www.theblueskitchen. com)

Vortex Jazz Club   Acclaimed hub for leftfield jazz since 1984, covering all of big band, free-impro, world music, gypsy and folk orientations, with Sardinian restaurant Il Bacio (11 Gillett Square, N16; 020 7254 4097; www.vortexjazz. co.uk)

indie and alternative…

12 Bar Club   Genuine, diminutive and thoroughly charming space with a ridiculous quantity of live acts daily and a late licence, on London's guitar mile (26 Denmark Street, WC2; 020 7240 2622; www.12barclub.com)

93 Feet East   Live indie and electro bands daily for Shoreditch trendies in this bare-brick, shabby-chic 650-capacity space; live acts make way for popular club nights on Fridays and Saturdays (150 Brick Lane, E1; 020 7770 6006; www.93feeteast.co.uk)

100 Club   Playing since 1942, this 350-capacity club has seen it all: The Sex Pistols and the birth of punk, George Melly's last hurrah and regular secret gigs of big-name bands. Everything but a refurb (100 Oxford Street, W1; 020 7636 0933; www.the100club.co.uk)

Buffalo Bar   Cosy dive bar with eclectic heard-it-here-first programming, from art punk to noisy garage to acoustic 1960s harmonies (259 Upper Street, Islington, N1; 020 7359 6191; www.buffalobar.co.uk)

Café OTO Lauded leftfield warehouse for sonic experiment, run by Anglo/Japanese couple Hamish and Keiko since 2008, impressively serious about music and drink: organic juices, craft beers, sake, shochu (18 Ashwin Street, E8; 020 7923 1231; www.cafeoto.co.uk)

New Empowering Church Exciting warehouse space with DIY/underground vibe playing world music every Friday and Saturday, and also on random other nights; check their Facebook page for details (1a Westgate Street, Hackney, E8)

The Troubadour Wonky and lovely boho coffeehouse since 1954 that's heard the likes of Led Zep, Hendrix and Bob Dylan; now unsigned and acoustic, indie, blues and folk (263–7 Old Brompton Road, Earl's Court, SW5; 020 7370 1434; www.troubadour.co.uk)

Windmill The lo-fi but right-on-it gig venue right on the edge of a Brixton council estate that's bursting with character, charm and up-and-coming bands (22 Blenheim Gardens, SW2; 020 8671 0700; www.windmillbrixton.co.uk)

commercial fun factories...

Brixton Academy One-time Art Deco picture palace opened in 1929, now technically the O2 Academy, but marketing can't trump the legacy of NME's best venue on 12 occasions (211 Stockwell Road, SW9; 0844 477 2000; www.o2academybrixton.co.uk)

KOKO Standing for 'Keep On Keeping On', this fabulously baroque five-tiered ex-Victorian theatre hosts club nights and one-off, sell-out gigs (1a Camden High Street, NW1; 0870 432 5527; www.koko.uk.com)

The O2 Arena Née The Millennium Dome, this space is finally fit for purpose as a world-class gig venue for international superstars (Peninsula Square, Greenwich, SE10; 0844 856 0202; www.theo2.co.uk)

The Roundhouse A former Victorian steam-engine turning shed where Hendrix, Pink Floyd and The Doors have all played (Chalk Farm Road, NW1; 0844 482 8008; www.roundhouse.org.uk)

Adult Entertainment

London's adult entertainment scene ranges from the louchely retro to the downright seedy. Starting at the higher end of the spectrum are the likes of Stringfellows and The Windmill Club (evidently, there are no great heights to the scene). **The Windmill Club** (17 Great Windmill Street, W1; 020 7439 3558), in the heart of London's red light district of Soho, was London's first nude dancing bar, and the subject of the film Mrs Henderson Presents (starring Dame Judi Dench). Now it's a strangely alluring combination of a Weimar cabaret bar and a 1980s soft porn Playboy video, with pole-dancers and tableside action for tourists and businessmen. **Stringfellows** (16 Upper St Martin's Lane, WC2; 020 7240 5534) and Peter Stringfellow's Angels

(201 Wardour Street, W1; 020 7758 0670) are both owned and run by the legendary leathery lothario Peter Stringfellow. With half-decent restaurants and some of the more beautiful girls in town, it is a classier night out alongside London's suited and booted voyeurs. Slightly less exclusive and slightly more seedy is the **Secrets** chain – six in all with the Holborn branch arguably being the best (3 Grays Inn Road, WC1; 020 7242 6266). **Spearmint Rhino**, the American chain, has a large club in the West End (161 Tottenham Court Road, W1; 020 7209 4488), which is often rumoured to be close to closure for all sorts of shenanigans. Slipping a little further down the greasy pole is the likes of **Metropolis** (234 Cambridge Heath Road, E2; 020 8980 2917), three floors located on the edge of Hackney Road's 'Titty Mile'. Finally, at the bottom of the pile, at the end of the mile, are the pubs that offer lunchtime strips, where punters put a pound in the pint pot for the privilege of watching – for example **Browns** (1 Hackney Road, E2; 020 7739 4653), amusingly right in the heart of hipster central.

Casinos

The recession has had a mixed effect on baize behaviour: smaller stakes and smaller dicks, just more of them taking shots for easy money. That means, at the top end, only the stalwarts have survived (bye-bye flashy Fifty of St James's), with the cards being stacked in the supermarket-style casino's favour. And since London's gaming laws changed in 2004, allowing instant access (with the production of a passport, driving licence, or, for UK residents, simply a credit card), London's casinos have become something of a casual drop-in, rather than an occasion. Most are located in the West End, are open till 6am, and offer a similar variety of games – blackjack, roulette and poker, all ringed by a glittering and noisy array of slot machines. Some have begun to jump on the Texas hold'em poker bandwagon and hold regular tournaments where players can 'buy-in' for around £100. Hard Rock's 24-hour **G Casino** (3 Coventry Street, W1; 020 7287 7887) is in the neon tourist hell of Leicester Square and, accordingly, attracts the lowest common denominator of clientele, but there is at least no dress code or pretensions. The 24-hour, 55,000-square-foot **Casino at the Empire** (London's largest), promising 'a touch of Vegas' has glam aspirations and the smart-casual dress code to boot (5 Leicester Square, WC2; 0870 870 7731). Slightly more upmarket, which also means higher minimum bets and a smart-casual dress code is **The Sportsman** (Old Quebec Street, Marble Arch, W1; 020 7414 0061). The Sportsman offers regular poker nights on Thursdays and Saturdays, and free poker tuition for those who ask nicely. **Palm Beach Casino** at the star-crazy May Fair hotel (see Sleep) offers the promise of free celeb-spotting with your chips, as well as some of London's larger gaming rooms in the former Art Deco ballroom (open till 6am; 30 Berkeley Street, Mayfair, W1; 020 7493 6585); in summer, both The Sportsman and Palm Beach are open 24 hours. Those wanting to don a tux and play with the high-rollers should try **The Ritz Club Casino** in the hotel's former ballroom (150 Piccadilly, W1; 020 7499 1818) or

Aspinalls (27 Curzon Street, Mayfair, W1; 020 7499 4599), but be warned – there's no such democracy here, but a large annual membership fee and a tight screening process. Time to start making friends in high places.

Members' Clubs

One commodity that really proves you've made it (apparently) is club membership, since it requires many hundreds of pounds and powerful friends – the recession has only seemed to encourage people to substantiate their solvency, justify their mingling or perhaps keep up appearances. The ultimate collection of membership cards would include **Shoreditch House**, the recent satellite of corporate media haunt Soho House, which has upped the ante with its East End location, rooftop swimming pool overlooking the Gherkin, private bowling lanes, bar and restaurant, plus high-fashion and high-camp regulars. **The Groucho** in Dean Street, Soho, is the playground of more mature media luvvies with a bar and restaurant, and especially useful for its bedrooms. Also in Dean Street is **Quo Vadis**, Damien Hirst's erstwhile folly, and now in the more entrepreneurial hands of Sam and Eddie Hart of Fino (see Eat), with private dining rooms, billiards room and martini trolleys. **The Hospital** in Endell Street, Covent Garden, is Dave Stewart's incubator of creativity and harbour for the hungrily ambitious, with its own cinema, recording studios, bar, restaurant and games room. And when hunger actually hits, it's all about Piers Adam and Nick House's **Brompton Club** in South Kensington, a Mahiki warm-up supperclub for slebs

and Sloanes with dancing on tables and boozy weekend brunches. Those thirsting for a perfectly mixed martini flash their **Milk & Honey** card for entry into Jonathan Downey's speakeasy-style temple to cocktails (though free day membership is available early in the week; Poland Street, Soho, W1; 020 7065 6840). For shaking the old money-maker, **Maddox** in Mayfair (from the team behind Movida) caters for the Eurotrash for whom dropping a grand in your common or garden table club looks a bit cheap (also with an Italian restaurant and smokers' courtyard), while **Bungalow 8**, Amy Sacco's New York outpost at St Martin's Lane Hotel (see Sleep), attracts the out-of-towners perhaps believing it will be as rockingly Studio 54 as the New York mothership (it usually isn't). Then there are the nightclubs for daddies and their darlings – **Annabel's** on Berkeley Square, Mayfair, **Raffles** on the King's Road, and **Tramp** on Jermyn Street, St James's are all old-school, 1960s vestiges that play comforting cheese to the society set (many of whom started partying in the 1960s); absolutely worth the blag for the comedy value and odd stray celeb.

party…

culture…

Warning: this chapter may cause serious harm to a hedonist's partying programme. London is a veritable heritage theme park. It's taken a few knocks, such as with the Great Fire in 1666, and the Blitz – though these only add to its rich history, and has been continually added to ever since the Roman invasion in AD43 (if you're visiting the Tower of London, check out the remnants of Londinium's city walls at Tower Hill). Rome's legacy didn't stretch to town planning, however: blame the capital's haphazard layout on the merrymakers of medieval times – though its distinct lack of right angles makes for a quirky charm with surprises around every corner.

Getting lost in London's 2,000-year history is another hazard. A visit to the triumvirate of the Tower of London, the Houses of Parliament and Westminster Abbey will provide a crash course in British history, while tombstones in the Abbey, St Paul's Cathedral and Highgate Cemetery present a near-full pack of flash-cards of the city's VIPs. Also look out for the blue circular plaques on buildings, denoting famous Londoners' residences. The most famous residence of all needs no such introduction – the seat of the British monarch, Buckingham Palace.

Architecture anoraks will find plenty to forage on in London's chaotic patchwork of fashions – Gothic, Romanesque, neoclassical, Art Deco, modernist, postmodernist, High Tech, post-capitalism's shambles-chic even. But indulging in London's culture needn't involve excessive brain engagement. There are plenty of handsome buildings to gaze at idly – such as those royal residences (including Clarence House, Prince Charles' present home, and Kensington Palace, home of the late Princess of Wales). An amble along the river's South Bank offers a fine vantage point – not least if you take the London Eye, or there are all manner of tours that will do the hard work for you (see Play). And don't forget to look up. Unsung treats await above street level.

London's contemporary arts scene offers yet more (world-class) passive entertainment of all genres, and has proved remarkably resilient in the recession – be that about escapism, a quest for meaning, or simply a desire, finally, for experience over materialism and real life over the ubiquitous virtual world. And while London's national institutions and historical monuments add gravitas to the city, much of its cultural character comes from its independent enterprises, from the house museums of Sir John Soane and Dennis Severs to the hothouses of avant-

The British Museum

garde arts such as the Vyner Street gallery scene. Indeed, while London has a rich heritage of monarchy and aristocracy, empire and industry, it maintains a progressive outlook – and a sharp edge. The new guard – including Dalston's fringe art scene making something out of nothing, an ever-rolling wave of rebel rock stars and all those steel-and-glass-loving architects – is redefining London's cultural and physical landscape.

What follows are edited highlights of London old and new, with, inevitably, glaring omissions that could fill this section many times over – namely, Trafalgar Square and Nelson's Column, the National Gallery, the National Portrait Gallery, the art collections of Somerset House, the war museums, the Museum of London, the Old Bailey, Number 1 London (the residence of the Dukes of Wellington past and present), Temple Church (now a tourist destination thanks to The Da Vinci Code) and so on and on and on. Save these for a rainy day – though with London's inclement climate, that might obliterate any chance of hedonism whatsoever.

Sightseeing

■ **The British Museum** *(top)*
Great Russell Street,
Bloomsbury, WC1
Tel: 020 7323 8000
www.thebritishmuseum.ac.uk
Open: daily, 10am–5.30pm (8.30pm
Thurs/Fri). Free

So important are the collections in the vast neoclassical British Museum that it seems that every schoolchild in the land is required by law to see them firsthand. Our advice is to hire an audio guide to block out their unrestrained awe when they see the Egyptian mummies, the Lindow Man (a peat-preserved 1st-century body) or 'Ginger' (a sand-preserved 3,400-year-old man with, yup, ginger hair). Thankfully there are quieter wonders of antiquity, including the Rosetta Stone, that lump of rock dated 196BC that unlocked the code of Egyptian hieroglyphics, and the Elgin Marbles, those friezes and statues c.440BC controversially taken by Lord Elgin from the Parthenon in Athens in 1816 – in fact the British Museum has so much, it's a wonder what can be left in the countries of origin. Less contentious is Norman Foster's masterful architecture in the Great Court, Europe's largest covered square with 3,300 triangular glass panels that shed a magical luminescence onto the pale limestone courtyard, and the domed Reading Room where Lenin, Marx, Dickens and Hardy once studied, and where you can almost hear the sound of silence.

■ **Buckingham Palace** *(bottom)*
The Mall, Green Park, SW1

Tel: 020 7766 7300
www.royalcollection.org.uk
State Rooms: daily, 9.45am–6pm (last admission 3.45pm) end July–end Sept (£17); Royal Mews: 11am–4pm Sat–Thurs end March–end July; daily, 10am–5pm end July–end Sept (£7.75); Queen's Gallery: daily, 10am–5.30pm (£8.75)

Britain's most famous house boasts something of a trophy case of super-latives – the world's largest working palace, London's largest private gardens and, to some, one of the worst places to visit because it's expensive and most is out of bounds. Freeloaders can witness the 40-minute Changing the Guard, a daily traffic-stopping tradition of pomp and circumstance where bear-skinned guards and a marching band parade up the Mall from Wellington Barracks to the palace forecourt (11.30am daily May–end July; otherwise on alternate days in clement weather). Access beyond that famous neoclassical façade (actually the back of the building) is limited – only the 19 State Rooms can be visited (which includes a generous view of the garden), and only when 'grandma' trots off to Balmoral Castle in the summer. The Royal Mews – home to the palace's beautiful horses and State carriages (including the ludicrously dazzling 24ct gold-plated Coronation Coach) – are open half the year; only the Queen's Gallery, which displays the Royal Collection – dour oil paintings by Dutch masters, gilt parade furniture and precious jewels – is open year round. Otherwise, try appropriating an invitation to one of her garden parties, or a knighthood.

Dennis Severs' House *(left)*
18 Folgate Street, Spitalfields, E1
Tel: 020 7247 4013
www.dennissevershouse.co.uk
Open: 6–9pm Mon; noon–4pm Sun;
noon–2pm Mon fortnightly. From
£5–12

We could advise visiting the National Gallery, the Wallace Collection or Somerset House, for reasons of extreme cultural importance, but dragging your museum legs around acres of passive art won't improve your life. A far more engaging – if obscure – occasion may be found at the home/museum/'experience' of the late American artist Dennis Severs, who lived here from 1979 to his death in 1999. The cultural significance is twofold: firstly, the building, dating from 1725, is a Huguenot townhouse, originally inhabited by French silk weavers. Secondly – this is where the eccentric Severs comes in – its 11 beautiful rooms, from cellar to parlour to smoking room to bedrooms, are atmospherically set-designed (variously Hogarthian, rococo, baroque) to conjure an authentic picture of domestic life from 1725 to 1919, with ghosts still lingering around half-drunk coffee cups, open books and burning fires. But this is no twee pastiche; rather, you – in strict silence and, after dark, by candlelight – become part of the theatre. Enough – it doesn't do to know too much. However, if you count the fact that artists such as Gilbert & George, Tracey Emin and Gillian Wearing also live in these historic Spitalfields houses, that brings its significance up to two-and-a-half-fold.

The Design Museum *(bottom)*
Shad Thames, SE1
Tel: 020 7403 6933
www.designmuseum.org
Open: daily, 10am–5.45pm. £8.50

With a museum that champions the equal merits of style and substance, form and function, there are high expectations for its own architecture. Needless to say, the Design Museum is the apotheosis of good taste – an angular, whitewashed former warehouse in the style of the Bauhaus Dessau, built in 1989 under the direction and financial support of Sir Terence Conran (the man behind Habitat, the Conran Shop and, now, The Boundary Project). Now under the dynamic stewardship of Blueprint founder and one-time Domus editor Dejan Sudjic, this temple to design pays tribute to the best of all areas – product design, graphics, fashion, architecture and engineering – and hosts the annual Designer of the Year award (previously won by Apple's Jonathan Ive). For recharging one's batteries, there's the excellent Blueprint Café (a restaurant established by Conran, no less) with binoculars set out on the tables for spying on design in the distance – being riverside, there are panoramic views of architectural feats old and new, from Tower Bridge to the Gherkin.

Institute of *(right)* Contemporary Arts (ICA)
The Mall, Trafalgar Square, SW1
Tel: 020 7930 3647
www.ica.org.uk
Open: noon–11pm (1am Thurs–Sat, 9pm Sun) Weds–Sun. Exhibitions free; gigs/talks/films ticketed

culture...

Somewhat out of place plonked literally on the Queen's front drive is the ICA, a homage to experimental and cutting-edge art, music, film and people, founded in 1947 and still very much at the forefront of modern culture (and – following a recent financial battering – the news). Step inside away from the grandeur of The Mall into this minimal, whitewashed space to be surprised and challenged by its packed programme of exhibitions, film, performance, live music, talks and club nights, under the artistic direction of one of London's most influential operators, the writer and broadcaster Ekow Eshun. Previous eye-openers have included a talk on Nazism, an art exhibition posing as a car boot sale, and debut London performances from the likes of Franz Ferdinand, Scissor Sisters and a Japanese guitar band in drag. If that fails to inspire, tasty snacks by Peyton & Byrne in the bar and a cool, clever crowd in horn-rimmed specs and tomorrow's trends chin-stroking about the socio-political implications of Nazi car boot salesmen in drag should entertain.

Parliament Square *(left)*
Westminster, SW1
Houses of Parliament
Tel: 020 7219 4272
www.parliament.uk/visiting
Tours: Saturdays: 9.15am–4.30pm. During summer recess (August, possibly September) 9.15am–4.30pm Mon/Tues/Fri/Sat; ticket office opposite Parliament by College Green; £14, free for UK residents who must go through their MP
Lords'/Commons' Public Galleries: Commons open Sept/Oct–July (not during school holidays), 2.30–10.30pm Mon/Tues; 11.30am–7.30pm Weds; 10.30am–6.30pm Thurs; Lords' Chambers open: Mon/ Tues 2.30–10pmMon/Tues; 3–10pm Weds; 11am–7.30pm Thurs
Westminster Abbey Tel: 020 7222 5152 www.westminster-abbey.org Open: 9.30am–4.30pm Mon–Fri (7pm Weds); 9.30–4.30pm Sat (2.30pm Oct–April); Sundays worship only. £15 (NB: the evensong, 5pm Mon/Tues/ Thurs/Fri is free and goose-bumpily breathtaking)

Order, order! Here lies the seat of British politics. Access to the spiky neo-Gothic Palace of Westminster (aka the Houses of Parliament) is restricted but worth the bother – although the activists who camp outside it are alone quite a sight, not always a pretty one after sleeping rough but a valid barometer of political dissent. The House of Lords resembles a ridiculously pompous gentlemen's club (not far off, actually): all red leather, damask walls, gilt panelling and heavy oil paintings. The Commons (where government presides) is rather more humble, and green colour-coded. History is made and lived out in both – this was the target of Guy Fawkes' 1605 Gunpowder Plot, and its idiosyncrasies (eg, 'toeing the party line') have become common parlance. The Palace also features the 96.3m (306ft) clock tower better known as Big Ben (which actually refers to the clock's biggest bell, named after the clock's commissioner Sir Benjamin Hall). Meanwhile, Westminster Abbey, a majestic Gothic cathedral that dates back to 1245 (not to be confused with the nearby Westminster Cathedral on Victoria Street, mother church to

England and Wales' Catholic community), is the final resting place for over 3,000 British kings and queens, statesmen, academics, musicians, actors and writers, and the site of all British coronations (38 to date). Its ceiling is so detailed that there is even a mirrored table on wheels for avoiding neck strain. Nowt to salve brain strain, sadly.

The Photographers' Gallery *(top)*

9–11 Ramillies Street, Soho, W1
Tel: 0845 262 1618
www.photonet.org.uk
Open: 11am (noon Sun)–6pm (8pm Thurs/Fri). Closed Mondays. Check website for site-specific times. Free

Depending on when you read this, The Photographers' Gallery will either be a very progressive 'location-independent' space (up till late 2011), or (from winter 2011, we are promised) resident in its vast, gleamingly whitewashed new home with three galleries, a space for talks and events, a café and its excellent shop selling collectors' photography books and hard-to-find equipment (handmade pinhole cameras and, yay, Polaroid paraphernalia). Until then, director Brett Rogers, ex-British Council curator, will be having much fun hosting the public gallery's typically wide-angle (groan) programme of contemporary British and international photography – including its acclaimed Photography Prize (previous winners include Richard Billingham, Juergen Teller and Paul Graham), photographers' talks, screenings and seminars, as well as 2011's 40th anniversary celebrations – all offsite. It could even be more exciting than what's promised

in bricks and mortar, with access to edgy, original spaces (check website). Perhaps that promise will be delayed.

Also recommended:
Magnum Print Room The exhibition space of Henri Cartier-Bresson's photographic co-operative, Magnum Studios, only open to the public during exhibitions; check website first (63 Gee Street, EC1; 020 7490 1771 www. events.magnumphotos.com)
Proud Galleries Alex Proud's brace of commercial 'popular culture' galleries offering rock'n'roll Kodak moments (Proud Camden: Horse Hospital, Stables Market, Chalk Farm Road, NW1; 020 7482 3867; Proud Chelsea: 161 King's Road, SW3; 020 7349 0822 www.proud.co.uk)

The Royal Academy *(bottom)*

Burlington House,
Piccadilly, W1
Tel: 020 7300 8000
www.royalacademy.org.uk
Open: daily, 10am–6pm (10pm Fri).
Some free rooms, most £8–12

culture...

The Royal Academy of Arts is rather like an order of knights for the art world. Founded in 1768 by King George III, there's room around the proverbial table for 80 elected Academicians – sculptors, architects, printmakers and painters – who must be professionally active in Britain. Past Academicians include Sir Joshua Reynolds (its first president), Constable, Gainsborough and Turner; current members include Peter Blake, Norman Foster, David Hockney, Elizabeth Blackadder, Anish Kapoor, and, since 2007, Tracey Emin. Academicians' privileges include choosing its major loan exhibitions (recently featuring such art stars as John Singer Sargent, Van Gogh and Schiele), curating the famous Summer Exhibition (plus tickets to its society party), and of course hanging their own masterpieces ('Whoops – that's a whole wall taken out; no room for non-members. Oh well – our club'). And with the RA's architectural pedigree, the building itself is a work of art (and a welcome sanctuary, set back from Piccadilly) – built in 1668 for the Earl of Burlington, it's since been embellished by numerous Academicians including Sidney Smirke (who with his brother designed The British Museum) and Lord Foster, Knight of modern London.

Royal Albert Hall *(top)*
Kensington Gore, South Kensington, SW7
Tel: 020 7838 3105
www.royalalberthall.com
Open: daily, 9am–9pm. Tours 10am–3.30pm Fri–Tues. Tours £8

London has much to thank Queen Victoria and Prince Albert for, a lot of which can be found in 'Albertopolis' – a veritable village of epic national institutions (including the Royal Geographical Society and the Royal Colleges of Art and Music) designed to bring arts and sciences to the people. Its symbolic heart is the Albert Hall, a love story in red brick built in Albert's memory after he died of typhoid in 1861. Victoria mourned his death till her own and apparently always drew the curtains of her carriage when driving past as she couldn't bear to look; at the opening ceremony in 1871 she was

too emotional to speak, and the then Prince of Wales had to do the honours. For more heartache – and eyestrain – cross the road into Kensington Gardens to see the dazzlingly gaudy Albert Memorial, some 176ft of gilded Gothic revival. The Albert Hall – a 6,000 capacity rotunda – is vastly more tasteful and is affectionately known as the nation's village hall, thanks to a diverse programme including boxing, tennis and concerts; it's also famously home to the BBC Proms. It's even available for hire, so any secret ambitions of performing in the Albert Hall could be just a rather large cheque away.

St Paul's Cathedral *(bottom)*
Ludgate Hill, EC4
Tel: 020 7246 8350
www.stpauls.co.uk
Open: 8.30am–4pm Mon–Sat; £12.50. Sunday services at 8am, 10.15am, 11.30am, 3.15pm and 6pm; all welcome (NB: God doesn't charge for worship – services are free)

While Westminster Abbey is the 'House of Kings', St Paul's is the people's cathedral, and where, in 1981, Lady Diana Spencer married Prince Charles. It was built in 1710 by Sir Christopher Wren – as the first ever Protestant cathedral, Wren was instructed not to make it too 'Catholic'; blame Queen Victoria for its lavish gold artwork, after she complained that it was 'most dreary, dingy and undevotional'. During World War II, Churchill famously insisted on saving St Paul's 'at all costs'. It was relatively safe though – its Portland stone dome can be seen from all over London, and thus served as a German landmark.

And from its vertigo-inducing external galleries (via some 530 steps), one can see a breathtaking bird's-eye view of London (plus the odd architectural photographer taking advantage of it); visitors can also climb to the base of its massive freestanding dome, so-called the Whispering Gallery since a whisper can be heard on the opposite side. And those with OBEs or upwards can get married here – so really a cathedral for people who happen to be Very Important.

Serpentine Gallery *(top)*
West Carriage Drive,
Kensington Gardens, W2
Tel: 020 7402 6075
www.serpentinegallery.org
Open: daily, 10am–6pm. Free

Much of the Serpentine's appeal is in its snack size compared with some of London's cultural heavyweights. Indeed its setting – in a Grade II-listed tea pavilion (built in 1934 in the heart of Hyde Park for the park's 'poorer visitors' because the authorities thought there might be trouble if left without refreshments) – is also a pleasing antidote to the pandemonium of planet London. However, since becoming a contemporary art gallery in 1970 (and now co-directed by Hans Ulrich Obrist, named in 2009 as the most influential figure in the art world, and Julia Peyton-Jones OBE), its provocative exhibitions – from the likes of Jeff Koons, Richard Hamilton and Cindy Sherman – have stood in pleasing counterpoint to the tranquillity of the park. Each year from July to September the gallery reclaims some parkland with its Pavilion – always an exciting, and temporary showcase for pioneering and internationally acclaimed architects (previously, Frank Gehry, Zaha Hadid and Rem Koolhaas) under which a café operates, and in July, the social calendar's highlight, the Serpentine Summer Party. Park Nights runs throughout August showing open-air films, talks and 'sound' events in the Pavilion. Awfully refreshing indeed.

Shakespeare's Globe *(bottom)*
21 New Globe Walk,
Bankside, SE1
Tel: 020 7902 1400
www.shakespeares-globe.org
Open: daily, 10am–5pm Oct–April;
9am–12.30pm May–Sept; exhibition and tour only £10.50; performances only May–Sept

They say they don't make them like they used to, but here on the riverside, a group of thesps led by the late American actor Sam Wanamaker did just that. Shakespeare's Globe Theatre, originally built at the end of the 16th century, was authentically reconstructed in 1997 right down to the 12 million wooden pegs used to hold the playhouse together, and has the only thatched roof in London since the Great Fire in 1666 – needless to say, the original burnt down (daily tours and an exhibition tell the full story). Even if you despise olde-worlde theatre, the polygonal amphitheatre is incontestably spectacular, with its elaborate jewel-box stage and repro Tudor exterior of oak beams and whitewash. The auditorium comprises the pit for 700 'groundlings' and tiered benches for 900 (though the bard would have packed in a riotous 3,000). The pro-

gramme is Shakespearean, plus some plays by his contemporaries, as it would have been in Elizabethan times, and those relating to the Tudor era. In fact the most dramatic change to the experience is you, the audience – the throwing of rotten eggs has sadly been consigned to history.

 Sir John Soane's Museum *(top)*

13 Lincoln's Inn Fields, WC2
Tel: 020 7405 2107
www.soane.org
Open: 10am–5pm Tues–Sat (candlelit opening 6pm–9pm first Tues of every month). Free

Sir John Soane was a popular British architect of the 19th century, not least for bequeathing his house as a museum to the nation when he died in 1837. His greatest work was his design of the Bank of England – sadly this was later replaced, but since he used his home as a test-bed for his grand designs (produced in miniature and crammed into every inch), it has become a pilgrimage for architects and historians alike. Indeed, as a prolific collector with considerable taste – and a fabulous eccentric streak – he also attracts art lovers with his Hogarth series (including The Rake's Progress) and his Turners (he was great friends with the artist), and attracts archaeologists with his sarcophagus of Pharaoh Seti I (c.1,370 BC) that at the time was deemed too pricey for the British Museum. None of the above? You still count! Soane's appeal for all is in the townhouse's original (and mostly preserved) function as a home, so also on view are his breakfast parlour, drawing rooms, kitchen and study – all of course designed by Soane's gifted hand.

 Southbank Centre *(bottom)*

Belvedere Road,
South Bank, SE1
Tel: 020 7960 4200
www.southbankcentre.co.uk
Open: daily, 10am–10.30pm (times and costs vary for individual venues)

It's arguable that the Southbank Centre's concrete 'carpark-itecture' (aka Brutalism) is a strategy to repel the hordes of zombie tourists that invade the scenic South Bank. For this is a no-frills, highbrow culture bunker built in 1951 to celebrate the Festival of Britain (an enterprise to kick-start British post-war culture), and now largely populated by London's elite intelligentsia. Over some 21 acres are the Royal Festival Hall (now a Grade I-listed building – no doubt much to Prince Charles' consternation, as an avowed architectural classicist), which hosts ballet, dance and gigs; the Queen Elizabeth Hall and the Purcell Room – smaller venues for dance, concerts, 'live' art and talks; and the Hayward Gallery, a fine arts and photography exhibition space; nearby are the independently managed National Theatre and National Film Theatre. All around are cultural phenomena, official and otherwise – there are free exhibitions and concerts in its open foyers, a skate park in the complex's graffiti-ed underbelly, secondhand book stalls huddled under Waterloo Bridge, and temporary sculptures variously dotted about. Plus those unwitting tourists – aka 'live' art, perhaps.

BFI SOUTHBANK

Showing in M
Optronica

Jennifer & Ke
Tiny, Funny, F

Mediatheque
London Callin

21st London
Film Festival

Tate Galleries *(top)*
Tel: 020 7887 8000
www.tate.org.uk Free, except for
special exhibitions
Tate Britain Millbank, SW1. Open:
daily, 10am–6pm (10pm first Friday of
each month)
Tate Modern 53 Bankside, SE1.
Open: daily, 10am–6pm (10pm Fri/
Sat)

Tate has had various associations over
time. Today the name paints a picture
of contemporary art, as in its flagship
Tate Modern: an immense, riverside
ex-power station designed by Sir Giles
Gilbert Scott (he of Battersea Power
Station) and re-opened in 2000 as the
national gallery for international modern art under the direction of Sir Nicholas Serota. Within some 4.2 million
bricks, it holds works by, like, everyone:
Picasso, Matisse, Dalí, Magritte, Mirò,
Rothko, Lichtenstein, Warhol; the star
attraction is whatever annual installation is exhibited in the colossal Tur-
bine Hall (in 2010/11, Ai Weiwei). But
before Swiss architects Herzog & de
Meuron created Tate Modern (they're
also behind its skyline-altering exten-
sion), if you said 'Tate', you would
mean what is now known as Tate
Britain on Millbank, which since 1897
has been the national gallery of British
art from 1500 to the present day, with
works by, like, everyone: Turner, Blake,
Constable, Gainsborough, Hogarth,
Bacon, plus all those YBAs, and is host
to the annual Turner prize exhibition
for contemporary art. And preceding
the original Tate gallery, the name was
simply associated with its benefactor,
Sir Henry Tate, as in Tate & Lyle sugar
– we surely have him to thank for many
pleasures.

Tower of London *(bottom)*
Tower Hill, EC3
Tel: 020 3166 6000
www.hrp.org.uk/TowerOfLondon
Open: daily, 9am (10am Sun/Mon)–
5.30pm. £17

Only Britain's most esteemed villains
– among them, royals, high-society
traitors, and those notorious cockney
gangsters, the Kray Brothers – have
been behind bars at the Tower of London. The Krays were among the few
to leave alive – most (including two of
Henry VIII's wives) were subjected to
gruesome torture and bloody execu-
tion. The last prisoner is long gone,
leaving a well-preserved medieval
fortress originally built over 900 years
ago for William the Conqueror. Actually it's an entire town of towers, with
charming cobbled lanes, cottages and
a chapel. Add to that the jolly Beefeat-
ers carrying out arcane traditions, the
royal ravens and the Crown Jewels
(yes, they are the real deal, apparently),
and the result is rather like a Disney
film set. Except for the bloodstains.
If stamina allows, visit Tower Bridge
– that iconic landmark so often (and
occasionally expensively) confused
with London Bridge. Opened in 1894,
the upper walkway (45m/148ft up; intended for crossing the bridge while its
drawbridges were raised) is still accessible, as is the Engine Room's original
steam-powered machinery. Now, however, electric motors lift the two 1,200-
ton arms in 90 seconds, and since it's
one of the Thames' lowest crossings,
do so over 500 times a year (020 7403
3761 www.towerbridge.org.uk).

culture...

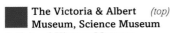 **The Victoria & Albert** *(top)* **Museum, Science Museum & Natural History Museum**
South Kensington, SW7
V&A Cromwell Road.
Tel: 020 7942 2000
www.vam.ac.uk;
Open: daily, 10am–5.45pm (10pm Fri).
Free, except special exhibitions.
Science Museum Exhibition Road.
Tel: 020 7942 4000 www.sciencemuseum.org.uk; open: daily, 10am–6pm.
Free, except special exhibitions.
Natural History Museum Cromwell Road. Tel: 020 7942 5000 www.nhm.ac.uk; open: daily, 10am–5.50pm. Free, except special exhibitions.

Built, as part of 'Albertopolis', in Queen Victoria's reign as an initiative to make information available to all – take comfort: tackling Museum Central does not require Tefal-headed learnedness – these world-class museums cater for dilettantes and PhD types alike. The 'V&A' specializes in decorative art and design, fashion and textiles, and its seven miles of galleries, halls and corridors hold over 4.5 million historic items (the lawns of its grand Italianate courtyard and the new Benugo café both provide good slumping spots). The Science Museum is rather more left-brain and among its treasures are patent models of Stephenson's Rocket and Arkwright's textile machinery, plus medical artefacts (some necessarily pickled) from Ancient Greece to the present day, flight simulators and, for those in need of a brain break, an IMAX cinema. The Natural History Museum, with its grand Romanesque architecture, is hailed as 'the animal's Westminster Abbey'. Its most famous inhabitant is the diplodocus cast but it

boasts over 70 million other exhibits, from microscopic cells to mammoth skeletons and Martian meteorites. Sometimes small children can be found feigning slumber at their sleepovers.

 Whitechapel Gallery *(bottom)*
77–82 Whitechapel
High Street, E1
Tel: 020 7522 7888
www.whitechapel.org
Open: 11am–6pm Tues–Sun (9pm Thurs; 11pm Fri). Free for most exhibitions.

That the East End is now a major centre for fine art, the Whitechapel has come to be its unofficial flagship gallery, despite arriving long before the bandwagon. Founded in 1901, it introduced artists into the UK such as Rothko, Pollock, Kahlo and Picasso (whose Guernica had its first and only showing there, in 1939). And it was the first to showcase Hockney, Gilbert & George and Freud – eat that, establishment! It's now having such a moment that, following an ambitious Lottery Fund-supported £13.5m expansion completed in 2009, it has increased its gallery space by 78%, and, via the vision of director Iwona Blazwick OBE, its programme also stretches to talks, film and Friday night fun with live music and the obligatory art tarts and attitudinal haircuts.

Also recommended:

Close behind the flagship is the commercial gallery **White Cube** (48 Hoxton Square, N1; 020 7930 5373 www.whitecube.com) run by art dealer Jay Jopling who has a near-monopoly

on YBAs (or BAs): Quinn, Gilbert & George, Emin, the Chapman brothers... Such is the eminence of White Cube that there is even a rip-off/tribute 'gallery space' in epicentre-of-cool The George & Dragon pub (see Pubs), called **White Cubicle** (yes, housed in the ladies' toilet, measuring precisely 1.4m by 1.4m) curated by Mexican artist Pablo Leon de la Barra who has persuaded all of Wolfgang Tillmans, Terence Koh and Julie Verhoeven to exhibit there. Certainly not bog standard.

The Gallery Scene

Mayfair Galleries

Once rife with stuffy galleries run by old Etonians, Mayfair has seen a steady invasion of international commercial galleries only too happy to feed It-art to uber-rich non-doms and hedge-funders with bonuses to blow – they're free to enter, of course, though not always free to leave. From Zurich came **Hauser & Wirth** to 196a Piccadilly (020 7287 2300), opening in 2003 in an old Lutyens-designed bank, representing Louise Bourgeois, Martin Creed and co. They then went into business with the old master dealer, Colnaghi, creating – you guessed it – **Hauser & Wirth, Colnaghi** (15 Old Bond Street; 020 7399 9770). The formidable **Sadie Coles HQ** runs her mini-empire (that looks after the likes of Sarah Lucas and Matthew Barney) from her flagship gallery at 69 South Audley Street (020 7493 8611) plus a showing space at 9 Balfour Mews. Nearby is the British dealer **Timothy Taylor** who sells, among others, Alex Katz and Craigie Aitchison (15 Carlos Place; 020 7409 3344). Then from the Big Apple with big ideas and big names (like Jeff Koons and Carsten Höller) is **Gagosian**, at 17 Davies Street (020 7493 3020). Meanwhile, in their spatially challenged ex-bag/glove shop is the German power-duo Monika Sprüth and Philomene Magers (**Sprüth Magers**, 7a Grafton Street; 020 7408 1613) who represent artists such as Andreas Gursky, Cindy Sherman and Karen Kilimnik. Previously they were in business with **Simon Lee** who still sells Larry Clark et al at 12 Berkeley Street (020 7491 0100). Returning to its shiny new refurb in **Haunch of Venison** mews in spring 2011 (entrance on Bond Street) is the gallery of the same name with outposts in Berlin, New York and Zurich (020 7495 5050) – once the residence of Nelson and now of art, by the likes of Bill Viola, Mat Collishaw and M/M. Meanwhile at 25 Mason's Yard is Jay Jopling's **White Cube** (020 7930 5373), a satellite gallery to Hoxton Square's mothership that is equally white and cube-shaped, and at 106 New Bond Street is **Max Wigram**'s gallery (aka Mr Phoebe Philo; 020 7495 4960). Revealingly, both Jopling and Wigram, both 'new guard', happen to be old Etonians. Over at 34 Bruton Street, run by Rolling Stones scion Tyrone Wood and representing Robert Crumb and daddy Tyrone, Ronnie Wood, is **Scream** (020 7493 7388). Which is what you might feel like doing after all that.

Vyner Street Galleries

Ever since grande-dame gallerists **Maureen Paley** (21 Herald Street, E2;

020 7729 4112, representing the likes of Gillian Wearing, Liam Gillick and Banks Violette) and **Victoria Miro** (16 Wharf Road, N1; 020 7336 8109, selling Grayson Perry, Peter Doig, Conrad Shawcross et al, in her incredible, immense gallery and gardens, worth visiting in their own right) paved the way to the Hackney art scene, dealers, collectors, artists and budding art students have descended on East London in their droves, largely settling in Vyner Street and Herald Street. In fact, it's spawned a social phenomenon. 'First Thursdays' – some 100-odd East End galleries' private views ('PVs') on the first Thursday of every month, offering free warm white wine and hobnobbing opportunities, from roughly 6–9pm – has become the art-mob's mecca, and as such, sees a mass of studied scruffiness spill out onto Vyner Street; quite the contrast to the low-key, monochrome daytime vibe (NB: most galleries are open noon–6pm Weds–Sun; by appointment at other times). But let's not forget the art, which over here is necessarily in yer face, experimental and 'challenging'. The dominating statement at the end of the street is **Wilkinson** (50–58 Vyner Street; 020 8980 2662). Having moved from just around the corner, this is the first purpose-built gallery in E2, covering 6,000 sq ft and representing George Shaw, Phoebe Unwin, Joan Jonas et al. Over the way, set back off the road, No.45 is home to both Dutch artist Suzanne Schurgers' **Vegas Gallery** (020 3022 5850), which having relocated from Redchurch Street, continues to promote Dutch, Belgian and Swiss artists; and Fred Mann's **Fred [London]** (020 8981 2987), which focuses, among other areas, on

that unrepresented genre of African art (and, er, art rock: Mann's record label is also based here). Committed to showing young, emerging artists is art photographer-couple Tony Taglianetti and Danielle Horn's **Nettie Horn** (25b Vyner Street; 020 8980 1568) – its emphasis on experimental techniques and materials makes for a consistently good show. Somewhat trumping them on youth is **DegreeArt.com**, Isobel Beauchamp and Elinor Olisa's incubator for UK-wide art students and recent graduates (in London alone, from Goldsmiths, St Martin's, Slade, Chelsea, RCA...), which moved from the Edwardian chapel at No.30 to a typical Vyner Street warehouse at No.12a (020 8980 0395) so as to be able to get those bigger pieces through the door. Finally, look for the fabulously unprepossessing brown-tiled gallery at 1 Vyner Street, **Madder139**, named after a Pantone colour by founder-curator Debbie Carslaw, who supports emerging British talent, plus at least one international artist a year who has not previously had a UK solo show (020 8980 9154).

London's Best Art Nights

First Thursday See Vyner Street Galleries entry.

Late at Tate Britain The older Tate's bid for modernity, with themed evenings (previously on comedy, East London and other more abstract, inscrutable concepts) featuring special screenings, talks and other treats (first

Friday of the month till 10pm, free but first come, first served; NB: Tate Modern is open late Fri/Sat till 10pm, but with less structure).

Serpentine Park Nights Outdoors but under the cover of the annual architect-designed Pavilion, with artists' talks, arty films, music, performances, a bar and the backdrop of Hyde Park (Fridays 7–9/10pm, from late June till early Oct; tickets from www.serpentinegallery.org).

Somerset House Summer Series 10-day music festival in July with big, cool acts (previously Mystery Jets, Air, The xx; from £25); **Film 4 Screen** 11 nights in early August showing modern classics plus premieres, also discussions and directors' Q&A (£12.50). **Ice Rink** with DJ nights (Fri/Sat till 11pm, Nov–Jan; check website first, from £10.50).

V&A Friday Late Popular interactive evenings themed on such topics as Renaissance masked balls, gay cruising and playgrounds, with guest DJs, one-to-one performances and beer; avoid the queues by taking advantage of the late-night exhibition opening (last Friday of every month except December; 6.30–10pm; free).

Whitechapel Art Gallery Late Nights Experimental, arty lock-ins with might-be-big bands playing acoustically (previously Florence and the Machine), live art and spoken word (£6–8, 8–11pm 'officially', monthly Fridays, sometimes more frequently; check website). Also open till 9pm every Thursday for film and talks.

the best of the rest...

Barbican Centre Arguably London's finest example of the 'Marmite' metaphor (a classic British yeasty spread that's either loved or loathed) – its seven acres of Grade II-listed Brutalist architecture is revered by some (mostly leftie liberals swayed by its socially utopian aims), and scorned by everyone else. Whatever – as Europe's largest performing arts centre, its programming is consistently progressive and its facilities impressive (a 2,000-seat concert hall, two theatres, two art galleries and three cinemas; Silk Street, Barbican, EC2; 020 7638 4141; www.barbican.org.uk).

Freemasons' Hall No need to wait for the special squeeze: tours are available Mon–Fri of the Art Deco Grand Temple – the other 23 onsite are in 'constant demand' (free; 60 Great Queen Street, WC2; 020 7395 9257; www.freemasonry.london.museum).

Hampton Court Palace The beautiful red-brick residence built for Cardinal Wolsey in 1514 (they think), who was pushed aside by Henry VIII; also with grand gardens and ghosts (£14; Hampton Court, Surrey; 020 3166 6000; www.hrp.org.uk/hamptoncourtpalace).

Highgate Cemetery Step into an eerie Victorian gothic underworld, all overgrown vines gripping the ornate tombs and headstones of the age (including those of Karl Marx, George Eliot and Michael Faraday), and newer arrivals including Malcolm McLaren and Alexander Litvinenko. The older, western half is only accessible by guided tour (£7); the eastern half, opened 1854, can be roamed unguided (£3). Dress appropriately and don't bait the ghosts (Swain's Lane, West Hampstead, NW6; 020 8340 1834; www.highgate-cemetery.org).

Kew Gardens Forget oxygen tents: here's 300 acres of glorious green arcadia, with 30,000 different kinds of living plants (the world's largest collection) and a 250th birthday in 2009 (£13.50; Kew, Richmond, TW9; 020 8332 5655; www.kew.org).

King's Place Extravagant regeneration of King's Cross wasteland with top-spec concert halls and three galleries, plus The Guardian newspaper's book clubs, who also share the building (some free events; 90 York Way, N1; 020 7520 1440; www.kingsplace.co.uk).

Rivington Place The striking David Adjaye-designed home to both Iniva (Institute of International Visual Arts) and Autograph (the association for black photographers), showing 'diversity issues' in exhibitions, films, talks and performance (Rivington Place, EC2; 020 7749 1240; www.rivington-place.org).

Royal Courts of Justice Glorious gothic castle built of Portland stone in 1882 that's also a publicly accessible court with 88 court rooms, fascinating civic and criminal trials and bad wigs (free; The Strand, WC2; 020 7947 6000 www.hmcourts-service.gov.uk)

Saatchi Gallery Arch art collector Charles Saatchi's latest toys at the grand old Duke of York's HQ, with 70,000 whitewashed square feet of contemporary art, plus snacking sanctuary; see Snack (free; King's Road, Chelsea, SW3; www.saatchi-gallery.co.uk).

The Wapping Project Housed in an ex-power station, it's Tate Modern's mini-me (with bar/restaurant), but with more performance, original industrial fixtures and authentic grease smells (free; Wapping Wall, E1; 020 7680 2080; www.thewappingproject.com).

Wilton's Music Hall An evocative Victorian timewarp: commissioned by John Wilton in 1858, this is the world's oldest surviving Grand Music Hall (just – it's now semi-derelict, and rudely authentic for it). Its programme is pretty inspiring too: avant-garde revues, talks by eminent talking heads, powerful theatre and moving music (recently, a Creole choir). The atmospheric Mahogany bar (open Mon–Fri) hosts romping, troubadour-style bands every Monday; £5 tours monthly (Graces Alley, Cable Street, E1 020 7702 2789; www.wiltons.org.uk).

Theatre

London's answer to Broadway essentially straddles Leicester Square and Covent Garden, and is where all the big-budget productions, long-running musicals and cheesy pantos sell out by the coachload (check Time Out, London's listings magazine; for tickets, 0844 277 4321; www.ticketmaster.co.uk). Rival impresarios (and friends) Sir Andrew Lloyd Webber and Sir

Cameron Mackintosh own the lion's share, Cameron having in 2010 vowed to keep his seven well-respected 'children' running forever (Prince Edward Theatre, Prince of Wales, Novello, Queen's Theatre, Gielgud, Wyndham's and Noel Coward Theatre; www.delfontmackintosh.co.uk). London awaits news of whether Lloyd Webber will match the gesture (for Cambridge Theatre, Theatre Royal, Her Majesty's Theatre, London Palladium, the New London Theatre and the Palace Theatre; www.reallyuseful.com). However, honouring Britain's rich heritage of playwrights – including Shakespeare (see The Globe), Alan Bennett, David Hare, David Mamet and the late Nobel Prize-winning Harold Pinter – are plenty more challenging theatres, as follows.

The Almeida Under the artistic direction of Michael Attenborough, son of veteran actor Lord Richard Attenborough, this celebrated studio theatre fills its 325 rather fashionable seats with 'bold and adventurous' classical and contemporary plays (Almeida Street, Islington, N1; 020 7359 4404; www.almeida.co.uk).

Arcola Pioneering studio theatre in Dalston, founded in 2000 in an ex-textile factory, with a taste for socio-political themes, multiculturalism and experimentation – so Dalston (23 Arcola Street, E8; 020 7503 1646; www.arcolatheatre.com).

Battersea Arts Centre For some, the BAC is the only reason to go to Battersea (or even South London): always an innovative line-up of alternative theatre, cabaret and comedy in this characterful Grade II-listed ex-town hall, with a delightful café/bar to boot (Lavender Hill, SW11; 020 7223 2223; www.bac.org.uk).

Donmar Warehouse Named after theatre impresario Donald Albery and his friend, the ballerina Margot Fonteyn (Don and Mar, see?), who in 1961 together set up this space in an old warehouse, the Donmar is an internationally acclaimed yet intimate studio theatre with just 250 seats, renowned for its edgy, new productions (41 Earlham Street, Covent Garden, WC2; 0844 871 7624; www.donmarwarehouse.com).

Old Vic With Kevin Spacey as artistic director, the historic theatre, first opened in 1818 and later renamed after Queen Victoria, has seen its fair share of drama – and Spacey – on its stage. The programme is an eclectic mix of old classics and brave new theatre, and thanks to Spacey's friends in high places, sees many a star tread the boards (The Cut, Waterloo, SE1; 0844 871 7628; www.oldvictheatre.com).

Open Air Theatre A magical (if risky) combination of theatre and fresh air, in the idyllic inner circle of Regent's Park, weather permitting – sensibly, it's only open May–Sept; genres range from Shakespeare to family plays (The Ironworks, Inner Circle, Regent's Park, NW1; 0844 826 4242; www.openairtheatre.org).

Royal National Theatre Widely regarded as London's leading playhouse with a diverse programme of new and classical plays over three auditoriums overseen by the acclaimed artistic director Nicholas Hytner, the National (or, to luvvies, the 'Nash'), is also considered its ugliest – built in 1976 according to Brutalist principles, Prince Charles once described it as 'a clever way of building a nuclear power station in the middle of London without anyone objecting' (South Bank, SE1; 020 7452 3000; www.nationaltheatre. org.uk).

St Martin's Theatre The home of the world's longest running show, Agatha Christie's The Mousetrap, going since 1952 (more than 23,000 times), and a national treasure from one of Britain's greatest crime writers; most Londoners know whodunit (West Street, Covent Garden, WC2; 020 7836 1443; www.the-mousetrap.co.uk).

Soho Theatre Modern mistress in amongst the West End mainstream, showing contemporary plays and alternative comedy and cabaret. Its ground-floor bar is an excellent refuge from Soho's chaos (21 Dean Street, W1; 020 7478 0100; www.sohotheatre. com).

Tricycle Theatre The one with the conscience: its agenda-setting programme reacts to contemporary and political issues with an emphasis on cultural diversity; also has a cinema and art gallery (269 Kilburn High Road 020 7372 6611; www.tricycle.co.uk).

Opera, Ballet & Dance

In the heart of theatreland is the seat of both the Royal Ballet Company and the Royal Opera – the **Royal Opera House** (Bow Street, Covent Garden, WC2; 020 7304 4000; www. roh.org.uk) is actually in its third incarnation after the first (built 1732) and second (built 1809) both burnt down. Backstage tours (often filled with entertainingly obnoxious stage school kids; booking recommended) usually cover much of the 2.5-acre site and 10 floors, including the Grade I-listed auditorium in splendid 24ct gilt and red velvet, the Fame-style dance studios that are maintained at 80°F so that dancers' muscles stay warm, and the bewitching prop-making room. If your take on opera and ballet is more sedentary, be sure to snap up one of the 67 tickets made available each day for that evening's performance, take lunch at Mondays' free recitals in the ornate Victorian Crush Room, or tea in the gorgeous Floral Hall, a Victorian crystal arcade where monthly tea dances are held (third Friday of every month; check website). Meanwhile, the **London Coliseum** (St Martin's Lane, Covent Garden, WC2; 020 7632 8300; www.eno.org) has been home to the English National Opera since 1968 in a splendidly plush structure that since 1904 has variously been a music hall, cinema and a greyhound track. The ENO Company is rival only to the Royal Opera but is the more populist since all performances at the 'Coli' are sung in English and surtitles are provided (to the disdain of elitists). Blowing a little fresh air through the fusty world of opera is **Opera Holland Park**, the respected summer opera company (June–mid-Aug) that stages classic and verismo opera in original language with surtitles for up to a thousand under a smart temporary canopy in the glorious grounds of Holland Park, and accompanied by the City of London Sinfonia orchestra (Holland Park, W11; 020 7361 3570; www.operahollandpark.com). For dance, with its 300-year heritage, **Sadler's Wells** (Rosebery Avenue, Islington, EC1; 020 7863 8198; www.sadlerswells.com) is considered London's premier contemporary dance venue (even calling itself 'London's Dance House'). Its portfolio comprises three theatres – two onsite (the main auditorium and the more experimental Lilian Baylis Theatre) and the Peacock Theatre in Portugal Street, WC2. All show international and UK dance of all varieties, from the Shaolin Monks to disabled troupes.

Cinemas

Leicester Square is Cinema Central, showing the latest popcorn movies at the highest prices – it's also where all the premieres take place. **Odeon** (0871 224 4007; www.odeon.co.uk) and **Vue** (0871 224 0240; www.myvue.com) cover most mainstream releases, with branches in Leicester Square (if you must) and across London (of particular note is **Vue Westfield's** new 14-screen cinema, opened in 2010 with five 3-D screens).

But the capital has plenty of independent cinemas and lovingly restored picture palaces that show art house and world films and films that haven't cost $100m to make (see also the ICA and the Barbican). Not least the independent, two-screen **Prince Charles Cinema**, which, bang in the middle of Leicester Square, subverts those premiums with classic films at £5.50–6.50 (plus new releases at £8–10; 7 Leicester Place, WC2; 020 7494 3654; www.princecharlescinema.com). Meanwhile, **Curzon Cinemas** specialize in European and art house films, though also show select Hollywood movies. Curzon Soho, built in the 1950s, has three screens, while Curzon Mayfair, built in 1934, is a Grade II-listed building with two screens. Curzon has recently acquired the Chelsea and Renoir cinemas – a sign of the times for independent picture houses (**Chelsea Cinema** 206 King's Road, SW3; 0871 7033 990; **Curzon Mayfair** 38 Curzon Street, W1; 0871 7033 989; **Curzon Soho** 99 Shaftesbury Avenue, W1; 0871 7033 988; **Renoir Cinema** The Brunswick Centre, WC1; 0871 7033 991; www.curzoncinemas.com).

Similarly, **The Picturehouses** chain is slowly gobbling up independent cinemas, which might sound like the plot of, say, Nightmare at the Cinema but this group has trodden carefully. Expect a programme of cult, foreign language and independent films, select commercial films and themed festivals: **Clapham Picturehouse** (76 Venn St, SW4; 0871 704 2055); **The Gate** (87 Notting Hill Gate, W11; 0871 704 2058); **The Ritzy** (Brixton Oval, Coldharbour Lane, SW2; 0871 704 2065; www.picturehouses.co.uk). The see-and-be-seen screen at **The Electric** (191 Portobello Road, Notting Hill, W11; 020 7908 9696; www.electriccinema.co.uk) is decked out like a modern gentleman's club with the baroque backdrop of one of London's oldest cinemas (built 1905) – all chunky leather armchairs, footstools and kissing couches. The bar serves cocktails, champagne and swanky snacks; the programme leans towards the critically acclaimed mainstream.

The Roxy Bar and Screen over in Borough does all that (the tasty food, proper drinks, the sofas; see Bars), but without people looking over their shoulders to see who's around, while **Cinéphilia West,** a small independent project with a café, bookshop, gallery and screening space is for West Londoners who want to (or can) intellectualise film, with themed weeks on cinema's most modern developments (171 Westbourne Grove, W11; 020 7792 4433; www.cinephilia.co.uk/west). Cinéphilia East, sadly, is just a book shop, though there is **Rich Mix** (35–47 Bethnal Green Road, E1; 020 7613 7490; www.richmix.org.uk), the epitome of East End gentrification that saw, in 2006, a six-storey cultural centre move into an ex-garment factory. Three cinema screens (showing documentaries, art house and respected major releases), an exhibition space and a 200-seat auditorium comprise, yes, a 'creative arts factory'.

But for the ultimate big screen experience, try the **BFI London IMAX Cinema** (1 Charlie Chaplin Walk, Waterloo, SE1; 020 7199 6000; www.bfi.org.uk). Inside a dramatic cylindrical glass building situated on a busy roundabout is the UK's largest cinema screen. It typically screens films set in extraordinary landscapes – such as the North

Pole, the moon, the summit of Everest – in 2- or 3-D, and with such steeply raked rows, even getting to your seat is a thrill. Also under the administration of the British Film Institute and as part of the Southbank Centre is the **BFI Southbank** (Belvedere Road, South Bank, SE1; 020 7928 3232; www.bfi.org.uk), London's leading art house cinema with four screens (including a 35-seat studio screen), directors' talks, the London Film Festival in October and an awful lot of film buffs cerebrating in its lovely bars.

shop...

'I shop therefore I am' is the mantra of London's power-tribe of compulsive ma-
terialists. 'Buy, buy, buy!' hums the ambient noise on the frenzied drags of Oxford
Street, Regent Street and Knightsbridge. 'I predict a riot!' is the spiritual soundtrack
at the latest over-hyped launch of a designer's diffusion range on the high street.
Fact: police marshalling smash-and-grab fashion victims at such launches frequently makes the evening news.

So retail resisted the recession? While the enlightened may now claim to eschew
greed, the hordes have not diminished. That's no doubt due to commercial enterprises working ever harder to lure the footfall, with fashion shows, in-store gigs, and
the ubiquitous pop-up shop – 'now you see it, now you don't' temporary spaces
that encourage shoppers to shop now, not later, housed in newly defunct commercial space (created as the recession separated the wheat from the chaff). Out on
the fringes, jumble sales and cottage industries mushroom, as people try to make
money on the side. There's more to buy than ever.

Meanwhile, London's fashion industry fights on: as one of the four fashion capitals,
where New York is commercial, Milan is high-glamour and Paris sophisticated,
London is considered the experimenter. Fuelled by the capital's renowned design
schools and a much-vaunted stable of agents provocateurs (Vivienne Westwood,
John Galliano, Gareth Pugh), London is seeing a hothouse of young, out-there designers actually turning concept into commerce, as experiment comes of age. Flavours of the month are Christopher Kane, now designing for Versace, and Marios
Schwab, who brings an intellectual rigour to rags, while London's enduring innova-
tors include Stella McCartney, Christopher Bailey at Burberry, and Phoebe Philo,
redefining fashion's landscape at Celine.

All this experimentation is a symptom of something much more core to Britishness: eccentricity, and it's for this reason that London's vintage scene is so well
established, since originality comes so much more naturally with one-off pieces.
John Galliano pops back from Paris to draw inspiration from Virginia in Notting
Hill, and Paul Smith from Portobello Market; but it's the East End, with its glut of
empty warehouses and (relatively) cheap rents, that has become the main destination for vintage vultures and bold new ventures.

As ever, Bond Street and Sloane Street offer everything any label slave could ask
for, while the fiercely competitive British high street – Top Shop, Warehouse, Oasis
and Primark (which, in irony, we call 'Primarni' because it is so low-grade) – is
known and loved for replicating the catwalks in a matter of weeks, plus London is
host to all the key high street imports including H&M, Mango, Uniqlo and Zara.

For fast, affordable fashion, sharpen your elbows, pack your patience and head for Oxford Street, Regent Street, Kensington High Street and the King's Road. For a high concentration of edgy and urban boutiques, beat a path to Soho, Covent Garden and the East End. But for calmer consumption, there are numerous lovely villagey streets (Marylebone High Street, Walton Street, Chelsea Green, Exmouth Market, Broadway Market), where you'll find one-off boutiques, bijou jewellers and local delis and cafés that, with admittedly some knowingness, hark back to a more old-fashioned era of shopping: a world apart from the mayhem and mass production of the homogenous high street.

Then there are London's specialist streets – rummage for literature in Charing Cross Road, guitars and rock music in Denmark Street, diamonds in Hatton Garden, and antiques in Pimlico Road and Portobello Road. There are also the fabulously elegant Victorian and Edwardian arcades of Piccadilly and Mayfair (The Royal Arcade, Princes Arcade, Royal Opera Arcade, Burlington Arcade) where dainty shops sell fine jewellery, art and chocolates.

The best example of anachronism (and, sadly, fighting the biggest battle against the developers) is London's hallowed heritage of classic craftsmanship and fine tailoring, located in the bespoke shops of Savile Row and Jermyn Street (even the very word bespoke originated in Savile Row, meaning that a suit is 'spoken for'). Many of these historic stores have been trading for generations and offer a wonderfully personalized and refined service – now you don't get that in Primarni.

COVENT GARDEN

The enormous flower, fruit and vegetable market of My Fair Lady days is long gone but Covent Garden still has a quirky character and vibrant atmosphere. Serious shoppers ignore the rejuvenated picturesque piazza, a tourist- and brand-magnet, and head to the more subdued cobblestone pedestrian side streets stemming from the Seven Dials roundabout (featuring, er, six sundials) where independent fashion boutiques are interspersed with vintage shops and London's best streetwear and surf shops.

Earlham Street

Carhartt American streetwear: sweatshirts, jackets, jeans and their trademark carpenter jeans

Diesel Two floors of Renzo Rosso's Italian denim and streetwear

Fenchurch Skateboard clothing label plus headphones (of course) for girls and boys

Fopp Saved by HMV, this once-indie chain is ever popular: records (both indie and mainstream), CDs, books and art house films

Kidrobot Art toys for kidults, plus tees, hoodies and jackets

Magma Two outlets of the specialist store selling deeply cool arty mags and design books

Reworks The Vintage Showroom's exciting reworking of old threads

Urban Outfitters Industrial-style American emporium for retro/modern culture, music, clothing and homeware

Floral Street

Agnès B Understated but original French fashion design for hommes et femmes

Betsey Johnson Loud pinks, flirty dresses and playful jewels for coquettes

Camper Curious, cultish shoes for men and women from Barcelona

Nicole Farhi High-end, understated menswear with subtle French chic

Paul Smith The historic first shop from Britain's reigning knight of fashion Sir Paul Smith, who lends a quirky spin and colour to classic English tailoring

The Tintin Shop Because one never quite grows out of the Belgian cub reporter

Monmouth Street

Coco de Mer Classy yet kinky lingerie and erotica from Sam Roddick, daughter of Body Shop founder Anita Roddick

Kiehl's Flagship store for slick American cosmetics line

Miller Harris Nose Lyn Harris' outpost for her clean, luxe scents

Orla Kiely The Irish designer's 1970s-style prints in muted colours on bags and womenswear

Pop Retro relics (clothes and kitsch curios) from the disco era, beloved by scores of stars whose photos pepper the walls

Poste Mistress Eccentric designer shoes in a kitsch 1950s boudoir

Tatty Devine Witty pieces laser-cut from colourful acrylics

Shorts Gardens

Benefit Cosmetics with the rare combination of brains and beauty, plus brow bar

Baracuta Mod-ish menswear including the classic Harrington jacket

Fred Perry The laurel-logoed British heritage sportswear brand with of-the-moment guest designers

G-Star Raw Blokey streetwear and trainers for boys and tomboys

Size? Multi-brand treasure trove for trainer-heads: old school, limited editions and the latest treads

Neal Street

American Apparel Effortless cool with colourful teeshirty clothing and accessories for all

Dr Martens 8-holes, 16-holes, metallic blue, steel-capped, patent pink, leopard-print…

MAC Cosmetics New York's little black magic loved by pros, queens, everyone

Shu Uemura Top-spec Japanese make-up in extraordinarily fashionable colours

Tabio For all you sock obsessives that fly to Japan for your fix – now there's no need

Terra Plana Eco-friendly, original shoes for men and women from Clarks scion Galahad Clark

THE EAST END

Despite a steady corporate invasion and now even a shiny new mall at Spitalfields, the East End is less commercially adulterated than most of London.

Still outnumbering the multinationals are thrift and vintage shops, innovative independent ventures posing as 'installations' and street markets where enterprising young designers sell their kitchen-table-produced wares. For that, its treasures are not neatly town-planned along one convenient street, but scattered around in among the knock-off designer shops of the old East End. On your wander, keep your radar tuned for the area's many sample outlets and pop-up shops.

1948 (Arches, 477 Bateman's Row) Nike goes concept with this specialist sportswear pop-up store that did so well it stayed (open Thurs–Sat)

Albam (111a Commercial St) Own-brand 'modern crafted' menswear with an old mindset and forward outlook

Blondie (114 Commercial St) Absolute Vintage's classier sister where quality trumps quality. Head to AV on Hanbury Street for the reverse

Bordello (55 Great Eastern St) Boudoir boutique stocking Myla, Damaris and Pistol Panties

A Child of the Jago (10 Great Eastern St) Vivienne Westwood's son Joe Corré scales back to make artisan menswear

Columbia Road A dear old East End lane lined with tiny cafés and cottage-industry shops variously selling ceramics, cupcakes and jewellery, plus a long-running Sunday flower market

M.Goldstein (67 Hackney Road) Retaining the previous incarnation's name (so East End), this 'installation'/shop sells fashionable antiques, art and clothes, expensively

Hoxton Boutique (2 Hoxton St) The first boutique on the block, selling current and vintage staples for self-respecting Hoxtonites

No-One (1 Kingsland Rd) Tight edit of mens- and womenswear, art and lifestyle with Shoreditch sensibility

Present (140 Shoreditch High St) Highly rated multi-brand menswear from Duffer of St George founders, plus awesome coffee

Relax Garden (40 Kingsland Rd) Shoebox fashion store full of little independent labels and charm

SCP (135 Curtain Rd) Modern, upscale interiors emporium

Sh! (57 Hoxton Sq) Pink and perky erotica for women; an East End institution

Start (42 Rivington St) Probably Hoxton's glossiest boutique – key men's and women's fashion, plus jeans solutions for all

The Three Threads (47 Charlotte Rd) Rare streetwear brands (and Edwin, YMC, Paul & Joe) for boys and girls, plus free beer

WAH Nails (420 Kingsland Rd) Sharmadean Reid's badass nail bar/boutique, tagging nails with Chanel logos, leopard-print and crystals

Brick Lane

Bernstock Speirs Witty, modern millinery for sharp boys and girls

The Laden Showroom A platform for young designers who have outgrown their market stalls, plus vintage treats

Rokit A well-edited selection of vintage clothing, all according to the trends of the season

Tatty Devine Playful plastic accessories, plus art, fashion and zines from all their clever and creative friends

Cheshire Street
(off Brick Lane)

Beyond Retro Over 10,000 pieces of secondhand American clothes and accessories in a good old East End warehouse

Labour & Wait Resembling an old-fashioned general store, L&W sells fashionably trad clothes, interiors and gardenware

Mar Mar Co Scandinavian design: lamps, ceramics, prints and stationery

Shelf Charming and quirky shopette selling English retrorama – wooden, tin, ceramic and paper knick-knacks

Dray Walk
(off Brick Lane)

A Butcher of Distinction Boys' boutique selling cool, casual menswear from underground, overground and traditional labels

Gloria's A sneaker freak's fantasy – all sorts of rare, collectible trainers

Rough Trade East Indie heaven: records, live stage, fresh coffee

Redchurch Street

Aubin & Wills Jack Wills' 'Gap-luxe' line for men and women, plus onsite gallery in collaboration with artist Stuart Semple and cinema in collaboration with Shoreditch House

Caravan Interiors Stylist/author Emily Chalmers' cool home store with quirky and vintage finds – bambi heads, bugs, birdcages

Sick Ex-BOY owner Steph Rayner's 'anti-retail' secondhand clothes store sums up the post-capitalist East End vibe

Speedie Speedie Gazelle's grungy installation/vintage store with monthly gigs sets itself apart from all the competition

KNIGHTSBRIDGE & CHELSEA

These pretty, posh neighbourhoods are where many well-heeled shoppers aim for, and where reassuringly large price tags hang from comfortably conservative objects of desire. Ladies who lunch worship in the holy houses of Harrods and Harvey Nichols, and the numerous other shrines to designer fashion on Sloane Street (a less busy – more staid – version of Bond Street), and take their communion in San Lorenzo on Beauchamp Place; for a more villagey vibe, explore Brompton Cross and Chelsea Green. The King's Road may have lost its mojo of the Swinging Sixties, but the further west you walk down it, the more originality you'll find.

Brompton Cross

Joseph Stylish womens- and menswear designer and own-brand clothes and shoes spread over three boutiques

The Conran Shop British designer Sir Terence Conran's flagship store, selling furniture, kitchenware, books and gadgets, all housed within the magnificent Art Deco Michelin Building

The Library Menswear boutique selling cool, casual labels including Dries Van Noten, Alexander McQueen and Martin Margiela

King's Road

Anthropologie Urban Outfitters' upscale homesy shop, also with womenswear

Austique Girly heaven selling fashion and accessories by niche labels and the Austique sisters, Lindy Lopes and Katie Canvin

Comptoir des Cotonniers Quiet, timeless French fashion for women

Designers Guild Tricia Guild's longserving interiors and lifestyle emporium

Duke of York Square Don't overlook this 'retail court' including Zara, Joseph, Myla, Agnès B and All Saints

Graham & Green Pretty interiors, trinkets and fashion that make Chelsea types happy

Peter Jones The iconic one-stop shop for all matters home, wardrobe, life; an amusing window onto wedding-list shopping

Neal's Yard Remedies Organic skin-, hair- and bodycare in signature blueglass apothecary bottles

R. Soles Cowboy boots in every conceivable style (note the naughty pun in the name)

Rococo Chocolate heaven, from traditional violet creams to vegetableshaped pralines, all beautifully packaged

The Shop at Bluebird Inside the original 1920s Bluebird garage is impeccably edited fashion from the fashion capitals, plus Antwerp, LA and well-preserved attics; next-door in the Bluebird Epicerie is impeccably made (and presented) food

shop…

Vivienne Westwood The queen of punk's original store, the one-time SEX with its anticlockwise clock, down at World's End

Sloane Street

Chloé Glamorous French fashion: wishlist frocks and trophy handbags
Marni Future Systems-designed boutique selling Consuelo Castiglioni's sublimely non-fashiony fashion
Jo Malone Beautifully packaged and deliciously scented bathroom goodies
Paule Ka Stylish fashion from a French designer with an aunt named Paule
Pickett Eclectic treasure trove of gloves, jewellery and handmade leather luggage
Shanghai Tang Elegant Chinese-inspired clothing, from silk pyjamas to velvet Mao jackets, plus chinoiserie home furnishings
Zadig & Voltaire Insouciant French chic in rockster jeans, effortless tees, and their renowned cashmere knits

Also on Sloane Street:

Alberta Ferretti, Bottega Veneta, Chanel, Dior, Fendi, Dolce & Gabbana, Giorgio Armani, Gucci, Hermès, Jimmy Choo, Louis Vuitton, Missoni, Prada, Pucci, Versace and YSL

Walton Street

Bentleys Antique gallery/shop selling vintage luggage, bowler hats and 1920s aeroplane propellers
Blossom Gorgeous maternity shop, with exclusive pieces by top designers. Surplus to requirements? Get a head start next door in luxury lingerie store Myla
Dragons Hand-painted nursery furniture for little darlings who wouldn't settle for less
Louise Bradley London-based interior designer showcases her favourite stylish furniture and knick-knacks for the home
Monogrammed Linen Shop Lovely sheet sets, table linen and nightwear, for those who have everything

Department Stores

 Harrods
87 Brompton Road, SW1

The mumma of London's department stores comes with a caveat – as the UK's biggest shop (at 1 million sq ft), it's one massive maze crawling with tourists and arrivistes. There are 23 restaurants and countless (OK, 330 to be precise) different departments including fashion, furniture, food, sports, antiques and toys, not to mention two Dodi and Diana memorials (though maybe they'll go now that Al Fayed has sold up for £1.5 billion). Just opposite is the new Harrods 102, selling 'gourmet food on the go'. Undoubtedly, Harrods' best (and cheapest) angle is from the outside after dark, when its splendid terracotta façade sparkles with 11,500 light bulbs.

 Harvey Nichols
109–125 Knightsbridge, SW1

With a champagne nail bar, botox, fake tanning and Daniel Hersheson's blow dry bar, Harvey Nicks has become something of an Ab Fab parody: a one-stop shop to satisfy all of a narcissist's needs. Of course the daily trawl around the shop floor really is awfully hard work, what with four floors of all the top names in women's fashion, from red-carpet gowns to ready-to-wear to jeans, tees and lingerie, plus an ample accessories and beauty hall, interiors floor and two men's floors, so thankfully there are outposts of Daylesford Organic, Yo! Sushi, Wagamama and Fushi organic juice bar, plus the jet-set Fifth Floor restaurant, champagne café and bar.

MARYLEBONE HIGH STREET

Brora Gorgeous cosy cashmere, in a range of mouthwatering colours

Cath Kidston All you need for a chintzy-chic existence: from petal-patterned tents to vintage-inspired clothing

Daunt Books Everything you ever wanted to know about travel and more

Divertimenti Luxury kitchen emporium selling the domestic goddess lifestyle

Kabiri Jewellery 'gallery' selling Me&Ro, Alexis Bittar, Scott Wilson et al

KJ's Laundry Unusual international fashion including YMC, Filippa K and American Retro

Oxfam Music and Books One of the charity's specialist stores with an excellent, cheap selection

Matches Regarded as one of London's best: fast-moving, multi-brand designer boutique for men and women

Sixty 6 Tiny boutique with a variety

of fashion-forward, original labels for women

Space NK Cult beauty shop selling the coolest names in cosmetics

SOUTH

The OXO Tower
Barge House Street, South Bank, SE1

One of the South Bank's most famous landmarks, the OXO Tower (an ex-power station and later the HQ of OXO beef stock cubes) is an essential address for fans of original works from little-known design labels – and crowd-phobes. Many designers work onsite, making and selling fashion, jewellery, ceramics, art and photography. On the eighth floor is the OXO Tower Restaurant, Bar and Brasserie, under the management of Harvey Nichols, with panoramic river views, while the (original) red-brick barge house opposite the OXO Tower's south side hosts interesting exhibitions. If you like this, you'll also like Gabriel's Wharf, nearby (Upper Ground, SE1).

THE WEST END

The West End is scored with exclusive shopping streets – none more so than New and Old Bond Street, which are lined with designer boutiques (and big spenders' attendant limos), and are said to have more royal 'By Appointment' warrants than any other thoroughfare. Savile Row is the golden mile of men's tailoring (increasingly infiltrated by women and fashion brands), while Jermyn Street is for shirts what Savile Row is for suits. Bruton Street and Conduit Street add a younger, more hip edge, while Brewer Street and Broadwick Street take shoppers into the seedier realms of Soho. Meanwhile, South Molton Street provides the low-key antidote, with characterful independent stores and eateries.

MAYFAIR

Bond Street

Alexander McQueen So strong is the DNA that the brand continues in his name after his tragic suicide in 2010

Fenwick A department store full of good sense in amongst the excess: mid-range clothing/shoes/beauty

Louis Vuitton Ridiculous, gilt-clad superstore for logo obsessives

Mulberry British bastion whose trad-with-a-twist fashion ranges from interesting tweeds to the latest It-bag

Pringle Scottish sweater brand long associated with golfers, now competing on the catwalks with archive-inspired designs

Smythson The Queen's favourite purveyor of luxury leather stationery, now linked with First Lady Sam Cam

Solange Azagury-Partridge Fine jewellery with creative, modern edge

Watches of Switzerland Multi-brand horology emporium

Also on Bond Street:

Anya Hindmarch, Asprey, Breguet, Bulgari, Cartier, Chanel, Chaumet, De Beers, DKNY, Emporio Armani, Georgina Goodman, Gucci, Jimmy Choo, Lora Piana, Mappin & Webb, Miu Miu, Mont Blanc, Nicole Farhi, Patek Philippe, Prada, Ralph Lauren, Tiffany and YSL

Bruton Street

Holland & Holland Historic gun company established 1835, with chic outerwear for yomping in the country (or parading in the city)

Maison Martin Margiela Highbrow Belgian fashion for those in the know

Matthew Williamson Whimsical, colourful clothing – his sexy, flowing frocks for socialites are a speciality

Miller Harris The origin of many haute hotels' toiletries, plus beautiful scents and bijou tearoom serving Lyn Harris' own blends

Stella McCartney Delicious daywear, understated eveningwear and vegetarian shoes from the daughter of a Beatle

Conduit Street

Burberry Finally shaken off the chav association with super-pricey, superluxe men's and women's fashion

Rigby & Peller Made-to-measure lingerie with a royal warrant to the Queen. Guaranteed to find your perfect fit

Vivienne Westwood High drama meets outrageous tailoring from the punk queen

Dover Street Market

17–18 Dover Street, W1

When the intellectual Japanese label Comme des Garçons decided to open a London store, it shunned the obvious (ie ego and logo), instead opting for 'concept' and collaboration. On six floors of stark, spiky architecture (with sheds for cash desks and birdcages and Portaloos for changing rooms), DSM is the exemplar of curated consumption, with a thoughtful (if at times boggling) selection of fashion's darkest, edgiest offerings from Alaïa, Lanvin, Boudicca and of course Comme des Garçons and protégé, Junya Watanabe. Sufferers of fashion fatigue may reward themselves at the in-store outpost of Paris's excellent Rose Bakery café.

Jermyn Street

Dunhill British stalwart with in-store barber, made-to-measure shirts and suits, iconic lighters and all sorts of other accoutrements to make ladies swoon

Emma Willis One of the few female shirt-makers, renowned for her craftsmanship and fabrics

Taylors Everything a gentleman would need for grooming: badger shaving brushes, cut-throat razors, colognes

Trickers Traditional British footwear still handmade by the Tricker family in Northampton, Britain's artisan shoe centre

Turnbull & Asser Sharp shirts cut from a choice of 400 fabrics good enough, apparently, for Prince Charles, Al Pacino and James Bond

Mount Street

Balenciaga Fierce French fashion for whippets from demi-god Nicolas Ghesquière

Christian Louboutin The red-soled shoes that make women weak at the knees

Lanvin The London flagship for French fashion designer Alber Elbaz's masterful drapery and dresses

Marc by Marc Jacobs The designer's diffusion emporium with pretty girly pieces and affordable tat

Wunderkind Cool ready-to-wear dresses from feted German designer Wolfgang Joop

Savile Row

Abercrombie & Fitch Preppy American casualwear with a strict insistence on beautiful staff

b Store The Row's first fashion infiltrator: young, cutting-edge designers such as Peter Jensen, Bless and Bernhard Willhelm and their own label for fashion mavens

Evisu Subaro High-end indigo Japanese denim and streetwear with obsessive attention to detail

Gieves & Hawkes Has occupied the prized No.1 Savile Row address for over 90 years. Exemplary bespoke tailoring with design-led collections

Huntsman One of the most expensive on the Row and famous for its tweeds

Kilgour (pronounced 'Kilgar') Cary Grant's erstwhile tailor, straddling tradition and modernity; the modern poster-boy is Jude Law

Lanvin Luxe menswear with suiting, coats and casual stuff from the unfaultable French fashion house

Richard James An elegant, modern take on classic designs

South Molton Street

Browns Cult men's and women's fashion emporium with over 40 years' service, deemed one of London's best. **Browns Focus**, opposite, is younger and yet more fashionable, while **Labels For Less** is just that

Butler & Wilson A twinkling treasure box of vintage and new costume jewellery plus unusual, amusing fashion and frills

Poste Eccentric designer shoe shop for men, styled like a gentlemen's club

Tartine et Chocolate Luxurious French baby clothing

Wolford When only the best hosiery will do

SOHO

Agent Provocateur (6 Broadwick Street) Classy crotchless panties? Only at AP, sold by staff wearing saucy nurses' outfits

American Retro (35 Old Compton Street) Classy blokey clothes and jokey stuff that continues to surprise after all these years

Beyond the Valley (2 Newburgh St) Creative cradle for recent fashion grads: fashion, accessories, lifestyle, to rousing effect

Kokon To Zai (57 Greek St) Marjan Pejoski's avant-garde boutique/drop-in centre for trendatrons

Carnaby Street

American Apparel Cheap and cheerful, colourful stuff for teens and twentysomethings

Howies Active/fashionwear made with a conscience in Cardigan Bay. Looks nice too

Levi's Jeans (also on the street: G-Star Raw, Replay, Energie, Pepe, Diesel, Lee)

Puma Sportwear/trainer brand does concept store (also on the street: Vans, Size?, Office)

Soccer Scene For all things footy – if you must

Topshop
Oxford Circus, W1

For virtually all female Londoners (and visitors), Top Shop's flagship is the ultimate fashion honeypot – there are 1,000 staff working at any one time, 200 changing rooms and around 200,000 visitors a week. With 90,000 sq ft of cheap (yeah, best not to ask why), fast fashion, 'ToSho' is always ahead of the game with more, bigger, better concessions, vintage collections and designer ranges by fashion's most current names (Marios Schwab, Richard Nicoll, and the unfeasibly popular 'designer' Kate Moss). And with a nail bar, blowdry bar, and candy shop even, resistance is futile.

Department Stores

Fortnum & Mason
181 Piccadilly, W1

Established in 1707, Fortnum's is the grandmama of London's department stores. Beyond its eau-de-nil frontage is a taste of genteel, olde-worlde England (and now with a sympathetic David Collins facelift). With a clutch of royal warrants, the Queen's grocer sells tasty comestibles – handmade chocolates, British cheeses, fine teas and coffees, charcuterie etc – at right royal prices. Escape the tourist stampede by buying one of Fortnum's signature hampers or by retreating to the sleepy upper floors selling women's accessories, lingerie, perfume and homeware: granny would approve.

Hamleys
188–196 Regent Street,
London W1

London's gigantic, seven-storey toy store is loud and frantic, with swarms of over-excited kids and model planes circling overhead. The enormous selection ranges from tin soldiers and a sweet factory to the latest in Jedi fighting equipment and remote-control choppers. There are dressing-up departments, a Lego World, mountains of stuffed toys, in-store magicians and a café for birthday parties. Everything, in fact, except peace.

Liberty
214–220 Regent Street, W1
This iconic Tudor revival store started life in 1875 as a repository for Arthur Liberty's goods shipped in from the Orient. It still exudes a unique charm with its gorgeous panelled interior, Tudor-style beamed exterior, and eclectic, original buying throughout. Fashion labels span the top Brits, Belgians, French, Italians, Americans and Japanese, plus there are Arts and Crafts antiques, linens and homeware, and the store's famous Art Nouveau prints on any textile that will take it. Tea and scones and oysters and champagne await the weary, at its various cafés.

Selfridges
400 Oxford Street, W1
With its grand neoclassical façade, Selfridges is something of a temple to consumerism. Many place their faith in its problem-solving powers: 'Argh: want cool outfit, need clever present, run out of aftershave and I'm starving… Selfridges!' As Britain's second biggest shop (after Harrods), there's room to please everyone: fashion from McTopshop to McQueen, books, toys, electrics, homeware, and food to satifsy the pickiest of eaters. It's arguably the most progressive department store, and hosts in-store festivals, previously themed on Bollywood, Punk and Surrealism. If that requires a human window display, so be it.

WEST LONDON & NOTTING HILL

For a more bohemian vibe, head to Notting Hill, an area which exudes a laidback, villagey atmosphere and offers a mix of vintage, urban and high-end shops. It is also home to Portobello Market, one of London's most famous street markets, which stretches down the area's geographic backbone, Portobello Road – a cute, colourful road beloved for its rugged character, and dotted with charming antiques shops, pubs, and fruit and veg stalls.

Ledbury Road

Aimé Young-thinking boutique showcasing the brightest French labels
Anya Hindmarch Beautifully finished luxury handbags loved by Tory tottie

shop…

Bamford & Sons Lifestyle solutions – cashmere, casuals and gadgetry – for the cash-rich, time-poor modern gentleman

Fiona Knapp Bold, modern statement jewellery using coloured gemstones for bold, modern women

Matches A perennial favourite selling the season's key pieces from Azzedine Alaïa to Zandra Rhodes

Melissa Odabash Glamorous swimwear for yummy mummies

Wolf & Badger Innovative retail concept that rents micro-space to young British fashion designers

Portland Road

Summerill & Bishop Stylish, unusual kitchen shop with a vintage French look

The Cross Bohemian fashion boutique loved for its girly atmosphere and unusual trinkets

Virginia Antiques Virginia Bates' ravishingly romantic vintage boudoir specializing in Victorian and Edwardian frocks

Portobello Road

Banger Bros Chef Julian Dyer's original takeaway sausage shop on Bangerbello Road

Honeyjam Retro/eco toyshop co-owned by MILF model Jasmine Guinness

Hummingbird Bakery Cutesy cupcake cottage industry: so Notting Hill

One of a Kind Cult vintage store stuffed to the rafters with rare designer treasures

Portobello Green Arcade for 20-odd up-and-coming designers: womenswear, menswear and kidswear, including Preen's darkly romantic, stompy British fashion

Westbourne Grove

Daylesford Organic Lady Bamford's aspirational lifestyle store selling organic produce and immaculate good taste

Diptyque Because there's a big demand for luxury scented candles here

Feathers Womenswear boutique bursting with a global selection of current labels

Heidi Klein A one-stop holiday shop, with flattering bikinis, cool kaftans and wafty resort-chic clothing

JoJo Maman Bébé Cool kicks for mums, kids and mums-to-be, made well and sustainably

Nicole Farhi Interiors, menswear, womenswear and a great brasserie (202), from which to watch Notting Hill's socialites float by

Question Air Multi-brand fashion, plus the answer to your denim dilemmas: whichever jeans people want this week, they have it

Tom's As in Tom Conran, foodie offspring of Sir Terence – this sit-in/takeaway deli is perennially popular

Twenty8Twelve Admittedly likeable fashion from Sienna and Savannah Miller

 Westfield London
Shepherd's Bush, W12

For some, it's a heaven on earth – the size of 30 football pitches and built at a cost of £1.6 billion in 2008, London's largest shopping centre spans the market, from Debenhams to Dior, Levi's to Louis Vuitton, Mango to Miu Miu – 265 retailers, 80% fashion, and 40 of 'em within the designer apartheid, The Village (offering 'handsfree shopping', with valets doing the dirty work). Others revile it as nothing more than a cloneville, with identikit chains, climate control and piped music, not to mention it taking so long to get anywhere, it obstructs one's three meals a day. Just as well there are nearly 50 eateries (including The Real Greek, Wahaca, Yo Sushi!), and, of course, a champagne bar. NB: **Westfield Stratford City**, due to open in 2011 next to the Olympic Park in East London, aims to trump Westfield London, with all of the above, spread over some 1.9 million sq ft of retail space

MARKETS

Borough Market
Southwark Street, SE1

The 'Larder of London' is a gigantic covered food market endorsed by many a celebrity chef, selling organic/artisanal/local fare, often with the farmers/bakers/gardeners in attendance themselves (11am–5pm Thurs; noon–6pm Fri; 8am–5pm Sat when it tends to be overrun with foodies).

Brick Lane Market E1
What was once just a fleamarket now also encompasses reasonably priced fashion, art, homeware and vintage, plus random weirdos hawking whatever comes to hand, and generally excellent live local bands busking (9am–5pm on Sundays). Don't miss Sunday's (Up) Market inside the Old Truman Brewery for more up-and-coming creativity plus grub.

Camden Market, NW1
Anthropologically historic market that spans various subcultures (Goth, punk, hippy, biker, cyber), selling fashion, music, antiques and tat (open daily, 10am–6pm).

Gray's Antiques Market
Davies Street, W1

Over 200 dealers selling antiques, vintage fashion, sporting memorabilia and jewellery in a historic building with an indoor 'river' (open 10am–6pm Mon–Fri; 11am–5pm Sat).

Old Spitalfields Market
Commercial Street, E1

A hip, buzzy market all under an original Victorian structure selling everything from crafts, food and flowers to quirky creations by budding designers (open: 11am–5.30pm Sun–Fri. Mon–Weds: low-key, mostly fashion. Thurs: antiques and vintage. Fri: fashion, art, general. Sun (its busiest day): fashion, music, art, food).

Portobello Road Market,
W11

Pick your way through all the tourists and hundreds of antique dealers for clothes, collectibles and curios (9am–4pm Fri; 9am–5pm Sat). Monday to Thursday sees the street lined with fruit and veg stalls.

River Thames at Richmond

play...

'When a man is tired of London, he is tired of life' – so goes the now clichéd quote of 18th-century writer Samuel Johnson. And like any respectable cliché, it's entirely true – unless you've lost the will to live, it's impossible to be bored in the capital. Indeed, in a time when many are seeking rather more meaningful memories than beaches and binge-drinking, inventive and thoughtful entertainment is flourishing (see, in particular, our new section, Academic Amusements). Distractions range from the conventional to the quirky to the extreme – from de-stressing spas to a swim in frozen waters, from a walking tour with a London architect to the Chap Olympiad's Hop, Skip and G&T race, from 'Meet the Monkeys' at London Zoo to learning the trapeze at circus school.

Nature still holds ground in the metropolis, which boasts over 5,000 acres of royal parks. Hyde Park is London's answer to New York's Central Park and caters for both the hyperactive (with 'black run' roller-blading, horse-riding, swimming and space to run and run) and the heavy-footed (with open-air concerts, picnics and a spot of boating on the lake). Further afield at Hampstead Heath, Kew Gardens and Richmond Park are the rewards of larger horizons and fewer people.

While the Thames struggles to support aquatic life, it remains the city's backbone, and as such is rushing with energy and studded with landmarks. Take a river cruise, a stroll down the Thames Path, or a 'flight' on the London Eye, or put away a pitcher of Pimm's while cheering on the annual Oxford and Cambridge Boat Race. This boat battle, held in late March, essentially starts London's social calendar. Follow the aristocrats and arrivistes through the social whirl – the Grand National in April, Royal Ascot and Wimbledon in June, July's Henley Royal Regatta, polo at Windsor and Glorious Goodwood, and sailing at Cowes Week in August – and not only will you catch the season's main sporting events but you'll also gain an insight into this top-hatted and tailed breed that travels the land to quaff champers from the back of their Range Rovers and assert their Englishness.

For inverse snobs, there is greyhound racing – a much more proletarian pastime fuelled by lager, chicken-in-a-basket and a cheeky flutter. While we await the success or otherwise of the 'Save our Stow' Facebook campaign to stop the infamous Walthamstow Stadium from, erm, going to the dogs (well, property developers), one last track in London remains active: Wimbledon Stadium. As well as host to May's annual English Greyhound Derby (the Grand National for greyhounds), there are twice-weekly race nights (Friday and Saturday), and in between the galloping greyhounds is stockcar racing, ie dodgems with clapped-out cars ready for the scrapheap. Of course, any good boozer (pub) will offer a game of arras (arrows – darts) and a few Britneys (Britney Spears – beers).

Since rugby, cricket, tennis and football all have their origins in England (with London serving as the spiritual home to rugby at Twickenham, to cricket at Lord's, tennis at Wimbledon, and footie at Wembley), such sports are understandably close to Londoners' hearts. Most males of the species support a local football team, even if few London teams are truly 'local' (Chelsea and Arsenal's teams, for example, are comprised of players of every nationality attracting five-figure weekly wage packets, trophy girlfriends and international fame). And beyond the most common sports, there are the more peculiar pursuits such as crown green bowling, croquet and fencing. With the twin trends of Britishness (admittedly perhaps only amongst us Brits) and novelty-seeking, such games are gaining popularity, and definitely deliver anecdotes to dine out on.

For those with a pathological aversion to sports, there are festivals (read: a good excuse for a mass piss-up) throughout the year – Chinese New Year in January, the Great Spitalfields Pancake Race on Shrove Tuesday, St Patrick's Day on 17 March, Gay Pride in July, the Notting Hill Carnival over August's bank holiday, the Brick Lane Festival in September, the Pearly Kings & Queens Harvest Festival in October, and Bonfire Night on 5 November – the day, if any, for a London Eye night flight; we've also added a festivals section in Play (and in Party for the more hedonistic variety). Check out Time Out, London's fortnightly listings magazine, for current highlights – but if all that fails to leave you smiling, check out London's comedy scene for a 'giraffe' (laugh).

Academic Amusements

Thinking is in fashion! The post-materialist set has replaced 'stuff' with cerebral pursuits – talks, debates, philosophical ponderings.

The Book Club Think while you drink is the idea here (well, it is in Shoreditch, after all), with book launches, panel discussions, life drawing and laughing workshops (100 Leonard Street, Shoreditch, EC2; 020 7684 8618; www.wearetbc.com). Free–£6

Frontline Club Set up in 2003 by war correspondents in honour of colleagues who lost their lives during 1989's Romanian Revolution, it is committed to championing freedom of expression and independent journalism. As such, its programme of debates, discussions, quizzes, documentary and film screenings (with a focus on conflict reporting) has seen the likes of Christina Lamb, John Simpson and Boris Berezovsky, as well as the late Benazir Bhutto and Alexander Litvinenko, spill the beans to Frontline members and the public alike (13 Norfolk Place, W2; 020 7479 8950; www.frontlineclub.com). £12.50

ICA Regular, reactionary programme of talks and panel debates on art (recently on outsider art with Jarvis Cocker), philosophy (with, for example, the ICA's firm friend Slovenian Slavoj Žižek), current concerns (such as feminism, with Sam Roddick), and plenty of wildcards (Shere Hite on sexual purity, Martin Amis on radical Islam, Patti Smith reciting her poetry). £12

Intelligence Squared Britain's brainiacs have all shared their inner workings here at IQ2's debates, lectures and discussions so loved by the chattering classes: Will Self, Martin Amis, Yasmin Alibhai-Brown, variously on such highbrow issues as the economy, geo-politics and moral scruples (usually held at the Royal Geographical Society, South Kensington, SW7 and Methodist Central Hall, Westminster, SW1; 020 7792 4830; www.intelligencesquared.com). £25

The School of Life Established in 2008 by Britain's favourite pop philosopher Alain de Botton, its winning formula is equally focused on fun and thought. Sunday sermons (£12.50) see the 'congregation' stand to sing themed hymns (The Man in the Mirror for Ruby Wax's talk on ego, for example); its conversation dinners are held at the kind of restaurants you've always meant to go to (Providores, Konstam; £55), and its excellent classes (£30) bring intellectual insights to everyday issues – How to be Cool, for example, points students to the black power struggle (70 Marchmont Street, Bloomsbury, WC1; 020 7833 1010; www.theschooloflife.com).

Bike Hire

We may mock London mayor Boris Johnson as a bike buffoon (frequently papped wobbling on two wheels sans hat), but he is at least championing cyclists' rights, bringing new cycle superhighways (from Merton to the City, and Barking to Tower Gateway; see www.lcc.org.uk for cycle route maps), plus an ambitious Paris-style urban bike scheme (see below). He's even taken part in **Sky Rides**, regular mass- and mini-bike rides every Sunday designed to encourage fun times on a bike (www.goskyride.com). Unlikely, however, that he's jumped aboard that rather more anarchic bandwagon, **Critical Mass**, that takes to the streets at 6pm on the last Friday of every month (starting underneath Waterloo Bridge by the National Film Theatre, South Bank) to assert cyclists' rights: 'we aren't blocking traffic; we are traffic'. Indeed, it can be something of a traffic-stopper with numbers in the thousands. There's a lively carnival spirit with fancy dress and noisy sound systems strapped onto bikes; it can get political and the police are always seemingly on the verge of a crackdown – all the more motivation to attend (www.criticalmasslondon.org.uk). Boris could learn a lot.

The London
Bicycle Tour Company
1a Gabriel's Wharf, 56 Upper Ground, SE1
Tel: 020 7928 6838
www.londonbicycle.com
Open: daily, 10am–6pm. £20/day

Before Boris (BB), London Bicycle could boast that its fleet of 200 bikes was one of the largest; a good mix of mountain bikes, hybrids, traditional models, folding bikes, tandems and kids' bikes. Plus real people to help you choose the right bike.

London Cycle Hire Scheme
BoJo's £140 million hire scheme launched summer 2010, with 6,000 bikes and 400 self-service docking stations across Zone One, mainly at tube stations and 'key destinations'. The first half-hour is 'free' (ish: there's also an access charge to unlock the bike – £1 for a day, £5 for a week), and then a usage charge of £1 for one hour, £5 for 24 hours; docking stations happily take credit cards (www.tfl.gov.uk). It could spell a lot of alcohol-artists buoyed with liquid confidence trying to cycle home.

Velorution
18 Great Titchfield Street, W1
Tel: 020 7637 4004
www.velorution.biz
Open: 8.30am–6.45pm Mon–Fri;
10.30am–6.30pm Sat. £17/day

A bike shop hot for Dutch-style bikes and folding bikes, which also has 10 Brompton folding bikes (excellent for train tours) and will deliver within central London for a charge.

Canals

Still waters run deep – alongside some 100 miles of canals is a London that most Londoners don't even know. The waterways are a vestige of the Industrial Revolution – shire horses have not trotted the towpaths since 1956 – but they now provide a behind-the-scenes window on the gracious Regency architecture around Regent's Park, Hackney's forgotten industrial landscapes and the enviable backyards of Primrose Hill. It's a tranquil hiding place for anglers, 'yuvs', and houseboat-dwelling bohemia, with floating restaurants and

play...

canalside pubs aplenty, most scenically between Camden and Little Venice. The London Waterbus Company (020 7482 2550 www.londonwaterbus.com) offers short trips between Camden Lock, Little Venice (£6.50 one way) and London Zoo (includes admission through its own canal gate; £19.50), as well as day trips (£21) 'following in the footsteps of a forgotten way of life', eastwards to Limehouse Basin, or westwards along the Grand Union Canal to Greenford, both from Camden Lock on its fleet of four historic narrow boats (weekends Oct–Mar, daily April–Sept) – pack a picnic and Pimm's.

Circus Training

Circus Space
Coronet Street, Hoxton, N1
Tel: 020 7729 9522
www.thecircusspace.co.uk

In an old Hoxton power station (so plenty of room to swing a cat), the Circus Space runs evening classes (drop-in £13.50), half- (£55) and full-days (£95) in trapeze, juggling, tightrope-walking, stilt-walking, acrobatics and general clowning around. For those ready to remove the safety net, there's even a degree in circus arts on offer.

Comedy

London is the Hollywood of comedy (without the looks), and jokesmiths from around the world gravitate towards this rare platform for political incorrectness where heckling is actively encouraged. Apart from during August (when all migrate to Edinburgh's Fringe festival), comedians little and large can be seen rattling off their routines, from pub backrooms to purpose-built comedy club chains.

Comedy Café
66 Rivington Street, Hoxton, EC2
Tel: 020 7739 5706
www.comedycafe.co.uk
Open: 7pm–1am Weds–Sat (from 6pm Fri). From £8–15

The popular Comedy Café has followed the failsafe template – stand-up comedy served to seated punters plied with table service and predictable snackage (of the nachos/meze/burgers variety), followed by floor-filling disco music on the weekend; entry is free to Wednesdays' new acts night.

The Comedy Store
Haymarket House,
1a Oxendon Street, SW1
Tel: 020 7930 2949
www.thecomedystore.co.uk
Open: daily, 6.30pm–3am; shows 8pm (also midnight Fri/Sat). From £14–20

London's premier comedy venue is arguably the most sanitized, and often with a famous line-up (Mike Myers, Ruby Wax and Graham Norton have all trodden its boards) performing stand-up, improv and topical satire. Its house troupe, The Comedy Store Players (a team of seven including Paul Merton, Josie Lawrence and Neil Mullarkey plus guest stars), performs improv on Sundays and Wednesdays. But all is not lost for sell-out shows, as they often are – 70–100 tickets are made available on the door. And if heckling from the back is not enough, there are open slots for the public at the King Gong show, the last Monday of every month.

Jongleurs
Tel: 08700 111960
www.jongleurs.com
Hammersmith (Rutland Grove, W6; 7pm–midnight Fri/Sat)
Notting Hill Gate (The Tabernacle, Powis Square, W11; 6.30pm—midnight Fri/Sat)
Covent Garden (Sway Club, 61 Great Queen Street, WC2; 5–3am Fri/Sat). £17

'Eat, drink, laugh, dance' is Jongleurs' motto. Just as well they can see the funny side – after Jongleurs' backers went into administration in 2009, their three London venues were lost, and the brand (once the UK's biggest chain) has moved into hosting weekend parties at borrowed locations. The vibe remains the same, however, and, as such, is often swarming with hen/stag parties and office nights out, all creating their own unintentional comedy.

Cookery

Books for Cooks
4 Blenheim Crescent, W11
Tel: 020 7221 1992
www.booksforcooks.com
Closed: Sun/Mon, the last three weeks in August, Christmas week
From £40–80

What started out as a bookshop now has two purpose-built kitchens for its workshops taught by French, Italian, Japanese, British and vegetarian chefs (previously featuring names such as Mark Hix, Skye Gyngell and Sam and Sam Clark). Most courses are demonstration only, plus a few hands-on classes. For instant gratification, its café serves fresh international meals, and for swots, books galore.

Leith's School of Food & Wine
16–20 Wendell Road, W12
Tel: 020 8749 6400
www.leiths.com
Closed: second and third weeks of August. From £110

Leith's is London's best-known cookery school, so waiting lists are often on the menu. It's right up-to-date with its demonstration theatre and teaching kitchens, but still retains a rather charming school-ma'amish manner. Cuisine is contemporary and international, but there's a British focus with workshops in marmalade and curd-making, fish and game. There are also wine and champagne appreciation courses, and for those wanting to go the whole hog, professional courses.

Divertimenti Cookery School
33 Marylebone High Street, W1
Tel: 020 7486 8020
www.divertimenti.co.uk/cookery-school
Closed: August. From £40

With hands-on masterclasses, demonstration classes, lunchtime express classes, classes for kids, and gastro tours around London's culinary hotspots (Borough Market, Marylebone Village), Divertimenti presents a full dinner set of options to rookie cooks, often featuring successful authors, indigenous international chefs and guest chefs from London's gastrodomes (previously Roka, Dehesa, The Modern Pantry). The Marylebone 'kitchen theatre' features TV screens for close-up details, while a more intimate space at the South Kensington store allows smaller groups to gather around the chef's table and beleaguer them with questions (227 Brompton Road, SW3; 020 7581 8065).

Cricket

The English cricket scene has found its mojo again thanks to its tabloid-friendly national team (and their WAGs), frequent streaking, and the new, more entertaining Twenty20 games (essentially speed cricket where you get much more bang for your buck). For that, it's lightened up, though some say the tone has been lowered – which is, of course, just not cricket.

The Brit Oval
Harleyford Road, Kennington, SE11
Tel: 020 7820 5700
www.britoval.com. Tickets £10–102

The Oval is home to Surrey Cricket Club – Middlesex's biggest rival (see below) and the venue and birthplace of the Ashes (although they are always kept at Lords). The Ashes, cricket's grand prix, are so-called from when England lost the Test Match to Australia on English turf in 1882, and The Sporting Times published a mock obituary to English cricket. When England won the Test in Australia, the English captain was presented with an urn of ashes. The ground is called The Oval after an oval road was laid round a cabbage patch in the 1790s, which was re-turfed as a cricket ground in 1845. Nowadays it's the scene of county and international Twenty20 and traditional test cricket, and while bringing a picnic and having an all-day bender in the sun has always been a tradition, the Oval has cracked down on people bringing their own booze. Tours are available by arrangement, but if you fancy a go yourself, book one of the bowling machines to see what it's really like facing the likes of Stuart Broad or Jimmy Anderson.

Lord's Cricket Ground
St John's Wood, NW8
Tel: 020 7616 8500
(tickets 020 7432 1000) www.lords.org
Open: tours at 10am, noon and 2pm daily except match/preparation days April–Sept; noon and 2pm Oct–Mar;
From £14 (tickets £15–80)

Lord's is 'the home of cricket' and also to both Marylebone and Middlesex cricket clubs (MCC), and remains the guardian of the Laws of Cricket. It hosts county cricket (for Middlesex's matches) and international test matches – often sell-out events. The easiest (and cheapest) tickets to get are for the last day of test matches (ditto for the Oval), since these are not sold in advance. Otherwise, book well ahead and then pack a picnic, a bottle of champagne and a bat and ball – Lords, still a much stuffier environment, can afford to be more laidback about drinking. At the end of play, there's usually an unofficial pitch walk-on, where fans have a knock-up on the hallowed ground. Tours of the beautiful Long Room and Pavilion are also available and a must for anyone who actually understands the rules of cricket.

Festivals

The Annual Chap Olympiad
Bedford Square Gardens, WC1
Tel: 0844 477 1000
www.thechapolympiad.com
One Saturday in mid-July. £15

Start growing your 'tache and practising your cucumber-sandwich discus-hurling, for an afternoon and evening of such jolly capers as umbrella jousting, 'bounders' and the grand steeplechase, where the jockeys are ladies, the beasts – predictably – men. Hosted by the merry men of the monthly Chap Magazine and Bourne & Hollingsworth (of Blitz etc; see Party), all are encouraged to don their three-piece tweed suits/plus-fours/antique crown green bowling garb, whatever. It's a vintage day out, in rather more ways than one.

Hampton Court Palace Festival
0844 811 0050
www.hamptoncourtfestival.com
From £45, mid-June

Enjoy a picnic in Hampton Court's gorgeous grounds and then listen to a concert under the stars in the magnificent Palace Courtyard (all properly seated; the classical concerts are accompanied by fireworks). Programming is aimed at a more mature crowd: the likes of Jools Holland, Nicola Benedetti and Van Morrison.

Kenwood House Picnic Concerts
Hampstead Lane, NW3
Tel: 0870 333 1181
www.picnicconcerts.com
Sat evenings (till 10pm) late June–late Aug. From £25

Bring your own picnic, lollop on Hampstead Heath after a bottle of bubbly, and then pass out during the concert. That's what we do, but far better to stay with it to appreciate Kenwood's excellent atmosphere and line-up, for example Blondie, Rufus Wainwright and Jamie Cullum – the kind of music that carries well across the gentle grassy slopes of Kenwood House's grounds, backed by the beautiful 18th-century stately home itself. Carluccio's picnics (three-course meals for two plus one bottle of wine; £45) and deckchairs can be pre-ordered and collected on the day.

Taste of London
www.tastefestivals.com/london
From £22 (not including food and wine), mid-June

Don't enter on a full stomach: this four-day outdoor restaurant festival in Regent's Park is a cheaper chance to sample the signature dishes of over 40 of London's top eateries (Bentley's

play...

Oyster Bar & Grill, Fino, Le Gavroche, Yauatcha, for example), cooked up on mini-kitchens onsite, and to see/hear/meet/buy the signed book from Britain's top table of celeb chefs (previously Heston Blumenthal, Angela Hartnett, Tom Aikens and Anna Hansen), plus shop for some of London's yummiest produce, from, among 150 others, Bea's of Bloomsbury, Oddone's Gelati and Daylesford Organic. Even cook yourself, if you can face any more food.

Football

Britain's Premiership League – practically a global brand like Coca-Cola and McDonalds – is known for its highly charged and fast-paced games; half of London's 11 professional clubs are in this top division (Chelsea, Arsenal, Fulham, Tottenham Hotspur and West Ham). Chelsea (or 'Chelski' since it's owned by Russian oligarch Roman Abramovitch) is one of the world's richest clubs – the apocryphal story goes that when the opposition is losing, the 'Blues' supporters wave wads of cash at them. Tickets – as for any premiership game – are harder to get than scoring against Petr Cech, though tours of Chelsea's century-old ground are available. Chelsea's main rival is Arsenal (or 'the Gunners' – since the club was started by a group of employees of the Woolwich Arsenal Armament Factory in 1886) – also right up there in football's rich list. Book tickets in advance, through www.ticketmaster.co.uk or directly from the clubs (see www.thefa.com); be wary of touts. Getting tickets for the gleaming, £798 million

Norman Foster-designed Wembley Stadium – home to English national team, that architecturally thrilling arch, and high-profile games such as the FA Cup Final – is going to take yet more dedication; tours (£15) might be a more realistic option. No less fun and far easier to access are the lesser leagues – the Coca-Cola Championship and Coca-Cola Leagues 1 and 2 (comprising east London's Leighton Orient and Charlton Athletic, west London's Queen's Park Rangers and south London's Crystal Palace; www.footballleague.co.uk). With all, expect fruity banter and abusive anthems on the terraces.

Arsenal Football Club, Emirates Stadium, Ashburton Grove, Highbury, N5
Tel: 020 7704 4040 www.arsenal.com
Chelsea Football Club, Stamford Bridge, Fulham Road, SW6
Tel: 020 7915 2900
www.chelseafc.com
Wembley Stadium, Wembley, HA9
Tel: 0844 800 2755
www.wembleystadium.com

Golf

Richmond Park Golf Courses
Roehampton Gate, Priory Lane, SW15
Tel: 020 8876 1795
www.richmondparkgolfclub.org.uk
From £21

Set in the gorgeous surroundings of Richmond Park are two public 18-hole golf courses, a driving range, club hire, and a restaurant and bar. Daily tuition is available from PGA professionals.

Urban Golf

33 Great Pulteney Street, Soho, W1
Tel: 020 7248 8600
www.urbangolf.co.uk. From £20/hr

What central London lacks in rolling golf courses, it makes up for with technology. Urban Golf is a virtual indoor course that digitally simulates over 50 of the world's most famous courses, providing full sets of Callaway clubs at each simulator. PGA professionals are on hand for guiding that swing, as are bar staff to bring the 19th hole right to your feet (also at 12 Smithfield Street, EC1, and a caddishly designed third branch – the UK's largest indoor golf venue – in Kensington High Street, at the Tube Station Shopping Arcade, W8).

Horse-Riding

Hyde Park Stables

63 Bathurst Mews, W2
Tel: 020 7723 2813
www.hydeparkstables.com
Open: 7.15am–5pm Mon–Fri;
9am–5pm Sat/Sun (last hack at 3pm Oct–Mar)
From £59/hr (hats/boots incl)

There are five miles of bridleways and two arenas in Hyde Park. Its most famous bridle path, Rotten Row (from 'Route de Roi'), runs the length of the south side and was once a royal short cut between Buckingham and Kensington Palaces. The Household Cavalry can still be seen on morning exercise here on their majestic, glossy mounts. Rather less glamorous nags can be rented from this British Horse Society-approved riding school, and note that it's safety first (read: 'quiet' horses, leading ropes across roads, and no cantering without prior tuition – as such, hen parties are 'catered for').

Stag Lodge Stables

Robin Hood Gate,
Kingston Vale, SW15
Tel: 020 8974 6066
www.ridinginlondon.com
Open: 8am–10pm Tues–Thurs; 8am–6pm Fri–Sun
From £30/hr (hats/boots incl)

For vast green horizons speckled with beautiful wild deer, the more accomplished rider should head out to Stag Lodge at Richmond Park, which offers group hacks for up to two hours; with an outdoor floodlit school, they run late lessons all year. Horses range from Shetland ponies to 16hh hunters (though most are middling); Madonna has previously hired the entire stables.

Ice Skating

Temporary ice rinks are set up each winter in London's most lovely historic settings (from mid-November to end January) – in the neoclassical courtyard of Somerset House (home to three art galleries), in front of the Natural History Museum, at Kew's Royal Botanic Gardens, and sometimes at Hampton Court Palace, the Tower of London and the O2 (okay, not historical). Ali McGraw scarf-and-hat sets, mulled wine and much hand-holding all paint a romantic, festive scene – thus it's a popular venue for office parties and first dates; book ahead. Fanatics and amateur anthropologists should check out Queens Ice Skating & Bowling (17 Queensway, W2; 020 7229 0172; www.queensiceandbowl.co.uk) – its diner, ten-pin bowling alley, games arcade and junk food attract a rather different social scene. **Somerset House**, Strand, WC2; 020 7845 4670; www.somersethouseicerink.org.uk; **Natural History Museum,** Cromwell Road, South Kensington, SW7; 020 7942 5000; www.nhm.ac.uk; **Kew Gardens** Kew, Richmond, TW9; 020 8332 5655; www.kew.org (tickets for all also available from www.ticketmaster.co.uk 0870 534 4444). From £10.50

Karaoke

Hot Breath Karaoke

Run by perky, quirky couple Mike'n'Jen Hot Breath, this is a cult (and roaming) night that reminds singers that collective fun is better than X Factor ambition. Defiantly unserious, free and vaguely in public, Hot Breath is adored by the fashiony, arty set (including the likes of the Tatty Devine girls and the Eley Kishimoto designers). Regular outings at the Bethnal Green Workingmen's Club (see Party) and The Stag's Head, 55 Orsman Road, N1, but check their website, www.hotbreathkaraoke.com.

Karaoke Box

www.karaokebox.co.uk
Soho: 18 Frith Street, W1;
020 7494 3878   £20–84/hr
Open: daily, noon–1am (11pm Sun);
later opening in December.
Smithfields: 12 Smithfield Street,

EC1; 020 7329 9991   £20–150
Open: noon–3am Mon–Sat

Private karaoke has much to answer for, given the better-than-drugs high that's experienced after a behind-closed-doors sesh here. Take a hit yourself at London's first Japanese-style karaoke booths (its age is starting to show in Soho – the Smithfields branch is much glossier, though can be costlier). Smithfields also features movieoke (act along with your friends to classic film scenes; third Wednesdays of every month) and **Rockaoke**, where a live band plays backing for you (second and last Wednesdays of every month; free – do check www.rockaoke.co.uk as they do other nights around London, eg at Punk and Proud Camden). Otherwise, it's all the guilty pleasures you could ask for, food and cocktails on demand, and tambourines to drown out the singing. Advance organisation advised.

Lucky Voice

www.luckyvoice.co.uk
Soho: 52 Poland Street, W1;
020 7439 3660   £20–130/hr
Open: 5.30pm–1am Mon–Weds;
3pm–1am Thurs–Sat; 3–10.30pm Sun
Islington: 173 Upper Street, N1;
020 7354 6280   £20–155/hr
Open: 5pm–midnight Mon–Thurs;
3pm–2am Fri/Sat; 3pm–midnight Sun

If uber-entrepreneur Martha Lane Fox is behind it, it must be a good idea. Private, sleekly designed 'pods', touch-screen technology, Japanese-influenced (and expensive) cocktails at the touch of a button (marked 'Thirst'), and over 4,500 songs including that hard-to-find Bros B-side. In fact, so genius is it that since opening in 2005, four more UK branches have opened, including one in Islington (revealingly, the pods are growing – Islington's goes up to 15. So much for private). Ditto on the organisation.

Lidos & Swimming Pools

A throwback to pre-jumbo jet days when holidaying in Britain was the only choice, lidos – large outdoor (unheated) pools, often still with Art Deco features, sunbathing decks and candy-coloured wooden changing cabins – bring a little bit of the seaside to the city. Fashionable in the 1920s and 1930s, they numbered around 30 in London; now just a third remain, and still represent the steely British spirit – lifelong regulars swim at the crack of dawn every day of the year. The weaker of will may prefer the new, sceney pools at Shoreditch House and Haymarket Hotel – though it may take booking a room to access them.

Hampstead Swimming Ponds & Lido
East Heath Road, NW3
Tel: 020 7332 3773/020 7485 5757
Ponds open: 7/8am–before sunset all year (mixed pond: 7am–6.30pm May–mid-Sept only for non-members). £2
Lido open: daily, 7–9am; 10am–6pm; 6.45–8pm Mon/Thurs/Fri (adults only) May–mid-Sept; 7am–noon Sept–April. £2–4.50

Among the lush, undulating hills of Hampstead Heath are three deep freshwater ponds (ladies', men's and mixed) and the 60-metre Parliament Hill Lido – the subject of a recent row between overzealous Health & Safety officials and locals over the dangers of unsupervised swimming in chilly waters. Now they recommend a medical check-up before taking to the waters – pah! Even worse, swimmers may be asked to perform a quick swim test 'to prove their competence'! Unaccompanied males should take note that the Heath is a cruising zone; its male pond is prone to 'shark infestation' and some swimmers prefer to be, ahem, at one with nature.

London Fields Lido
London Fields Westside, E8
Tel: 020 7254 9038 www.hackney.gov.uk/c-londonfields-lido.htm
Open: 9.30am–noon, 1.30–5.30pm (7pm Tues/Thurs) Mon–Fri; 10am–6pm Sat/Sun. £4.10

A heated outdoor pool! 50 metres long! Open all year, all weather, in one of London's sceniest parks! The London Fields lot were rightly smug when this long-dormant, functionally designed lido in the park's northwest corner was finally resurrected in 2007 and heated to 25°C, just to add to their smugness about being in Hipster Central. Plus there are three cafés servicing the swimmers (and on summer weekends, there needs to be, when the place turns into one big posing pageant). But it's perhaps most atmospheric in winter, in the rain, in solitude, with steam rising off the water, when you can almost imagine how it was in 1932 before the cool kids came along.

Oasis Sports Centre

32 Endell St, Covent Garden, WC2
Tel: 020 7831 1804
Open: 7.30am–9pm Mon–Fri;
9.30am–5.30pm Sat/Sun. £4.05

A literal oasis in the centre of town, and no need to bring bravado since its 27-metre (88ft) outdoor pool is heated, and there's a back-up indoor pool. Also with squash courts, a gym, exercise classes and lovely sun terraces – make like the proverbial German and his beach towel on summer weekends though.

The Porchester Spa

Queensway, W2
Tel: 020 7792 3980
Open: daily, 10am–10pm (women only: Tues/Thurs/Fri/Sun till 4pm; men only: Mon/Weds/Sat; couples (single-sex/mixed): 4–10pm Sun.
£23 for 3 hours

A magnificent Edwardian Turkish baths, built in 1929, with lots of Art Deco features (green and white tiles, porthole windows, soaring ceilings), that, as well as a huge pool, has excellent spa facilities – an ice-cold plunge pool, two Russian steam rooms, three Turkish hot rooms and a Finnish sauna cabin. Excellent treatments include Shmeisse massages and Moroccan scrubs, and because it's run by Westminster City Council, prices are very reasonable. But perhaps the real draw is the bohemian (if naked) West London crowd that sit around playing chess, backgammon or cards (NB: nudity is not an insistence – quaint gingham wraps are provided). It's a democratic, community spa that runs as it always would, before the likes of Chiva-Som came along. However, for that, some do complain that it's dirty, so bring flipflops and leave the OCD behind.

Serpentine Lido

Hyde Park, W2
Tel: 020 7706 3422
www.serpentinelido.com
Open: daily, 10am–6pm mid-June to mid-Sept. £4

A sectioned-off part of the Serpentine Lake, this freshwater lido has lured Londoners for over 100 years, despite the goose detritus. At its maximum, there are 100 metres of straight swimming; there are also deck chairs, a paddling pool, a sandpit, a slide and swings, and the Lido Café in the old pavilion. But the 'serps', members of the Serpentine Swimming Club, don't need any such bait – they swim here all year round from 6.30–9.30am. If you arrive early, you'll see that wetsuits would be laughed out of town whatever time of year – many of the wiry serps compete in the Peter Pan Christmas Day Race when the water temperature averages 4°C. Goose excrement pales into insignificance.

Tooting Bec Lido

Tooting Bec Road, SW16
Tel: 020 8871 7198
Open: daily, 6am–7.30pm June–August; 6am–4.30pm Sept. £4.75

Built in 1906, Tooting is London's earliest purpose-built lido and is still Europe's largest, at 91 metres by 30 (300 by 100ft); it's also one of London's prettiest, with candy-coloured changing rooms, reminiscent of Brighton beach huts, and a nest of surrounding trees from Tooting Bec Common. It remains unheated and swimmers have been known to break the ice rather than break their habit. For winter madness, swimmers require membership to the South London Swimming Club (running since 1908 and open to all for a small annual fee; 020 8871 7198). Just remember the promise of its Jacuzzis and saunas to keep you going.

London Eye

London Eye
County Hall, Westminster Bridge Road, South Bank, SE1
Tel: 0870 500 0600
www.londoneye.com
Open: daily, 10am–8pm (9pm April–Sept). £17.88

The London Eye has done for London what the Eiffel Tower did for Paris. This giant Ferris wheel serves both as a radical shake-up to London's skyline and as the city's tallest public viewing platform. At 135 metres (443ft) high and built to celebrate the new millennium, it was, for a time (in 1999) the world's largest observation wheel, but inevitably has since been trumped (by Singapore); on a clear day, it offers 20 miles' visibility. 32 glass eggs each hold up to 25 people; the 'flight' takes 30 minutes, and both champagne and, in summer, Pimm's flights are available (though this does mean one glass only). For thirstier types, whole pods can be booked out for champagne flights, which can take a second rota-tion, giving you an hour to get high.

Other places to get high

London's tallest building, at 235 metres (771ft), is the pyramid-topped One Canada Square in Canary Wharf, E14, but unfortunately we can't get you in there. And it's not easy or cheap to get into the 180 metre-high (591ft) Gherkin, Norman Foster's glass-and-steel torpedo at 30 St Mary Axe in the City, topped by the Searcy's-run **40/30** restaurant (020 7071 5009; www.4030.co.uk). Either befriend a resident, buy membership (like, £1,000), or book a private table (from £265, and £50/65 per person lunch/dinner). And there are plenty of other Towers of Babel offering design, fizz and giddiness. Originally a members' club, the 117metre-high (385ft) **Paramount Club** at the top of Centre Point (103 New Oxford Street, W1; 020 7420 2900; www.paramount.uk.net) is what you might expect of a members' club – a Tom Dixon-designed space, showpony food, posh'n'pricey cocktails, plus staggering 360° views from what seems, literally, the very centre of London. Now non-members can access it by booking dinner, or by going to club nights held there (sometimes till 6 or 7am, by, for example, Circus and Superfreak). Meanwhile, the entry requirement for Sir Christopher Wren's **Monument** is extreme fitness – inside are 311 dizzying steps to the top of a single Doric column (Monument Street, EC2; 020 7626 2717; www.themonument.info £3). At 65 metres (213ft), it's the world's tallest isolated stone column, and was built in 1677 to commemorate the Great Fire – its height is equal to its distance from Pudding Lane bakery where the fire started. Even worse, it's 530 steps up to the top of **St Paul's Cathedral** 85metres (278ft) up (see Culture). Those who'd prefer not to sweat for the view could take the lift direct to **Vertigo 42**, a champagne bar at the top of Tower 42 (née the Natwest Tower), situated 183 metres (600ft) up on the 42nd floor of London's seventh tallest (and dropping fast) building. Note that it's by reservation only, and because of its City location, is something of a bonus-blowing joint (25 Old Broad Street, EC2; 020 7877 7842; www.vertigo42.co.uk). Likewise, the much-anticipated **Heron Tower** (London's second tallest building, at 230 metres (755ft) at 110 Bishopsgate, EC2) will boast a restaurant and Sky Bar on the top three floors; the bankers are already buying up its bachelor pads.

London Zoo

London Zoo
Outer Circle, Regent's Park, NW1
Tel: 020 7722 3333 www.zsl.org
Open: daily, 10am–6pm mid-July–early Sept (5.30pm Sept–end Oct and Mar–mid-July); 10am–4pm Nov–Mar.
£17.20

The conservation work of the Zoological Society of London has thrown animal rights activists off their high horses. Of London Zoo's 721 species, over 100 are endangered and there are breeding programmes for over 130. It was founded in 1826 by Sir Stamford Raffles in Regent's Park as the world's first scientific zoo (Charles Darwin was a Fellow) and still retains some original Grade I- and II-listed structures, including the neoclassical Giraffe House (built in 1837) and Lord Snowdon's aviary (built in 1964). Its most famous inhabitants are the Komodo dragons that grow up to 3.5m (10ft) long and can eat up to 80% of their bodyweight in one sitting. Book ahead online to avoid that caged-animal feeling in its long, long queues.

Roller-Blading

Hyde Park sees most of the skate action – there's a hip black scene (complete with retro quad skates, legwarmers and ghetto blasters on shoulders – still!), snaking the Serpentine Road through DIY slalom courses, and sportos and skate punks who beat the life out of pucks and shins whilst playing street hockey next to the Albert Memorial – join in if you care/dare. For the social skater, there are various free congos to join: The 'green run' **Easy Peasy Skate** (traffic-free, one hour and two miles long) is every Saturday at 10.30am in Battersea Park (www.easypeasyskate.com); the seven-mile-plus 'blue run' **Rollerstroll** is every Sunday in Hyde Park, starting at 2pm from the east side of Serpentine Road (www.rollerstroll.com), and the 'black run' **Friday Night Skate** (FNS) charges all over town at speeds of 32mph over 12-plus miles (tuition available, thankfully; 020 7193 5866; www.citiskate.co.uk). There's also a roller-disco every Thursday, Friday and Saturday at **The Renaissance Rooms**, Vauxhall (0844 736 5375; www.renaissancerooms.co.uk; £10–16.50 entry includes skate hire).

Slick Willies

12 Gloucester Road,
South Kensington, SW7
Tel: 020 7225 0004
www.slickwillies.co.uk
Open: 10am–6.30pm
Mon–Sat; noon–5pm Sun

A skate shop just down the road from Hyde Park that rents skates (£10/day) and protective equipment.

Royal Parks

The 'lungs of London' were historically the playgrounds of kings and queens. Now they're open to all for picnics, play and oxygenating (020 7298 2000; www.royalparks.gov.uk). The romantic **St James's Park**, designed by Buckingham Palace's architect John Nash, is London's oldest Royal Park. Hire a stripy deckchair, sip on prosecco at Inn the Park (see Snack) or stroll along the lake to spot the scores of bird species there (the park's bird keeper even lives on site, at Duck House). **Hyde Park** is over 350 acres in size, with its own boating lake, lido and numerous cafés. Next to Marble Arch is Speakers' Corner where anyone is free to take to their soapbox (mostly though it's just ranting religious fanatics). Centuries ago, Hyde Park was cleaved in two to make, on the west side, **Kensington Gardens**, Kensington Palace's 260-acre back garden (the palace has been home to Princess Diana, Queen Victoria and Princess Anne and is open to the public). **Regent's Park** covers 487 acres (including Primrose Hill), again gloriously landscaped by John Nash. Within its ring of palatial white Nash-designed Regency terraces are London Zoo, the Central London Mosque and the Open Air Theatre.

Rugby

Twickenham Stadium

Rugby Road, Twickenham, Middlesex
Tel: 020 8892 2000
www.rfu.com; tickets from www.ticketmaster.co.uk

On London's southwest outskirts is Twickenham, HQ of the Rugby Football Union and the venue for England's most important matches. Most – from premiership to World Cup matches – are played Saturday and Sunday afternoons, and given its public school associations (Rugby was born at Rugby school), it's often frequented by the royal princes. The main premiership teams in London are London Irish, London Wasps, NEC Harlequins and Saracens. Smaller games are played on their home grounds in and around London.

Sight-Seeing

While lofty types may regard sight-seeing tours with some hauteur, taking a tour is undeniably a fast way of getting your bearings, as well as delivering an ample portion of tapas tourism – London's most important nuggets presented with bite-sized information – direct to your seat.

The Big Bus Company

Tel: 020 7233 9533
www.bigbustours.com
Open: daily, 8.30am–6pm (5pm Oct; 4.30pm Nov–March).   £26

Bus tours are not classy (the Queen has even banned them from passing in front of her house) but they are a pleasant, superficial and lazy way of nailing the key sights. The Big Bus Company has two hop-on, hop-off lines with stops every 15–20 minutes – the shorter red line has a live guide; the longer blue one has a recorded commentary in eight languages, with stops at Baker Street, Green Park, Marble Arch and Trafalgar Square. Get the top deck for top views. Also recommended is the Original London Sightseeing Tour (020 8877 1722; www.theoriginaltour.com £25).

Black Taxi Tours

Tel: 020 7935 9363
www.blacktaxitours.co.uk
Open: daily, 8am–midnight.
From £100 per taxi

A tourist attraction in their own right, cabbies train for at least three years to get the 'knowledge' – a comprehensive mental map of London. With their cockney chat and London-wide nous, it's kind of obvious that they'd make good guides. Black Taxi Tour cabbies are also trained guides and will conduct two-hour door-to-door tours for up to five people any time of day or year. Extras on request.

Duck Tours

Tel: 020 7928 3132
www.londonducktours.co.uk
Open: daily, 9.45am–1hr before sunset, or 6pm in summer. From £20

So-called because the tour covers both land and water in a World War II amphibious DUKW craft (used in the D-Day Landings), the route starts and finishes by the London Eye, takes 75 fun minutes and covers just the very central sites, with a rather dramatic launch into the Thames itself. Since it's such an odd-looking vehicle (painted a conspicuous, rubber-duck yellow), the Duck and its passengers become something of an attraction themselves.

Heli-tours

Tel: 020 8953 4411
www.cabairhelicopters.com
Open: 2–5pm Sat monthly; 10am–1pm Sun monthly, demand dependent. From £150

With an average speed of 100mph and with zero congestion, helicopter tours are by far the most efficient way of joining up the dots – and because Cabair's choppers have twin-props, they are permitted to fly right through London. In 30 minutes, the captain covers the Westminster, Buck Pal, the London Eye, the BT Tower, the Tower of London, the Emirates Stadium and the Thames Barrier, while giving a running commentary. However, you will have to negotiate London's traffic to get to your chopper – they're based in Elstree, Hertfordshire. Private charter also available.

The London Bicycle Tour Company

Gabriel's Wharf, SE1
Tel: 020 7928 6838
www.londonbicycle.com
Open: daily, 10am–6pm. From £15.95

While London is no Amsterdam, two-wheelers certainly have the advantage in traffic and it's the fast track to engaging with the city. The friendly folk at London Bicycle offer three different tours, the 6-mile central tour is available daily (2.5 hours), and the 9-mile east and west tours weekends only (3.5 hours). They're mostly quite leisurely, though sloths might appreciate the option to sit down for a fish'n'chips lunch. Bespoke rides also available.

London RIB Voyages
Tel: 020 7928 8933
www.londonribvoyages.com
Open: daily, 10am–7pm (4pm Fri–Sun in Nov–Mar). From £32.50–45

RIB being, of course, Rigid Inflatable Boat, this tour gets you very close to Thames Water indeed, in a very fast (35 knots/hr) 12-seater dinghy, travelling from the London Eye, and visiting all the riverside sights from the Houses of Parliament, out past Greenwich to the Thames Barrier (there are two tours, 50 and 90 mins). RIB Voyages also run the VIP O2 enclosed RIB shuttle that does O2 transfers from anywhere along the river, 24 hours a day, for £600/hr. Also available for private charter.

Tour Guides
Tel: 020 7495 5504
www.tourguides.co.uk. From £170

Walking tours are the best way to discover London's nooks and crannies. Of course, trotting en masse in matching cagoules after an erect umbrella is route one to loss of street cred, but why join a group when the guides can come to you? This agency offers expert, approved 'blue badge' guides for tailored half- or full-day walking tours on the subject of your choice, for example, a British Museum highlights tour, the 2012 Olympics, film locations such as the Da Vinci Code, Love Actually and Notting Hill, Royal London and Westminster, or general sightseeing. Driver guides are also available (from £275).

Urban Gentry
Tel: 020 8149 6253
www.urbangentry.com
From £149 per group

Finally, a company that grasps that curiosity doesn't only come from coaches. Giving a cool spin to walking tours, Urban Gentry covers London's hotspots for fashion and food to art and architecture, as well as running hip neighbourhood tours, street market tours and general London tours. Aiming to deliver the inside track, the East End tour, say, will introduce participants to local fashion designers; the architecture tour is led by a local architect with his own practice. Group size is on average just four (though bespoke tours can be arranged) and driving tours are also available.

Spas

Pity those poor Londoners. More specifically, those cash-rich, time-poor Londoners – so time-strapped are they that the trend now is to offer multiple pairs of hands to get hands, feet, hair and face sparkling all at once, carwash-style (try **Groom** at Selfridges, W1; 020 7499 1199; www.groomlondon.com, and the multitasking Cowgroom treatment at Soho House's sister spa **Cowshed**, 119 Portland Road, W11; 020 7078 1944, Shoreditch House, E1; 020 7749 4531, and 31 Foubert's Place, W1; 020 7534 0870; www.cowshedonline.com). And with the arrival of the destination spa to London, locals are increasingly holding off from going global to get their fix, and instead booking up at the heavenly Amanresorts (see separate entry), and **Six Senses** at Canary Wharf's Pan Peninsular skyscraper (020 7531 2320) – with its city panoramas from the infinity pool, mind-stilling Ila treatments and watsu (shiatsu massage in water), you'll feel a thousand miles from the metropolis. It's very new austerity – the scaled-back spend.

Aman Spa

The Connaught, Carlos Place, Mayfair, W1
Tel: 020 3147 7305/6
www.the-connaught.co.uk
Open: daily, 9am–9pm
From £110 (one-hour massage)

Amanresorts has taken a city break. The luxury Asian spa chain's first urban spa is found, fittingly, in the Connaught Hotel's new west wing (see Sleep). Like a sepia photograph, its understated neutral fittings and furnishings (gold silks against cool granite and white marble) give it a timelessly elegant feel. It is a boutique affair – just five treatment rooms (one for couples), a pool and a steam room – but its star treatments, the 2.5-hour 'Aman Experiences' (£280) take you to paradise and back ('Aman' is Sanskrit for peace). Based around holis-

tic Thai, Indian, Chinese and Navajo healing techniques, their grounding yet energizing capabilities make you feel you are partaking in a sacred ritual, while the organic Sodashi scrubs and oils applied make skin silkier than an emperor's robe. These treatments also give the golden ticket to the steam and pool facilities usually reserved for hotel guests – as the staff explain, 'Johnny Depp may not appreciate too many other people if he is taking a swim'. Now that's access.

The Dorchester Spa

Park Lane, W1
Tel: 020 7319 7109
www.thedorchester.com
Open: 7am–9pm Mon–Sat, 8am–9pm Sun. From £55 (manicure)

Surely the capital's most decadent spa experience, The Dorchester Spa echoes the hotel's Art Deco splendour with a chandelier of south Pacific pearls, swathes of ivory drapes and blue velvet chaise-longues for lazing like Romans. Plan an afternoon visit and, after detoxing with a facial designed by A-list favourite Vaishaly Patel (known for her meticulous pore-unplugging) or a botanical body treatment with the cosmeceutical line Kerstin Florien, you can re-tox on the fanciful bite-sized cakes served in the Spatisserie. And since its precious clientele (think foreign royalty and wealthy socialites) wouldn't be seen dead leaving with oil in their hair, there's also a hair salon, and a mani/pedi suite complete with ivory leather thrones and rainbowed walls of Essie polish, to provide the finishing gloss.

Method Spa

Home House, 21 Portman Square, W1
Tel: 020 7670 2037
www.homehouseclub.com
Open: 9am–8pm Mon–Fri, weekends
by appointment. From £35 (manicure)

Hankering after supermodel skin?
Then head to members' club Home
House, where Anastasia Achilleos, the
dexterous facialist famed for massag-
ing the gleam back into Kate Moss'
skin, has set up shop in the basement
of the Robert Adam-designed Georgian mansion. Having trotted around
the globe's best spas, Achilleos has
cherry-picked her favourite cult brands
(a mixture of holistic and high-tech)
for the many, varied treatments here.
Thus, in the womb-like domed treatment rooms, you can test out and stock
up on Australia's organic and Halal
skin range, Kusch, the biodynamic US
brand, Dr Alkaitis, and South Africa's
cosmetic surgeon-designed, skin-heal-
ing Environ line. Lazy spa-goers seeking a full-body beautifying experience
(scrub, massage and intense moisturi-
sation) can luxuriate on the space-age
Naussica treatment couch – with its
inbuilt shower and steamer hood, it
offers a complete wet spa experience
without you having to move. A facial
with Achilleos herself will set you
back a staggering £345 but includes
a full analysis and washbag overhaul,
and her special knack for making your
chakras sing. Must be Mossie's secret.

The Spa at Mandarin Oriental

66 Knightsbridge, SW1
Tel: 020 7838 9888
www.mandarinoriental.com/london
Open: daily, 7am–10pm

From £110 (one-hour massage)

The cosseting starts before even slipping out of one's clothes, thanks to
the sublimely soft spotlighting, dark
granite flooring and black walnut
wood fittings. Complete relaxation
is promised with a dip in the Vital-
ity Pool, while hydrotherapy jets give
muscles a satisfying massage. Toxins
are gently purged in the Amethyst
Crystal Steam Room and Sanarium
(cooler than a sauna), and in case of
any residual stress, there's chill-out in
the colour therapy relaxation area.
Holistic massages, facials and body
treatments (with E'SPA products) are
East-meets-West in philosophy. Full-
and half-day spa programmes are
available and include use of the gym
but recommended is the Two Hours
of Time Ritual – yes, a two-hour treatment (often Ayurvedic) matched to
your specific needs.

Spa Illuminata

63 South Audley Street, Mayfair, W1
Tel: 020 7499 7777
www.spailluminata.com
Open: daily, 10am–6pm (7pm Tues/
Fri/Sat; 9pm Weds/Thurs)
From £50 (manicure)

Classicists will appreciate the décor
of Spa Illuminata whose marble pillars, mosaic floors and mock gargoyle
fountains lend it the feel of an ancient Greek or Roman bath. However,
the emphasis of this women-only
sanctuary is not traditional wet spa
therapies but holistic skincare treatments courtesy of the sophisticated
French botanical brands Decléor and
Carita. Each treatment begins with a

diagnostic back massage that eases you into a deeply relaxed state, laying bare any troublesome areas. The facials are some of the most thorough around, while the deeply relaxing four-hand massage is almost enough to persuade the imagination its mistress is a goddess being tended by her cherubs.

Urban Retreat at Harrods
5th Floor, Harrods,
Knightsbridge, SW1
Tel: 020 7893 8333
www.urbanretreat.co.uk
Open: 10am–8pm Mon–Sat; 11.30am–6pm Sun. From £35 (blow dry)

The gargantuan proportions of Harrods' Urban Retreat (covering a whopping 2,320m^2/25,000ft^2) and its constant bustle may not make this the ultimate beauty utopia, but what it lacks in tranquillity it makes up for in choice. The Urban Retreat houses some of Britain's best beauty experts: there's a Shavata brow studio, a Leighton Denny nail salon, a Roja Dove haute perfumery, and facialist John Tsagaris on hand with his acclaimed acupuncture. There's a Medi-spa, with all the needlework and fat-melting technology, and it is also the only place in the country where you can indulge in the deluxe Crème de la Mer facial, administered in a suite with exotic fish tanks for windows. Perfunctory beautifiers such as waxing, laser hair removal and endermology (cellulite-busting) are not forgotten. And when you're finished with all that, there's beauty photographer Tony McGee's Lights, Camera, Beauty to snap you in soft focus. So Harrods.

Tennis

All England Lawn Tennis Club
Church Road, Wimbledon, SW19
Tel: 020 8946 2244
www.wimbledon.org
Open: daily, 10am–5pm
Museum and tour £18

For spectating, strawberries and cream, Wimbledon is the obvious venue (the fortnight-long championship starts in the last week of June). Access to Centre and Number One/Two courts requires corporate clout or obsessive-compulsive organization (such is the demand that there's even an online public ballot open from Aug–Dec of the preceding year, where you can enter a draw to buy tickets, with no choice of day, time or court). Day tickets for the outer courts can be queued for on the day, though 'the day' for many starts the night before with sleeping bags and gritted determination. Tours of the club and access to the museum, whose collection dates back to 1555, is available to all outside of the championship.

The Hyde Park Tennis Centre
South Carriage Drive, Hyde Park, W2
020 7262 3474
www.willtowin.co.uk/hyde-park
Open: daily, 7am–9pm summer; 9am–4pm winter. From £12–13/hr

Championing that very inclusive idea of public tennis, Will to Win manages two tennis centres, both in London's royal parks: Hyde Park's comprises six hard courts and two mini courts for kids (booking, up to three days in advance, is advised) plus changing rooms and showers, as well as bowling and putting greens. Ace.

Regent's Park Tennis Centre
York Bridge Road Inner Circle,
Regent's Park, NW1
Tel: 020 7486 4216
www.willtowin.co.uk/regents-park
Open: daily, 8am–9pm (8pm Sat/Sun)
From £9–11/hr

Calling it 'community tennis', this is a very reasonable 'turn up and play' affair, with 12 hard courts (four flood-lit), two mini courts, changing rooms and showers, and a café, plus tuition. Though given the nation's annual tennis fever, booking in advance (up to three days in advance) is recommended.

The Thames

The River Thames, at 215 miles long (rising in Gloucestershire), is no record-breaker – although the city authorities claim that it is the cleanest river in the world that runs through a city. Most Londoners wouldn't take a running jump, but it's certainly recognized as the city's most important feature, and harbours many historic landmarks – particularly striking after dark. The best and longest view is from **Waterloo Bridge** (sing it now: 'Dirty old River, must you keep rolling… Waterloo sunset's fine'). Some bridges are views in themselves (such as Tower Bridge), while others should be walked for posterity – for example, Norman Foster's **Millennium Bridge** (aka the Wobbly Bridge). Opened by the Queen in 2000, it was closed two days later, deemed unsafe due to the swaying motion pedestrians felt walking over it (all water under the bridge now). Take a river cruise from Westminster Pier to Greenwich (recommended is City Cruises, from £8, 020 7740 0400; www.citycruises.com). Most of the action is between Westminster and Tower Bridge, but in Greenwich is the line of longitude that marks GMT, plus maritime attractions including the Wren-designed **Old Royal Naval College** (020 8269 4747; www.old-royalnavalcollege.org) and the **Cutty Sark**, a 19th-century tea clipper (020 8858 2698; www.cuttysark.org.uk). The river is also home to other floating museums, including:

HMS Belfast
Morgan's Lane, SE1
Tel: 020 7940 6300
www.hmsbelfast.iwm.org.uk
Open: daily, 10am–6pm (5pm Nov–Feb). £12.95

Permanently moored just west of Tower Bridge, this 11,500-ton British war cruiser served as a flagship in World War II. Set over nine decks are variously the engine room, the ops rooms, officers' cabins and (unintentionally) creepy waxwork sailors. There's a poignant chill on board as its recent history unfurls itself – it opened the bombardment of the Normandy coast on D-Day.

The Golden Hinde
Cathedral Street, SE1
Tel: 0870 011 8700
www.goldenhinde.co.uk
Open: daily, 10am–5pm. £6

Just to the west of HMS Belfast is an authentic reconstruction of Sir Francis Drake's 16th-century wooden galleon that circumnavigated the world in three years. Essentially, it's a Peter Pan stage set on five decks, sometimes with costumed pirates and sailors on their pirate workshops and guided tours (check website for pirates' availability).

Tower Bridge

Notes…

info…

Driving

'The man who is tired of London is tired of looking for a parking space,' said Paul Theroux, paraphrasing Dr Johnson. Add to that a weekday congestion charge (by January 2011, £10/day, 0845 900 1234 www.cclondon.com), traffic that chugs along at 10mph, aggressive drivers (especially the notorious 'white van man') and a confusing road layout, and drivers are sure to knot their knickers. The undeterred should drive on the left and keep to 30mph in town – as if there's much chance of exceeding it. Many roads have bus lanes (the far left lane, clearly marked); you can incur a fine for driving in these at certain times, so check the road signs. Parking – if you can find it – is by the meter (many now activated by mobile phone), Pay and Display or in car parks – and pricey.

Money

Britain continues to resist the euro, and the proud pound lives on. The majority of British banknotes in circulation are issued by the Bank of England (in denominations of £5, £10, £20 and £50), but some Scottish banknotes (perfectly legal and spendable despite some people's protestations) can infiltrate London's system. If unfamiliar or uncertain, ask the cashier to swap them.

Navigation

No Londoner is without their A–Z map to get from A to B (see also www.street-map.co.uk) but with medieval town planning, it's rarely straightforward. London's alphanumeric postcodes follow about as little logic as its street layout. The initial letters indicate the compass orientation (C=Central, NW=North West etc) but the numbers can seem meaningless, so SW1 is central while SW2 is Brixton, considerably further south.

Public Holidays

Public holidays, aka bank holidays, land on 1 January, Good Friday, Easter Monday, the first and last Mondays in May, the last Monday in August, 25 and 26 December – many enterprises take this opportunity to close, so call ahead to check.

Public Transport

Forever a source of anguish to Londoners, this includes the Underground, bus, overland trains and river transport. The Underground, or tube, is largely the most efficient (or the best of a bad bunch until the Crossrail finally arrives in 2017) but rush hour by any mode is grim. Fares vary depending on how many zones (some six concentric circles, where Zone 1 is the bull's-eye) are travelled through. Allow three minutes between each station and if making two or more journeys in a day, buy a Day Travelcard or Oystercard (which can be used on the underground, buses and some trains). Tubes run 5.30am–12.30am Mon–Sat and 7am–11.30pm Sundays. London buses are good for getting your bearings but not so useful if you don't recognize your destination. London Transport's helpline is 020 7222 1234 and there's actually a very useful journey planner on Transport for London's homepage (www.tfl.gov.uk).

Smoking

Smoking is banned in all bars, restaurants and clubs. This has led to a spike in patio heater sales, pavement parties, and 'smirting' (smoking and flirting on the pavement).

Taxis

All black cab drivers have the 'knowledge' – a qualification that takes on average 34 months to prepare for, with some 25,000 London roads to memorise. Conventional cabs can take five passengers, though the new Mercedes 'minibus' black cabs can take six or seven; all are usually up for sharing cabbie politics. You can now tweet for a cab by tweeting your journey details to twitter.com/tweetalondoncab, though it might be more straightforward to look out for the yellow 'TAXI' light, signifying an empty cab. Cheaper taxis can be booked through Addison Lee (020 7387 8888). If alone and in a hurry, call for their traffic-busting motorbike taxi (try also www.passengerbikes.com, 020 7033 9600; and www.virginlimobike.com, 020 3126 3998). Ignore approaches from unlicensed minicabs.

Telephones

The international dialling code for the UK is +44. The code for London from within the UK (including from a UK mobile) is 020, followed by two sets of four digits. If calling London from abroad, the code is +44 20 and then two sets of four digits. Central London numbers are denoted with a 7 at the start of the first set of digits, outer London with 8, and newer numbers with 3.

Tipping

Taxis, restaurants and fancy bars expect a tip. For cabbies, it is polite to round up the fare (many Londoners don't tip any more than this since fares are so expensive). Bar tipping is discretionary, but expected with table service. Restaurants expect 12.5%, but check it's not already included on your bill; tipping in cash gives it a better chance of staying out of management's hands.

index...

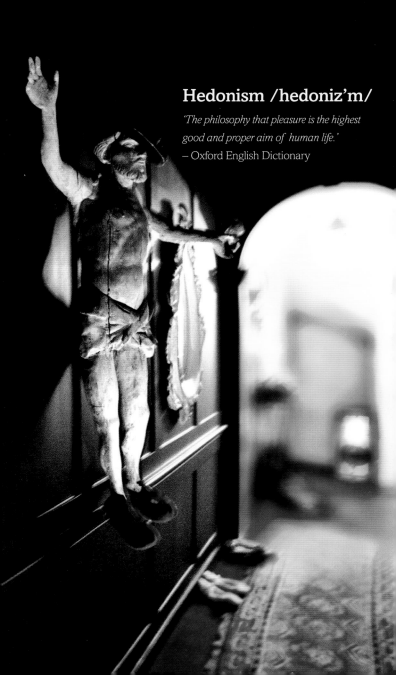

Hedonism /hedoniz'm/

'The philosophy that pleasure is the highest good and proper aim of human life.'
– Oxford English Dictionary

Hg2 Corporate

Branded Gifts....

Looking for a corporate gift with real value? Want to reinforce your company's presence at a conference or event? We can provide you with branded guides so recipients will explore their chosen city with your company's logo right under their nose.

Branding can go from a small logo discreetly embossed on to our standard cover, to a fully custom jacket in your company's colours and in a material of your choice. We can also include a letter from your CEO/Chairman/President and add or remove as much or as little other content as you require. We can create a smaller, 'best of' guide, branded with your company's livery in a format of your choice. Custom guides can also be researched and created from scratch to any destination not yet on our list.

For more information, please contact Tremayne at tremayne@hg2.com

Content licensing....

We can also populate your own website or other materials with our in-depth content, superb imagery and insider knowledge.

For more information, please contact Tremayne at tremayne@hg2.com

Hg-Who?

Welcome to the world of Hg2 – the UK's leading luxury city guide series. Launched in 2004 as the *A Hedonist's guide to…* series, we are pleased to announce a new look to our guides, now called simply Hg2. In response to customer feedback, the new Hg2 is 25% lighter, even more luxurious to look at or touch, and flexible, for greater portability. However, fear not, our content is still as meticulously researched and well-illustrated as ever and the spirit of hedonism still infuses our work. Our brand of hedonism taps into the spirit of 'Whatever Works for You' – from chic boutique hotels to well-kept-secret restaurants, to the very best cup of coffee in town. We do not mindlessly seek out the most expensive; instead, we search high and low for the very best each city has to offer.

So take Hg2 as your companion to a city. Written by well-regarded journalists and constantly updated online at www.Hg2.com (register this guide to get one year of free access), it will help you Sleep, Eat, Drink, Shop, Party and Play like a sophisticated local.

"Hg2 is about foreign life as art" **Vanity Fair**
"The new travel must-haves" **Daily Telegraph**
"Insight into what's really going on" **Tatler**
"A minor bible" **New York Times**
"Excellent guides for stylish travellers" **Harper's Bazaar**
"Discerning travellers, rejoice!" **Condé Nast Traveller**